THE

POOR

PAY

A Report of the
Bureau of Applied Social Research
Columbia University

DAVID CAPLOVITZ

THE
POOR
PAY
MORE

CONSUMER PRACTICES
OF LOW-INCOME FAMILIES

THE FREE PRESS, NEW YORK
COLLIER-MACMILLAN LIMITED, LONDON

Introduction

OF FEW BOOKS can it be truly said that they are pioneering works. Yet *The Poor Pay More* is such a book, for when it was first published it delineated with uncompromising, scientific evidence the brutal economic facts of existence for a group of low-income families in four New York City housing projects.

The families that speak of their consumer difficulties in David Caplovitz' book prove what sociologists have long known from observation: The spending habits which lead the poor to pay too much for too little are the direct result of their state of poverty. Dr. Caplovitz' book provides convincing documentation.

The dilemma of the low-income family is stated clearly and succinctly: Their need to possess major durable items is frustrated by a lack of cash and information that the wise shopper must have in our technological society. But, curiously, the poor have a marketable item—their own untenable credit position, which too often makes them good business for the salesman who sells a television set or washing machine at inflated prices and on inflated credit terms. As Dr. Caplovitz points out, even families on relief, still have a "pervasive need for credit" filled only too readily by the neighborhood credit store, or by the door-to-door peddler, who can provide the satisfaction that possession brings.

Dr. Caplovitz digs deeply. A majority of the families interviewed were aware to some degree of their plight in the marketplace. Three out of five said that they thought buying on credit was a bad idea. Three-quarters of *all* the families sampled used credit.

Some interesting facts are brought out. Families who bought

on credit owned more durable goods than those who paid cash. Why? ". . . some family heads felt that it was *easier* to buy on credit than to save and pay cash." They made it clear that they were referring to the discipline required for advance saving. Another fact: There are racial differences. White families are less apt than Negroes and Puerto Ricans to have credit problems, for they have a higher, steadier occupational status and a correspondingly more stable financial position. Yet when non-whites achieve a similar occupational status, they too show a greater financial responsibility.

The documentation in the book is thorough. Dr. Caplovitz probes the unfair selling practices that account for many consumer problems, noting that many families have financial problems not because of debts, but because of meager or nonexistent assets. The illness which meant a lost paycheck also meant missed payments; thus the half-paid-for furniture is repossessed, and the buyer cannot understand that he is also liable for additional interest charges, and legal fees, and court costs.

Every tactic of the unscrupulous seller is pinpointed. The workings of the *"deviant* system in which practices that violate prevailing moral standards are commonplace" are explained. Dr. Caplovitz' definitions of the "bait," and "switch," the "T.O.," and the "fifteen-month year" are classics.

The case is summed up explicitly. The marketplace for the poor "can exist because it fulfills certain functions that are presently not fulfilled by more legitimate institutions. . . . It may even be that under the present marketing arrangements in our society, unethical practices are an inevitable consequence of serving the wants of the poorest risks. Society now virtually presents the very poor risks with twin options: of foregoing major purchases or of being exploited."

It is this trenchant criticism of our society that gives *The Poor Pay More* its value, and that inspired corresponding studies in several other cities. Dr. Caplovitz says to the reader: This is the way it is. Surely, the reader's conscience must be touched now, as it was when the book was first published. We can justly boast that never have so many been so prosperous, yet we are forced to admit that a significant proportion of our urban and rural citizens not only fail to share our bounty, but are victimized in the attempt.

The message is clear in 1967. The War on Poverty has become an established part of our domestic policy, now that we realize the disease of poverty requires an immense effort of education, the opening up of job opportunities with decent incomes, and the end of discrimination.

I am glad that Dr. Caplovitz' words will receive a fresh hearing. His message, alas, is timely.

ESTHER PETERSON
Assistant Secretary of Labor
Former Special Assistant to the President for Consumer Affairs

September 1967

Foreword

THREE SETTLEMENTS situated on Manhattan's lower and upper East Sides found themselves, after World War II, in rapidly changing neighborhoods where vast programs of rebuilding and renewal were going on. One result of this physical change was the dislocation of many old patterns of life. Local independent merchants were uprooted in great numbers, which encouraged the development of a peddler economy. This brought high-pressure salesmen right into the home and the practice of buying on the dollar-down–dollar-a-week basis into the family economy. The two chief results of this new way of life are shoddy merchandise and greatly increased costs.

The Settlements, much concerned about this emerging pattern, planned first to get at the facts and second to evolve an effective consumer-education program. Most consumer programs are oriented principally to middle-income families, and not particularly to low-income families. Yet low-income families make up a very large percentage of the total population. It is estimated that 34 million Americans live in families with total incomes under $4,000, and that an additional 4 million people who live alone have incomes under $2,000. So the consumer problems of the Settlements' neighbors on Manhattan's upper and lower East Sides are likely to be typical of those confronting a broad segment of the population throughout the country. It is in the tradition of Settlements to undertake appropriate programs when there are conditions of special duress that seriously affect not only their neighbors but people like them in many other parts of the country.

Since World War II a great, concerted effort has been made to improve housing in marginal urban areas, through Federal, State, and City housing programs. There has been, however, a dearth of concern about such related matters as the consumer problems of low-income families. Out of our neighbors' experience comes a needed reminder that the building and rebuilding of neighborhoods is indeed complex. We see that some of the gains made in securing new and better housing can be offset by vulnerability to the peddler and to installment buying.

We would like to call attention to the contribution our neighbors made in providing the facts presented in this book. Many cooperated by conveying their experiences to Dr. Caplovitz. Their firsthand descriptions of consumer exploitation as it affected their lives give the study depth and perspective, and, more important, point up the urgency for carrying the *action* program forward. Our neighbors spent as much time as the interviewer needed to complete a complex, long, and intimate review of their personal economic circumstances. As at other times when the Settlements have turned to neighbors for firsthand, direct experience, they responded with an interest and good will without which the study would not have been possible.

That three dispersed Settlements were able to carry forward this joint undertaking was due in large measure to the interest and generosity of Consumers Union, the Fred L. Lavenburg Foundation, and The Flagg Fund. To them go our hearty thanks.

In the director of the study and author of this book, Dr. David Caplovitz, the Settlements encountered a sociologist who received the highest compliment our neighbors could accord him—acceptance and trust. We ourselves felt that Dr. Caplovitz brought to this project an impressive technical skill and an ability to combine academic hard-headedness with fresh perception and an underlying warmth and concern. In the Settlements' hierarchy of values this is a combination that is greatly appreciated and respected.

JOINT SETTLEMENT COMMITTEE
HELEN HALL
MILDRED ZUCKER
WILLIAM KIRK (*Chairman*)

Henry Street Settlement
James Weldon Johnson Community Center
Union Settlement

March, 1963

Preface to the 1967 Edition[1]

THIS BOOK appeared in September 1963, eleven months before President Johnson signed the Economic Opportunity Act, which marked the beginning of the "war on poverty." Ever since, "poverty amidst affluence" has been very much in the news and *The Poor Pay More* has benefited from this resonance. The primary objective of the war on poverty has been to overcome the obstacles that have prevented the poor from achieving a meaningful place in the productive sphere of society. The emphasis has been on how to expand the earning power of the poor through education, job training, and the creation of jobs. *The Poor Pay More* served as a reminder that the poor are consumers as well, and that their inability to earn a decent living is only one side of their economic plight. Also important is how they spend what little income they have. If the poor pay more for the goods they buy, they are being denied the benefits of their earning power. They are forced to live in a world of inflation that more well-to-do citizens are able to escape.

This perspective of the poor—as consumers—provides some balance to the view set forth by Michael Harrington in *The Other America*. Harrington's best seller shocked America by reminding it that the poor are still with us. But Harrington's poor were invisible, tucked away in urban slums, skid rows and migrant workers' camps. Existing on the fringes of society, his poor were very different from the rest of us. To see the poor as consumers is to see them as part of the main stream of America, participating, however marginally, in

1. I should like to thank Dr. Persia Campbell, Professor Terence Ison, and Father Robert McEwen for their helpful comments on an earlier draft of this preface.

what George Katona has called the "mass consumption society."
As Katona has pointed out, America is the first society in which the
great majority have discretionary income; that is, income above
that needed for the necessities of life. Since the poor presumably do
not have discretionary income, it is not immediately obvious that
they should have consumer problems. Perhaps the central contribution of this book has been to show that they too take part in the
consumption society, but at considerable cost.[2] Whereas the poor
at an earlier stage of development were viewed as exploited workers,
it makes some sense today to view the poor as exploited consumers.[3]

Apart from its relevance to the war on poverty, the subject matter of this book is germane to a central feature of the mass consumption society, the phenomenon of consumer credit. Consumer
credit has been the fuel for the new society. The word "explosion"
has become a cliche for describing events in the rapidly changing
world, but it is a particularly apt description of what has happened
to consumer credit. The expansion of consumer credit since World
War II has truly been explosive, far outstripping the growth in
population. In 1945, the amount of outstanding *installment* debt
was 2.5 billion dollars. A decade later, in 1955, it had climbed to 29
billion. By the end of 1965, it had soared to 66 billion and as of this
writing, in mid-1967, it stands at 75 billion. Growing at the rate of
about ten per cent a year, installment debt should surpass 100
billion by 1970.

The phenomenal growth of installment credit has brought in
its wake a sharp rise in deceptive and fraudulent marketing practices. Insofar as market transactions depended upon cash, sellers

---

2. The mechanism permitting even the poor to play the role of consumer is,
of course, installment credit. However, Katona's annual surveys of consumer
finances, carried out by the Survey Research Center of Michigan, fail to show
that the use of credit is widespread among low-income groups. Spending units
with incomes below $3000 are much less likely to have installment debts ac-
cording to these national surveys than spending units of higher income. This
would appear to contradict the findings presented in this book, but the contra-
diction readily disappears when we take into account the age of the household
head and the size of the family unit. My sample tends to be comprised of those
in the early stages of the family life cycle, whereas Katona's samples of the poor
include many aged and single-person households in which consumer activity is
known to be slight. In short, the people in my book are more representative of
poor families with young children than of the aged who comprise a large
segment of the poor.

3. This perspective is all the more appropriate when we consider that the
poor are consumers (clients) of a wide range of social services, such as health
care, legal services, welfare and housing programs. The inadequacies of these
services hardly need further documentation.

had less opportunity and incentive to employ deception and fraud. The consumer who could afford to pay cash for an automobile or an expensive appliance was probably more deliberate and sophisticated in his shopping behavior, and there was no point in trying to convince the person without cash to make an expensive purchase. All this changed with the advent of installment credit. Whether or not the consumer could afford the purchase became largely irrelevant. Once the contract was signed, the seller could count on the law to enforce his right to payment. Appropriate changes in contract law and regulations governing consumer credit have lagged far behind the growth of our credit economy. The signed contract is treated as sacrosanct in courts of law, and the fraudulent techniques used to obtain the consumer's signature, so difficult to prove in court, are largely ignored.[4]

Installment credit has thus been the door through which the poor have entered the mass consumption society, and they, more than any other group, have been victimized by the fraud and deception that have accompanied this method of selling. As I have tried to show in this book, the marketing system that has evolved in low-income areas is in many respects a deviant one in which exploitation and fraud are the norm rather than the exception.

Fraud and deception, however, are not the only bane of the low-income consumer. Once rent and food are provided for, the techniques of modern salesmanship tempt him almost inevitably to devote the balance of his earnings to installment purchases. Nothing is saved for emergencies, and the hazardous result is a total commitment of future income. If that income stops through sickness, injury, or unemployment—worse still if medical bills are added to debts—the family sinks into the despair of economic disaster.[5]

The Current Relevance of the Study

The study described in this book is now seven years old, and I am often asked whether these conditions are still with us today. Unfortunately, the answer is yes. If anything, the situation has grown worse. Garnishment orders against wages—symptomatic of break-

4. This situation is slowly beginning to change. A few years back, a suit against a poor consumer in Washington, D.C. was dismissed on the grounds that the transaction stemmed from an "unconscionable contract." The "unconscionable contract" doctrine is contained in the uniform commercial code, but until the Washington, D.C. decision, had never been applied to consumer credit. Whether this precedent will be widely applied remains to be seen.

5. For a solution to the problem posed by unexpected loss of income, see T. G. Ison, *The Forensic Lottery*, London: Staples Press, 1967.

downs in credit transactions—increase each year. In Chicago, where such statistics are readily available, the number of garnishments has increased from 59,000 in 1962 to 73,000 in 1966. The number of personal (nonbusiness) bankruptcies has mounted at alarming rates since World War II. In 1948 there were about 16,000; in 1958 there were 80,000, and in 1966 there were 176,000.

The exploitative schemes described in *The Poor Pay More,* such as bait advertising, the promise of free merchandise in return for finding customers, or the pretense of representing the school system when selling encyclopedias, are still being practiced. And still new schemes have evolved. The deep freezer that purportedly pays for itself out of savings from the accompanying food plan is currently a very popular racket. Many poor families sign contracts for these freezers, only to learn, when they later receive their copy of the contract and the payment book, that the quoted price was far below the price which they have to pay.[6] Moreover, instead of obtaining bargain buys on food, these families soon discover that the prices charged are actually higher than supermarket prices and that the quality of the food delivered each month deteriorates. Even the welfare poor are not immune. Some door-to-door salesmen specialize in selling appliances and television sets at exorbitant prices to families on welfare, coming around on the day of the welfare check to collect their payments. A particularly vicious racket only recently uncovered involved health care on the installment plan. A group of chiropractors in New York City solicited business by phoning low-income residents and informing them that they were entitled to a free medical examination. The examination would invariably reveal a health problem that could be "cured" by a series of treatments and the patient would be cajoled into signing an installment contract. Those patients who never returned would soon find their wages being garnisheed.

A related question that I am frequently asked is whether the conditions I found to exist in New York City occur in other parts of the country. The cumulative evidence seems to be that the practices and problems of low-income consumers in New York City are quite general. The Office of Economic Opportunity has funded consumer action components in a number of community action programs throughout the country. The investigations of the recent riots in Negro ghettos in various parts of the country have suggested

---

6. In New York and some other states, the law requires that the consumer be given a copy of the contract at the time of the sale, and yet this law is frequently violated with apparent impunity by the more unscrupulous merchants.

that resentment against consumer exploitation is one of the many grievances that find expression in riots.[7] From conversations with home economics in the Agricultural Extension Service in diverse parts of the country, I have learned that the poor in small towns and rural areas are also plagued by installment credit problems.

One topic that was not explored in *The Poor Pay More* is the cost of food in low-income areas. Since the publication of this book, a number of comparative shopping studies have been made by community action groups showing that the poor pay more for food as well as for durable goods. These studies have shown that supermarket chains often charge more for the same food items in low-income areas than in middle-income areas, and use the low-income outlets as dumping grounds for vegetables and meats that have begun to spoil. In short, the cumulative evidence seems to be that the themes of this book are not only applicable today, but that they are appropriate to areas of consumption not covered in this study.

Prospects for Reform

Perhaps no field better illustrates the contradictions and ironies of our democratic processes than the consumer area. Although nearly all Americans spend money as consumers—some 200 million of us—our interests as consumers have been submerged before the onslaught of the powerful lobbies of the business and financial communities. Consumer organizations are notoriously weak, and in spite of the justice of their cause—the impeccable values they espouse, such as truth, honesty, health, safety and free competition—they have been no match for the opposition. And yet the weakness of the consumer's lobby notwithstanding, the consumer's interests have been on the ascendency in the past few years. It is still too early to tell whether this is a temporary trend or a long-range one, but there are numerous signs that government is prepared, however haltingly, to increase the protection of consumers. The Kennedy administration was the first to provide for representation of the consumer with the creation of a Consumer Advisory Council within the Council of Economic Advisors. The Johnson administration has carried consumer representation further with the appointment of a Special Advisor on Consumer Affairs, and recent Presidential messages to Congress have raised hopes that measures increasing the protection of consumers will be passed. Congress has already

---

7. See Robert Fogelson, *The 1960s' Riots: Interpretations and Recommendations*, a report prepared for the President's Commission on Law Enforcement and Administration of Justice, soon to be published in book form.

taken action on the issue of automobile safety, and a "truth-in-packaging" bill, although greatly watered down, has been passed. Ex-Senator Douglas' long battle on behalf of "truth-in-lending" shows signs of coming to fruition. A number of states have made some efforts to reform their credit laws. By far the most progressive code was recently passed in Massachusetts. While the battle has raged in Congress over the disclosure of credit charges, whether they can and should be expressed in terms of a true annual interest rate, Massachusetts has already shown the way by enacting such a law.

The National Conference of Commissioners on Uniform State Laws, a prestigious organization whose members are appointed by the Governors of the States, has turned its attention to a model consumer credit law. The Commissioners have responded in part to the fear that the Federal Government will step in if the States do not provide the debtor-consumer with more protection. However, the committee working on this bill is financed by the credit industry and is industry-oriented, and it remains to be seen whether the resulting bill will strike an equitable balance between creditors' and debtors' rights.

A basic reason for this growing concern with the plight of the consumer has been the explosion in consumer credit and the burgeoning deception that has accompanied it. Interestingly enough, the experiences of low-income consumers have done much to expose the glaring inequities of the current legal structure. A number of efforts to reform the system touch upon matters that particularly affect the low-income consumer. The deficiency judgment is a case in point. As the law now operates in most states, the creditor can not only repossess the merchandise in default of payments, but he can collect the balance of the debt after the net value stemming from the resale is deducted. In most instances the amount realized is only a small fraction of the original sale price. The debtor is usually shocked to learn that even though he does not have the merchandise, he still owes the creditor considerable money. In some states, remedies are being proposed, and it is expected that the model state law now being drafted also will rescue the poor from this double jeopardy. One suggestion is to give the creditor the choice of either repossessing or suing for the balance of the debt, but not both. A second is to rule out repossession after a certain percentage of the debt has been paid.

Another consumer credit law that is now being re-examined concerns the sale of contracts to third parties. The person who buys the merchant's contracts—the "holder in due course," as he is called in legal language—is not now liable for any deception or fraud that might have been involved in the sale of the merchandise, and the contract that he has bought is binding upon the debtor.[8] In a few states, the debtor is supposed to receive notice of the contract sale informing him that he has a certain period of time, usually ten days, in which to register his complaints. Often these notices are not sent out on time and the key passage is hidden in the document, with the result that the consumer never knows of his opportunity to question the sale of his contract. (As this study disclosed, many poor people totally misunderstand this transaction and mistakenly think that the original creditor has gone out of business.) Moreover, the principle of notification fails to take into account the fact that the defect or fraud in the original sale may only become apparent some time after the contract is sold. For example, the gradual shifting to inferior brands in the food-freezer plan is not evident until some months after the transaction. The poor in particular are apt to suffer from the inequities of the "holder in due course" clause as the kinds of merchants they deal with are heavily dependent upon finance companies and banks buying their contracts.

As the survey reported in this book shows, the poor are particularly vulnerable to high-pressure door-to-door salesmen. Direct selling of this kind relies heavily upon misrepresentation and maximizes "impulse-buying," for the consumer usually has no intention of making a purchase before being approached by the salesman. As the system now operates, the consumer who signs a contract in response to this pressure has no recourse. Thus a third effort to reform the installment credit system is aimed at removing the abuses of direct selling by introducing a cooling-off period. England has adopted such a provision, giving the buyer seventy-two hours in which to re-think the transaction and rescind the contract if he so chooses. In Massachusetts, a twenty-four-hour cooling-off period has been passed into law and the model state law may recommend an equivalent grace period.

Garnishment laws are also coming under scrutiny in many states. It has been found that in states where large portions of wages can be attached by creditors, an increasing number of debt-ridden consumers are choosing personal bankruptcy.[9] In such states, ef-

---

8. This is true in every state except Massachusetts. The new law in that state specifically holds the financing agency liable for any defenses the buyer may have against the original seller.

9. See George Brunn, "Wage Garnishment in California: A Study and Recommendations," *California Law Review*, December 1965, v. 53, No. 5., pp. 1214-1253.

forts are now being made to increase the amount of income that is exempt from garnishment. Relatively little has been done to protect workers' jobs in garnishment cases, but even here there has been some progress. The New York legislature recently passed a law prohibiting employers from firing an employee for a single garnishment, and there are now efforts to extend the law to cover two or three garnishments. No other state that permits garnishments—and all but two do—has yet followed New York's example.

Finally, the passage of "truth-in-lending" legislation, if it includes disclosure in terms of a simple annual interest rate, will be a great benefit to all consumers, rich and poor alike. It will mean that consumers will for the first time have the necessary information to shop for credit. Since the poor tend to deal with those lenders and vendors who charge the highest interest rates, such legislation might well stimulate them to shop around before buying and borrowing. It might also discourage them from seeking credit at all, a possibility that I do not view with horror.

Perhaps another reason for the current ferment on consumer issues is that politicians have discovered that they can win votes by advocating the consumer's cause. In 1957, the Attorney General of New York State, Louis J. Lefkowitz, established a Division of Consumer Frauds and Protection within the Department of Law. This Division was soon elevated to the status of a Bureau. The Bureau, which has done much to combat fraud (although fraud is still prevalent in New York), has brought considerable publicity to the Attorney General who runs far ahead of the rest of his party in elections. Today, the Attorney Generals of 23 States have emulated the New York model by setting up Consumer Fraud Bureaus.

A further sign that consumer issues are becoming popular with politicians is the fact that six states have official consumer representation in their government. This takes the form of either an office of consumer advisor to the governor or consumer advisory boards and councils. Illinois, which is far from being in the vanguard of progressive consumer legislation, provides a good example of the trend of the times. A few years ago, the attempt by a Democratic state legislator to bring about credit reforms was defeated along strict party lines. Today, both Democrats and Republicans have submitted bills which, if enacted, will considerably strengthen consumer protection.

The cause of the consumer still has a long way to go, and it is not clear how far legislators and public officials will take it in the face of increasing opposition from the business community. Even representation for the consumer is far from institutionalized. In both New York and California, a change in administration has meant the end of consumer representation at the state level, and the advocates of a Federal Department of the Consumer see little hope for their goal in the near future.

Perhaps one small indication of the long road ahead is that the obviously fraudulent practice of turning back the odometer on used cars is not only widespread but is not illegal in most states. Only in 1966, after much controversy, did the consumer interests in Massachusetts succeed in passing a law that prohibited this deception. The used car dealers argued that such a law would result in a severe drop in used car prices, which is undoubtedly true. Since the poor overwhelmingly buy used rather than new cars, they stand to gain from this enforced honesty. Even more recently, the Department of Licenses in New York announced that it would amend its regulations so as to prohibit tampering with the mileage on used cars. But what, one wonders, protects the used car buyer in the less enlightened sections of the country?

The business community has done an enormously successful job in lulling the public into believing that such fraudulent practices are rare. After all, it has sponsored its own agency to police itself, the Better Business Bureau. The propaganda campaign has been so successful that the Better Business Bureau is the first agency that most people think of as a source of help when they have a consumer complaint. This is certainly true of the low-income families that we interviewed in New York, and a recent national survey shows that it is true generally. Yet the Better Business Bureau has no legal enforcement power to act against fraudulent merchants. Although it claims to be the nation's guardian against misleading advertising, such advertisements appear every day in the mass media. Its claims notwithstanding, the Better Business Bureau is little more than a businessman's protective association often syphoning off consumer complaints that would be better directed to other agencies. That it has less than the consumer's interest at heart is indicated by the fact that in many states it has lobbied against consumer representation in government on the false premise that the Bureau is already doing the job of protecting the consumer.

In the light of the powerful forces aligned against the consumer public, it remains to be seen how successful the current efforts at reform will be. It is noteworthy that in the few states where some progress has been made, such as Massachusetts, strong consumer groups had come into being to lobby on behalf of the consumer.

Until such groups form in other states, the prospects for reform are not good.

Consumer Action with Low-Income Groups

Apart from the efforts at legislative reform, there have been a number of attempts in the past few years to involve the poor in consumer education and action programs. Many of these programs have been sponsored by the Office of Economic Opportunity. So far, OEO has financed more than 80 consumer action programs. These include home management instruction, family financial counseling and low-cost credit services in low-income areas. But with a few exceptions, these programs have had limited success. Efforts to establish credit unions and other types of self-help institutions have been set back by the absence of seed money. Neither the Federal Government nor the State Credit Union Leagues have been eager to provide the capital and leadership to get these institutions established, and until such funds and leadership are available, there is little chance that these programs will get off the ground.

Somewhat more promising have been a few grass-root programs that have sprung up without the aid of federal funds. In Philadelphia, a group that calls itself the Consumer Education and Protective Association was founded a little over a year ago. Its membership, which has grown to about a thousand, is made up overwhelmingly of working-class and low-income persons. Its success stems from its readiness to take the militant action of picketing merchants who refuse to settle the grievances of customers who have been cheated. In the short time of its existence, CEPA has been able to work out a number of settlements for consumers who found that they could not get help elsewhere. Pennsylvania is one of the few states that prohibits garnishments, but its laws make it easy for the creditor to attach the property of a debtor, with the consequence that many debtors find themselves losing their homes. The work of CEPA has dramatized this practice, and its readiness to picket has prevented a number of Sheriff's auctions of the homes of working-class debtors.[10] Its work is beginning to attract attention in nearby communities, and there is some possibility that CEPA will spread to other places. But such a movement requires considerable funds and organizational talent, both of which are in short supply.[11]

---

10. It should be noted that the rate of working-class home ownership is very high in Philadelphia.

11. The value of mobilizing the poor for consumer action is vividly illus-

Another kind of grass-roots program that has taken hold in some low-income areas is the food-buying club. Under this arrangement, a number of families pool their resources and buy their food from wholesalers, thereby realizing substantial savings on their food bills. A number of these clubs exist in New York City and Baltimore and probably in other communities as well.

Some Reflections on *The Poor Pay More*

A new printing of a book provides the author with the opportunity to evaluate his own work and to share whatever second thoughts he has with the reader. Needless to say, second thoughts have been prompted by greater experience with the subject matter and the wisdom of hindsight. The first of these has to do with the neighborhood credit merchant who is cast pretty much as the villain in this book. I think it is a mistake to see the credit merchant only as a nefarious exploiter of the poor. A more thorough analysis than I undertook in this book would have to examine the economic constraints that operate on these men. In some respects the local merchants charge more for the simple reason that it costs them more to operate. I am not thinking only of the fact that being small businessmen, they cannot buy in bulk the way chain stores and large department stores can. In addition, these merchants frequently have to pay more for the money they borrow and the insurance they need. The insurance companies seem to be facing a crisis concerning insurance in ghetto areas. Even at the higher rates they charge, they claim that they are not finding it profitable to extend insurance to ghetto merchants. There is a need for new institutional arrangements to meet the needs of the local merchant as well as those of the local consumer. Why, for example, cannot there be some system of pooling insurance and sharing risk so that the local merchant can be protected at reasonable rates?

There is a second respect in which the portrait of the exploitative merchant needs to be clarified. In calling attention to the fraudulent schemes employed by the local merchants and, in par-

---

trated by the case of the fraudulent chiropractors mentioned earlier. The East Harlem community action agency known as MEND (Massive Economic Neighborhood Development) received a number of complaints from persons who were victims of this racket. The various governmental agencies that would seem to have jurisdiction in the matter were slow to respond, and as a last resort, MEND began picketing the chiropractors' office. The resulting publicity brought the case to the attention of the U.S. Attorney's office. After carrying out an investigation, the office arrested the chiropractors for, among other things, mail fraud.

ticular, by the door-to-door salesmen who work for companies located outside the neighborhood, I have unwittingly created the impression (one that the legitimate business community echoes) that these problems exist only because of a small class of disreputable sellers. Such a picture completely ignores the fact that these unscrupulous sellers could not exist without the finance companies and banks that buy their paper. These financial institutions must share the blame for the exploitation of the poor, for they know all too well (and if they don't, they should) that they are buying dishonestly obtained contracts. Yet they do so anyway.[12] Further, when we ask where the finance companies get the funds they need to operate, we soon discover that they often borrow from highly respectable banks. Thus, the respectable financial community is also a party to the exploitation of the poor.[13]

If I did less than full justice to the neighborhood merchant, there is one respect in which I also was less than just to the poor consumer. I greatly regret the use of the word "apathy" in the title of Chapter 12. "Apathy" implies "not caring," and this is not an accurate description of the response of the people we interviewed to their consumer problems. As I show in the chapter, the reasons why they did nothing about their problems were many, including their ignorance of sources of help, their inability to take time off from work to seek help, and for some, their cynicism based on experience about the efficacy of community agencies. I particularly regret the word "apathy" because it has been used often, and I believe mistakenly, to describe the poor's response to their situation. What is lacking is not so much the motivation of the poor to change their situation as meaningful courses of action for them to take in the face of unresponsive and frequently powerless community agencies. As some of the more successful poverty programs have shown, the poor are ready to respond when a meaningful opportunity is offered to them.

12. Changing the "holder in due course" provision so as to make the firm that buys the contract liable for the fraudulent practices employed in the transaction would do much to enforce responsibility in these third parties.

13. The extent to which the banking industry is involved with finance companies has been documented by Congressman Wright Patman, Chairman of The House Banking and Currency Committee. In an address before the New York Consumer Assembly on January 14, 1967, Congressman Patman reported that it has been estimated that the finance companies receive as much as 70 per cent of their funds from commercial banks. He cited a Federal Reserve Board weekly report of December 28, 1966 which stated that 350 large banks in this country had loans outstanding to finance companies in the amount of nearly 7 billion dollars.

Another second thought has to do with the notion of "compensatory consumption" that I introduced in this book. By this term, I mean to suggest that the motive to acquire expensive durable goods is quite strong among low-income groups, and that the ownership of such goods is apt to take on the symbolic significance of social progress for people whose chances for social mobility are blocked. But the existence of this motive is still more in the realm of hypothesis than demonstrable fact. What is needed is more research that would separate the various motives to buy among the poor and assess the importance of each. How much of the consumer behavior of the poor stems from their needs, how much from their vulnerability to unscrupulous merchants, and how much from the motive of compensatory consumption remains to be determined. Lacking systematic evidence to document the theme of "compensatory consumption," I had to resort to illustrative, suggestive materials. At one point I cite the presence of the more expensive colored telephone in many of the homes of these families as evidence of compensatory consumption. I have since come to realize that even this fact may have a different origin. The telephone companies also employ the hard sell to get their subscribers to buy the more expensive equipment, and even the colored telephone may be more indicative of vulnerability to sales practices than of compensatory consumption.

Finally, I cannot resist a few observations on the title of the book. It seems to have a life of its own and has become much better known than the book itself. It was used for a documentary film on the problems of poor consumers produced by National Educational Television. It may even have bestowed upon me fatherhood of an economic law, for a recent magazine article on food prices in low-income areas noted that the findings seem to support Caplovitz's "law" that the poor pay more. It will be a measure of social progress when this so-called "law" is no longer true, when the poor will not have to pay a special tax for being consumers in our affluent society. That the poor themselves are beginning to take action against their exploitation as consumers is perhaps the most encouraging sign that this desired state of affairs may yet come to pass.

DAVID CAPLOVITZ

Preface

THE STUDY reported in this volume grew out of the joint efforts of three settlement houses in New York City to develop a program of action directed toward the consumer problems of low-income families. All three, Union Settlement House (East Harlem), the James Weldon Johnson Community Center (East Harlem), and the Henry Street Settlement House (lower East Side), are located in slum areas which are being rapidly transformed by public housing projects. As an unanticipated consequence, these programs of redevelopment have enlarged the consumer problems of families in the neighborhood and have made these problems increasingly visible. Traditional economic relationships have tended to break down as hundreds of small shopkeepers have been forced to move and as many of the old residents have themselves had to move to other areas.

The old residents are being largely replaced by more recent migrants to the city: Negroes from the South and Puerto Ricans. Strangers to the neighborhood, the new residents find themselves with an unusual number of consumer needs as they move into the new housing developments. Many come from furnished rooms and must now fit out apartments of four, five, and six rooms. Most of them experience the move to public housing as a distinct improvement in their standard of living, and they want to furnish their new apartments with "nice" things. Even when they own furniture and appliances at the time of the move, they are apt to discard these, preferring to furnish their new place with new things.

Observing all this, the professional staffs of the settlement houses have become increasingly aware of the major problems facing these consumers. From the managers of housing projects they learned of maintenance trucks coming to the project grounds three times a week to collect discarded furniture. Some recently purchased pieces were shoddy enough to fall apart even before the completion of payments on them. Many of the new residents were so heavily burdened with installment debts that the strains made life difficult for them in their new environments. The staffs of the settlement houses uncovered facts of repossessions, wage assignments, and legal entanglements that the confused residents seemed powerless to cope with. As their observations cumulated, they became convinced that efforts to help these families would come to no avail until something could be done about their financial problems as consumers. The idea of a consumer action program took form.

The settlement groups submitted a proposal to the Fred L. Lavanburg Foundation for a consumer study and program of action. This called for an extensive survey of existing conditions that would identify both the major kinds of consumer problems in these areas and the types of families which were especially vulnerable to these problems. The survey was to provide a factual basis for developing a program of action. A grant for the program was provided by the Fred L. Lavanburg Foundation, the Flagg Foundation, and Consumers Union. These organizations turned to the Bureau of Applied Social Research of Columbia University for the first phase of the program, the survey of existing conditions. This book reports the results of that survey. It is based on an unpublished report by the Bureau of Applied Social Research completed in 1961.

The Role of the Local Community
in the Research Process

The research plan called for intensive interviews with families living in low-income housing projects in the neighborhoods of the sponsoring settlement houses. At the outset, there was much concern about whether it would be possible to conduct interviews with these families about such intimate details as debts and savings. The investigators were reminded by the settlements that many of the families were newcomers to the city, somewhat disturbed by both the big city and by the rules (often strange to them) that governed their residence in public housing. As a result, they would be suspicious of strangers at the door.

The first several months of the study were devoted to becoming acquainted with the tenants and their problems as consumers. The settlements had been working hard to develop a sense of community in the housing developments. Tenant groups had been organized. The relationships established between the tenants and the settlement staffs provided a basis of operation for the study. Doors were opened to the sociologists that might otherwise have been closed.

Exploratory interviews began at Washington Houses. In that project a group of housewives, known as the Coffee Hour Group, had been organized by Mr. Preston Wilcox, the director of a community service organization known as the East Harlem Project.[1] The sociologists attended weekly coffee hours, finding the members interested in the study and eager to talk about their experiences as consumers. The women volunteered to serve as subjects for pretest interviews in their homes, and as the questionnaire was being developed, the members of the Coffee Hour Group were interviewed time and again.

---

1. The East Harlem Project was created several years ago by the settlements in East Harlem with funds provided by the Lavanburg Foundation. The purpose of this organization is to stimulate community activities and to aid local residents in developing organizations to meet their needs.

This procedure for meeting families was used with equal success on the lower East Side. There, a group of social workers from the Henry Street Settlement House, under the direction of Mr. José Villegas, were at work developing organizations among the tenants of LaGuardia Houses.[2] Mr. Villegas and his coworkers arranged interviews for us with families active in the LaGuardia organizations.

When the study was ready to move into the phase of the formal interviews, the families with whom the settlements had established relations were again called upon for assistance. In Washington Houses and in LaGuardia Houses, the volunteers helped first by distributing copies of the project's newsletter[3] that announced the study and, again, by introducing the interviewers to the families in the sample.

The cooperation of the local community in the research effort was manifested in still another way. In the East Harlem area, a few local merchants known to Union Settlement generously gave of their time to answer questions about the problems of the small businessman in these neighborhoods. They were particularly helpful as consultants to a small survey of the merchants of durable goods in the East Harlem area. Their advice on appropriate approaches to the owners of appliance and furniture stores, on pertinent and taboo questions, proved to be sound and indispensable. In all these ways, the residents of the neighborhoods contributed to this study of a touchy and difficult subject.

DAVID CAPLOVITZ

---

2. This work, too, was made possible by a grant from the Lavanburg Foundation.

3. The existence of these newsletters is one example of the settlements' work with the tenant groups they helped organize.

Acknowledgments

MANY PEOPLE contributed to the study and helped in the preparation of this monograph, and it is a great pleasure to acknowledge my indebtedness to them.

The survey and the program of action now under way owe their existence to the inspiration and unflagging determination of the directors of the three sponsoring settlement houses. Helen Hall (Henry Street Settlement House), Mildred Zucker (James Weldon Johnson Community Center), and William Kirk (Union Settlement House) conceived of the program and patiently worked through the difficult organizational task of bringing it to fruition.

In the category of clients are three others whose interest and encouragement were appreciated: Janet Robbins and Carl Stern, then of the Lavanburg Foundation, and Colston Warne, president of Consumers Union.

Throughout the study I was most ably assisted by Louis Lieberman. Together, we carried out pretest interviews, struggled through the various drafts of the questionnaire, devised a sampling plan, and supervised the field work and data processing. The teamwork that developed between us was particularly rewarding, and I welcome this opportunity to thank him for a job well done.

A particularly important contribution to the study was made by two students of Columbia University's Graduate School of Business, Mr. Wolfram Arendt and Mr. Murray Caylay. They volunteered to undertake the small survey of local merchants, and Chapter 2 draws heavily upon their interviews.

Comments on the original report by several friends and colleagues were most helpful in planning the revisions. In particular, I would like to thank Bernard Berelson who was director of the Bureau at the time of the study, John Meyer, Carol Bowman, David Rogers, Nelson Foote, and Max Nadler.

Commissioner Ira S. Robbins, of the New York City Housing Authority, and Harry Fialkin, director of research of the Housing Authority, generously provided us with data on the tenants that permitted us to select a representative sample.

Mortimer Getzels, attorney-in-charge of the Legal Aid Society's uptown office, was kind enough to take time from his busy schedule to explain to me some of the legal aspects of consumer problems.

Pinpointing the contributions of my friend, Clara Shapiro, director of administration of the Bureau, poses a difficult task. Her constant encouragement and reassurance and her good advice on the hundreds of decisions that confront a project director come close to what I have in mind.

My greatest debt I save for last. Robert K. Merton painstakingly read the various drafts of this manuscript. His critical comments, his innumerable suggestions, and his extraordinary editorial skill, encompassing clarity of thought as well as style, have enriched this book enormously. Unfortunately only those who have had their manuscripts evaluated by this man can appreciate the full extent of my debt to him.

Of course, the responsibility for whatever errors remain in the book is wholly mine.

Contents

THE
POOR
PAY
MORE

CHAPTER 1

Introduction

THIS BOOK is about urban poor people in their role as consumers of major durable goods. A few generations ago, a book about low-income consumers would inevitably have focused on their problems in getting the necessities of life. Among other things, it would have found that the poor depended upon credit—credit from the land-lord, the corner grocer, and the second-hand clothing dealer. This would have been distinctive of the relatively poor. Today, the middle class has adopted the pattern of consumer credit from the poor and made it part of the American way of life. Every year, more and more Americans turn to installment credit in order to buy what they want.[1] Nor are low-income people excluded from this road to present purchases and better living through future payments. They are no longer limited to the informal, traditional credit pro-

---

1. The United States has seen installment buying since the middle of the nineteenth century. Until the advent of the automobile this practice was limited primarily to lower-income groups and was somewhat disreputable. After 1910 the automobile industry began to promote installment buying. During the twenties, this practice experienced a phenomenal growth and lost much of the stigma attached to it. See W. C. Plummer, "Installment Selling," in *The Encyclopedia of the Social Sciences.* Between 1920 and 1960 *installment* debt, exclusive of mortgages, rose from one billion to 42 billion dollars. Most of this increase occurred during the fifties. In this decade, installment debt increased by almost 30 billion dollars. In recent years installment debt has been increasing at the rate of 8 per cent a year. See *Consumer Credit Labeling Bill, Hearings before a Subcommittee of the Committee on Banking and Currency, United States Senate, 86th Congress* (Washington, D.C.: U. S. Government Printing Office, 1960).

vided by the corner grocer who will sell them food "on the book." They, too, have access to the more formal, "bureaucratic credit" symbolized by the installment contract. Through it, they reach out for the possessions that are taken to mark a *style* of life rather than life itself.

This book examines such consumer practices among low-income families in New York City. It describes the major durables they own, how they went about getting them, and the difficulties they encountered along the way. It also tells how these families are buffeted by high-powered advertising, exploitative salesmen, and debt entanglement. For many low-income families the road to "better living" through installment credit is an extremely hazardous one.

Plan of the Book

To understand these consumers and their problems fully would require a thorough study not only of the consumers but also of the merchants with whom they trade. Although the main emphasis of this study is upon consumers, some attention is given to the marketing situation as seen by local merchants. Under the direction of the Bureau of Applied Social Research, a limited study of the merchants in East Harlem was made by two graduate students of Columbia University's School of Business. Their interviews with fourteen furniture- and appliance-store owners provide an important supplement to the more systematic survey of consumers.

Drawing upon these interviews, Chapter 2 shows how merchants of high-cost durables are able to operate in low-income areas. They will be seen to be heavily dependent on a system of credit which involves close, personal control, as well as legal, impersonal control over consumers. This will be found to be only one element among many of a traditional economy existing in these urban low-income areas.

The main part of the book deals with various aspects of the consumer behavior of low-income families. Chapters 3

through 7 deal with the major components of their patterns
of consumption: what they own, where they shop, the prices
they pay, and the method of payment they use. Chapter 3
describes the kinds of goods they buy and aspire to own.
The next two chapters examine their patterns of shopping:
Chapter 4 describes the types of stores in which they shop,
the frequency with which they trade with local merchants,
and with major department and discount stores outside their
neighborhood; and Chapter 5 deals with a practice distinctive of low-income families—buying from door-to-door
credit peddlers. Who buys from these men, what they buy,
and their reasons for buying are described.

Credit, as we have noted, is of special importance to
low-income families. The need for credit and its extensive
use colors many facets of their consumer practices. It facilitates the accumulation of goods, affects their decisions
about where to shop, and, perhaps most importantly, has a
pronounced effect on the cost of what they buy. The factors
affecting the prices paid for durables are analyzed in Chapter
6 and the use of credit by these families is taken up in Chapter 7.

The next five chapters deal with the consumer problems of low-income families. Chapter 8 examines their financial position and their debts relative to assets. Here the
reader will find out how the finances of these families (all
of them living in low-income public housing) compare
with those of other low-income consumers throughout the
country.

Chapter 9 focuses on the families whose debts, in relation
to their income and savings, are so large that they border on
insolvency. The numbers of families in this difficult position
are estimated and their social characteristics examined.

The difficulties encountered by these consumers in their
dealings with merchants are set out in Chapters 10 and 11.
Their experiences with unscrupulously talented salesmen,
the resulting entanglement in debt, and the suffering imposed on many of them are described.

The reactions of low-income consumers to their troubles

are considered in Chapter 12. Here we shall find out how many families are aware of sources of help in the community and how many make use of them when they encounter a consumer problem.

Chapter 13 summarizes the main findings of the study and discusses their implications for a program of action.

Throughout the book it will be found that consumer practices and problems vary greatly *within* the low-income population. White, Negro, and Puerto Rican families, for example, differ greatly in their consumer practices and level of solvency. Other characteristics of families, notably their size and the age of the household head, also have a significant bearing on consumer behavior. In short, it will be seen that low-income families are by no means of a piece and that social characteristics of families, apart from income, affect their consumer practices and problems.

From this overview of what the book is about, we now turn to the people about which it is concerned, the sample of families under study.

The Projects

The sample was drawn from four low-income housing projects in New York City: Washington and Jefferson Houses in East Harlem and LaGuardia and Vladeck Houses on the lower East Side. These projects were selected because they were in the neighborhoods of the sponsoring settlements, and the proposed program of action would most immediately affect the families living in them. Although not selected to be representative of all low-income projects in the city, these projects differ enough from one another to provide a substantial range.

The two neighborhoods, East Harlem and the lower East Side, have long been areas in which the poor and disadvantaged have settled. Until recently, East Harlem had a predominantly Italian population. In the past several decades, Negroes from North Harlem and from the Southern

United States have migrated into the area in large numbers, and more recently there has been a heavy influx of Puerto Ricans. For many decades, the main ethnic group on the lower East Side has been East European Jews. In the last ten years or so, large numbers of Negroes and Puerto Ricans have moved into this area as well. The narrow streets of the old slum sections are now dotted with Pentacostal store churches, sandwiched between the synagogues of the older inhabitants.

Both neighborhoods are today the scene of vast programs of slum clearance. Within the past ten years, thirteen low-income and middle-income projects have been completed or are under construction in East Harlem, as have twelve on the lower East Side.

The two East Harlem projects differ from each other in several respects as do the two on the lower East Side. Washington Houses, on the fringe of East Harlem between 97th and 104th Streets and Third and Second Avenues, is about six years old. The first section was completed in 1955; the second, two years later. Its 1500 families consist mainly of recent migrants to the area. More than half the families are Puerto Rican and most of the rest are Negro. Only 7 per cent of the families are white.

About ten blocks to the north, in the heart of the old Italian section, is Jefferson Houses. Half of the project was ready for occupancy in 1955, but the other half was not completed until 1959. Thus Jefferson is somewhat newer than Washington. Unlike Washington Houses, Jefferson was rented under a policy of racial integration with the result that its population is more evenly divided among the three main racial groups. The white families of Jefferson consist mostly of Italians who had lived in the neighborhood before the project was built. Only one third of the Washington families in the sample lived in the neighborhood before moving to the project, but more than half of the Jefferson families had.

This difference in continuity with the past is reproduced in the two lower-East-Side projects. Like Washington Houses uptown, LaGuardia reflects the changing composition of the neighborhood over the past decade. About one third of its families are white, most of them Jewish; almost half are Puerto Rican and the rest are Negro. Like the two uptown projects, LaGuardia is fairly new, having been completed in 1957.

Vladeck Houses, only a short distance from LaGuardia, is quite different in character from the other three. Completed in 1940, it is one of the oldest projects in the city. It differs from the others both in design and composition. Unlike the very high-rise buildings of sixteen stories in the other three projects, the Vladeck buildings are only six stories high and are so arranged that they face each other along tree-shaded walks, lined with rows of benches. From an almost exclusively Jewish population in the forties, Vladeck has also come to reflect the changing composition of the neighborhood. More than one in every ten families today is Negro; another two in ten are Puerto Rican. The remaining 70 per cent are white, and most of these are elderly, retired Jews. An unusually high proportion of the households consist of either a single elderly person or a retired couple.

The Families

We wanted to select a sample of families that would be representative of these projects. However, the unusually large number of elderly residents living in Vladeck posed a problem. They are not typical of the residents in low-income projects and they are not likely to have the kinds of consumer problems with which the study was concerned. We decided to eliminate all single-person households from the study (a rule which primarily affected Vladeck rather than the other projects) and to undersample Vladeck's two-person households, most of which also contained elderly persons. This led to the Vladeck sample being more nearly comparable to those of the other three projects.

The sample was designed to reflect the composition of

families in each project in terms of race,[2] income, and size. With the cooperation of the New York City Housing Authority, all families in the projects were classified according to these three characteristics. The technique of stratified sampling was used to select an initial sample of 500 households, this being equal to one in every fifteen families living in the projects.

We were able to obtain interviews with 85 per cent of the initially selected. To minimize whatever biases might be introduced in the data by the families who either refused to be interviewed or were never home when the interviewer called, some fifty-five substitutes were added to the sample. Since the substitutes were so chosen as to have characteristics similar to those who could not be reached, it is not surprising that our efforts to interview them were somewhat less successful than with the original full sample. About 75 per cent of the substitutes were interviewed, bringing the overall response rate to 82 per cent.[3] Put in raw numbers, some 555 families were selected for interviewing, and of this number usable interviews were obtained from 464.[4]

Characteristics of the Sample

The racial composition of the sample is, of course, quite different from that of New York City as a whole. Only 25 per cent of the families are white exclusive of Puerto Ricans

2. The reader should keep in mind that "race" is used in this book to refer to whites, Negroes, and Puerto Ricans. This usage is, of course, incorrect since many Puerto Ricans are white. The only alternative would have been using the term "ethnicity," but this too is incorrect since the whites comprise a number of different ethnic groups.

3. White families were somewhat more difficult to contact than either the Puerto Rican or Negro families. Since the white families tend to be older than the others, it may be that it was their age rather than their race that led to the higher refusal rate. After all, the subject matter of the study was less meaningful to those families who consume relatively little. In any case, the final sample shows an underselection of white families amounting to about 5 per cent.

4. Five interviews were broken off when a suspicious spouse entered the apartment and refused to let the interview continue. These incomplete interviews were counted as refusals.

and most of these are concentrated in two ethnic groups, Italian and Jewish. Negroes make up 29 per cent of the sample, and Spanish-speaking residents another 46 per cent. Most of the latter are Puerto Ricans, but some are Cubans and a few are natives of other Latin American countries. We shall adopt the convention of referring to *all* the Spanish-speaking families as Puerto Ricans but the reader should remember that this group includes some from other Latin American countries.

Comparatively few, only 17 per cent, of the heads of the families are natives of New York City. About 20 per cent, mostly migrant Negroes, were born in the South. Forty-three per cent were born in Puerto Rico or Cuba, and 10 per cent, mostly Jews and Italians, were born in Europe.

The educational level of the household heads is in keeping with their low income and their places of origin. About half did not progress beyond elementary school. Another third had some high school education but did not graduate; 13 per cent completed high school, and 4 per cent had some advanced education.

The families in the sample tend to be much younger and larger in size than those in the city or nation at large. The median age of the household heads is about 38. Some 20 per cent of family heads are under 30 years of age and 54 per cent are under 40. The average family consists of four persons, and more than 40 per cent of these families have six or more members. Only 13 per cent consist of two people.[5]

The composition of the families also varies. Seventy-one per cent are "complete" families consisting of a mother, father, and children. Married couples without children constitute only 7 per cent of the sample. One fifth are broken families, 19 per cent consisting of a mother and children, and one per cent of a father and children. Young children are the rule. Only 9 per cent of the 464 households have

---

5. This includes four single-person households which got into the sample because other family members had left the household shortly before the interview took place.

no children living in them, and half have one or more under 6 years of age.

To understand the consumer behavior of these families, we must keep their characteristics in mind. Various studies have shown that it is the families in the early stages of the life-cycle—where the head is under 45 years of age and there are young children—that are the most active consumers of durable goods, and the ones most likely to have consumer debts.[6] In short, the typical family in the sample is one which has a number of characteristics generally associated with considerable consumer activity. But they differ from other families known to be active consumers in one important respect: they are exclusively low-income families. The various effects of this on consumption is, of course, a major question to be answered by the study.

Although all the families have incomes below the ceilings established by the Housing Authority, there is still considerable variation among them.[7] The median income for the families in the sample is approximately $3,500; 10 per cent have incomes below $2,000, and 12 per cent have incomes in excess of $5,000.[8]

As is to be expected in a low-income group, a good many families receive assistance from welfare. About 15 per cent derive all or part of their income from welfare, 13 per cent live on pensions, and the remaining 72 per cent obtain their income exclusively from earnings.

---

6. See Lincoln Clark (ed.), *Consumer Behavior*, Vol. II: *The Life Cycle and Consumer Behavior* (New York: New York University Press, 1955). See especially the article in this volume by John B. Lansing and James N. Morgan, "Consumer Finances Over the Life Cycle."

7. The data on income used in this study were obtained from the records of the Housing Authority. The interview data on income are not entirely accurate because of the confusion between take-home pay and gross salary. The Housing Authority makes great efforts to get accurate information in its annual investigations of family income. However, it is in the family's interest to conceal its income, and a number of families probably fail to report all sources of income. The data probably underestimate the true income of many families.

8. Family size is taken into account in establishing income ceilings. There are some families, presumably quite large ones, with incomes in excess of $6,000.

The statistics describing the sample are summarized in Table 1.1.

Table 1.1—Characteristics of the Sample
(In Per Cent)

Race		Income		Age of Head	
White	25	Under $2,000	10	20-29	20
Negro	29	$2,000-$2,999	27	30-39	34
Puerto Rican	46	$3,000-$3,999	30	40-49	24
		$4,000-$4,999	21	50-59	11
Total per cent	100	$5,000 and over	12	60 plus	11
		Total per cent	100	Total per cent	100

Education		Family Size		Family Composition	
Elementary school	49	1, 2 persons	13	Husband-wife, no children	7
Some high school	34	3 persons	19	Mother-father, children	71
High school graduate	13	4 persons	28	Mother, children	19
Beyond high school	4	5 persons	18	Father, children	1
		6, 7 persons	15	Other[a]	2
Total per cent	100	8 or more	7		
		Total per cent	100	Total per cent	100

Place of Birth		Source of Income	
New York City	17	Earnings only	72
U.S., South	21	Welfare, whole or part	15
U.S., Other	6	Pensions	13
Puerto Rico and Cuba	43	Total per cent	100
Europe and other foreign	13		
Total per cent	100		

a. Includes doubled-up families, siblings, and unmarried adults living with and supporting their parents.

Some of these characteristics are of course closely related. In particular, race is strongly associated with age of household head and family size, two characteristics that have important effects upon practices of consumption. Members of white families in the sample tend to be much older than either Negro or Puerto Rican families. More than half of the heads of white families, but only about one tenth of the heads of Negro and Puerto Rican families are over 50 years of age. The heads of Negro households are notably young; almost a third are in their twenties, compared with about a fifth of the Puerto Ricans and only a twentieth of the whites.

More than half of the white families have only two or three members; the great majority of the Negro and Puerto Rican families have at least four. The Puerto Rican families tend to be the largest; 50 per cent have at least five members, compared with 40 per cent of the Negroes and only 24 per cent of the white families.

These differences in the structure of the white, Negro, and Puerto Rican families will be taken into account in the analysis of their consumer practices and problems. Should it turn out, for example, that white families are less apt to use credit, we will consider the effect of family size and age of head on credit usage before concluding that race alone accounts for the finding.

As the statistical portrait of the sample indicates, these consumers are for the most part products of a comparatively traditional culture. Their place of origin, their race and ethnicity, and their level of education all suggest that their early training was not geared to life in highly urbanized and bureaucratic society. This fact underlies much of their behavior as consumers. It is perhaps not too farfetched to say that this book is the story of traditional consumers in a bureaucratic society, and of how merchants adjust to these consumers and take advantage of them. It is also the story of people with little money, with little competence as consumers, and with little chance of avoiding exploitation in the marketplace: consumers "poor" in three senses of the word.

CHAPTER 2

The Merchant and the Low-Income Consumer*

THE VISITOR to East Harlem cannot fail to notice the sixty or so furniture and appliance stores that mark the area, mostly around Third Avenue and 125th Street. At first this may seem surprising. After all, this is obviously a low-income area. Many of the residents are on relief. Many are employed in seasonal work and in marginal industries, such as the garment industry, which are the first to feel the effects of a recession in the economy. On the face of it, residents of the area would seem unable to afford the merchandise offered for sale in these stores.

That merchants nevertheless find it profitable to locate in these areas attests to a commonly overlooked fact: low-income families, like those of higher income, are consumers of many major durables. The popular image of the American as striving for the material possessions which bestow upon him both comfort and prestige in the eyes of his fellows does not hold only for the ever-increasing middle class. The cultural pressures to buy major durables reach low- as well as middle-income families. In some ways, consumption may

---

* This chapter is based in part on an unpublished research report by Wolfram Arendt and Murray Caylay.

take on even more significance for low-income families than for those in higher classes. Since many have small prospect of greatly improving their low social standing through occupational mobility, they are apt to turn to consumption as at least one sphere in which they can make some progress toward the American dream of success. If the upper strata that were observed by Veblen engaged in conspicuous consumption to symbolize their social superiority, it might be said that the lower classes today are apt to engage in *compensatory consumption*. Appliances, automobiles, and the dream of a home of their own can become compensations for blocked social mobility.[1]

---

1. I am indebted to Robert K. Merton for suggesting the apt phrase, "compensatory consumption." The idea expressed by this term figures prominently in the writings of Robert S. Lynd. Observing the workers in Middletown, Lynd noted that their declining opportunities for occupational advancement and even the depression did not make them class-conscious. Instead, their aspirations shifted to the realm of consumption.

> Fascinated by a rising standard of living offered them on every hand on the installment plan, they [the working class] do not readily segregate themselves from the rest of the city. They want what Middletown wants, so long as it gives them their great symbol of advancement—an automobile. Car ownership stands to them for a large share of the "American dream"; they cling to it as they cling to self respect, and it was not unusual to see a family drive up to the relief commissary in 1935 to stand in line for its four or five dollar weekly food dole. [The Lynds go on to quote a union official:] It's easy to see why our workers don't think much about joining unions. So long as they have a car and can borrow or steal a gallon of gas, they'll ride around and pay no attention to labor organization. . . . [Robert S. Lynd and Helen Merrill Lynd, *Middletown in Transition* (New York: Harcourt, Brace and Co., 1937), p. 26. See also pp. 447-448.]

It should be noted that the Lynds identify the installment plan as the mechanism through which workers are able to realize their consumption aspirations. Similar observations are to be found in *Knowledge for What?* (Princeton University Press: 1939), pp. 91, 198. Lynd's student, Eli Chinoy, also makes use of the idea of compensatory consumption in his study of automobile workers. He found that when confronted with the impossibility of rising to the ranks of management, workers shifted their aspirations from the occupational to the consumption sphere. "With their wants constantly stimulated by high powered advertising, they measure their success by what they are able to buy." Eli Chinoy, "Aspirations of Automobile Workers," *American Journal of Sociology*, 57 (1952), 453-459. For further discussion of the political implications of this process, see Daniel Bell, "Work and its

The dilemma of the low-income consumer lies in these facts. He is trained by society (and his position in it) to want the symbols and appurtenances of the "good life" at the same time that he lacks the means needed to fulfill these socially induced wants. People with small incomes lack not only the ready cash for consuming major durables but are also poorly qualified for that growing substitute for available cash—credit. Their low income, their negligible savings, their job insecurity all contribute to their being poor credit risks. Moreover, many low-income families in New York City are fairly recent migrants from the South or from Puerto Rico and so do not have other requisites of good credit, such as long-term residence at the same address and friends who meet the credit requirements and are willing to vouch for them.[2]

Not having enough cash and credit would seem to create a sufficient problem for low-income consumers. But they have other limitations as well. They tend to lack the information and training needed to be effective consumers in a bureaucratic society. Partly because of their limited education and partly because as migrants from more traditional societies they are unfamiliar with urban culture, they are not apt to follow the announcements of sales in the newspapers, to engage in comparative shopping, to know their way around the major department stores and bargain centers, to know how to evaluate the advice of salesmen—practices necessary for some degree of sophistication in the realm of consumption. The institution of credit introduces special complex requirements for intelligent consumption. Because of the diverse and frequently misleading ways in which charges for credit are stated, even the highly-educated consumer has difficulty knowing which set of terms is most economical.[3]

Discontents" in *The End of Ideology* (New York: The Free Press of Glencoe, 1960), pp. 246 ff.

2. A frequent practice in extending credit to poor risks is to have co-signers who will make good the debt should the original borrower default. The new arrivals are apt to be disadvantaged by their greater difficulty in finding cosigners.

3. Professor Samuel S. Myers of Morgan State College has studied the

These characteristics of the low-income consumer—his socially supported want for major durables, his small funds, his poor credit position, his lack of shopping sophistication—constitute the conditions under which durables are marketed in low-income areas. To understand the paradox set by the many stores selling high-cost durables in these areas it is necessary to know how the merchants adapt to these conditions. Clearly the normal marketing arrangements, based on a model of the "adequate" consumer (the consumer with funds, credit, and shopping sophistication), cannot prevail if these merchants are to stay in business.

On the basis of interviews with fourteen of these merchants, the broad outlines of this marketing system can be described. This picture, in turn, provides a backdrop for the more detailed examination in later chapters of the marketing relationship from the viewpoint of the consumer.

Merchandising in a Low-Income Area

The key to the marketing system in low-income areas lies in special adaptations of the institution of credit. The many merchants who locate in these areas and find it profitable to do so are prepared to offer credit in spite of the high risks involved. Moreover, their credit is tailored to the particular needs of the low-income consumer. All kinds of durable goods can be obtained in this market at terms not too different from the slogan, "a dollar down, a dollar a week." The consumer can buy furniture, a TV set, a stereophonic phonograph, or, if he is so minded, a combination phono-

---

credit terms of major department stores and appliance outlets in Baltimore. Visiting the ten most popular stores, he priced the same model of TV set and gathered information on down-payments and credit terms. He found that the cash price was practically the same in the various stores, but that there were wide variations in the credit terms leading to sizeable differences in the final cost to the consumer. (Based on personal communication with Professor Myers.)

In his statement to the Douglas Committee considering the "Truth in Interest" bill, George Katona presented findings from the consumer surveys carried out by the Survey Research Center of the University of Michigan. These studies show that people with high income and substantial education are no better informed about the costs of credit than people of low income and little education. See *Consumer Credit Labeling Bill, op. cit.*, p. 806.

graph-TV set, if not for a dollar a week then for only a few dollars a week. In practically every one of these stores, the availability of "easy credit" is announced to the customer in both English and Spanish by large signs in the windows and sometimes by neon signs over the doorways. Of the fourteen merchants interviewed, twelve claimed that from 75 to 90 per cent of their business consisted of credit and the other two said that credit made up half their business. That these merchants extend credit to their customers does not, of course, explain how they stay in business. They still face the problem of dealing with their risks.

THE MARKUP AND QUALITY OF GOODS

It might at first seem that the merchant would solve his problem by charging high rates of interest on the credit he extends. But the law in New York State now regulates the amount that can be charged for credit, and most of these merchants claim they use installment contracts which conform to the law. The fact is that they do not always use these contracts. Some merchants will give customers only a card on which payments are noted. In these transactions the cost of credit and the cash price are not specified as the law requires. The customer peddlers, whom we shall soon meet, seldom use installment contracts. In all these cases the consumer has no idea of how much he is paying for credit, for the cost of credit is not differentiated from the cost of the product.

Although credit charges are now regulated by law, no law regulates the merchant's markup on his goods. East Harlem is known to the merchants of furniture and appliances in New York City as the area in which pricing is done by "numbers." We first heard of the "number" system from a woman who had been employed as a bookkeeper in such a store. She illustrated a "one number" item by writing down a hypothetical wholesale price and then adding the same figure to it, a 100 per cent markup. Her frequent references to "two number" and "three number" prices indicated that prices are never less than "one number," and are often more.

The system of pricing in the low-income market differs from that in the bureaucratic market of the downtown stores in another respect: in East Harlem there are hardly any "one price" stores. In keeping with a multi-price policy, price tags are conspicuously absent from the merchandise. The customer has to ask, "how much?," and the answer he gets will depend on several things. If the merchant considers him a poor risk, if he thinks the customer is naive, or if the customer was referred to him by another merchant or a ped-dler to whom he must pay a commission, the price will be higher. The fact that prices can be affected by "referrals" calls attention to another peculiarity of the low-income mar-ket, what the merchants call the "T.O." system.

Anyone closely familiar with sales practices in a large retailing establishment probably understands the meaning of "T.O." When a salesman is confronted with a customer who is not responding to the "sales pitch," he will call over another salesman, signal the nature of the situation by whis-pering, "this is a T.O.," and then introduce him to the cus-tomer as the "assistant manager."[4] In East Harlem, as the interviewers learned, T.O.s extend beyond the store. When a merchant finds himself with a customer who seems to be a greater risk than he is prepared to accept, he does not send the customer away. Instead, he will tell the customer that he happens to be out of the item he wants, but that it can be obtained at the store of his "friend" or "cousin," just a few blocks away. The merchant will then take the cus-tomer to a storekeeper with a less conservative credit policy.[5]

---

4. The initials stand for "turn over." The "assistant manager" is ready to make a small concession to the customer, who is usually so flattered by this gesture that he offers no further resistance to the sale. For further de-scriptions of the "T.O.," see Cecil L. French, "Correlates of Success in Retail Selling," *American Journal of Sociology*, 66 (September, 1960), 128-134; and Erving Goffman, *Presentation of Self in Everyday Life* (New York: Double-day, Anchor Books, 1959), pp. 178-180.

5. The interviewers found that the stores closer to the main shopping area of 125th Street generally had more conservative credit policies than those somewhat farther away. This was indicated by the percentage of credit sales the merchants reported as defaults. The higher-rental stores

The second merchant fully understands that his colleague expects a commission and takes this into account in fixing the price.[6] As a result, the customer who happens to walk into the "wrong" store ends up paying more. In essence, he is being charged for the service of having his credit potential matched with the risk policy of a merchant.

As for the merchandise sold in these stores, the interviewers noticed that the furniture on display was of obviously poor quality. Most of all, they were struck by the absence of well-known brands of appliances in most of the stores. To find out about the sales of better-known brands, they initially asked about the volume of sales of "high-*price* lines." But this question had little meaning for the merchants, because high prices were being charged for the low-quality goods in evidence. The question had to be rephrased in terms of "high *quality*" merchandise or, as the merchants themselves refer to such goods, "custom lines." To quote from the report of these interviews:

> It became apparent that the question raised a problem of communication. We were familiar with the prices generally charged for high quality lines and began to notice that the same prices were charged for much lower quality merchandise. The markup was obviously quite different from that in other areas. The local merchants said that the sale of "custom" merchandise was limited by a slow turnover. In fact, a comparable markup on the higher quality lines would make the final price so prohibitively high that they could not be moved at all. A lower markup would be inconsistent with the risk and would result in such small profits that the business could not be continued.

The high markup on low-quality goods is thus a major device used by the merchants to protect themselves against the risks of their credit business. This policy represents a marked departure from the "normal" marketing situation. In the "normal" market, competition between merchants

near 125th Street reported default rates of 5 and 6 per cent, those six or seven blocks away, as high as 20 per cent.

6. The referring merchant does not receive his commission right away. Whether he gets it at all depends upon the customer's payment record. He will keep a record of his referrals and check on them after several months. When the merchant who has made the sale has received a certain percentage of the payments, he will give the referring merchant his commission.

results in a pricing policy roughly commensurate with the quality of the goods. It is apparent, then, that these merchants do not see themselves competing with stores outside the neighborhood. This results in the irony that the people who can least afford the goods they buy are required to pay high prices relative to quality, thus receiving a comparatively low return for their consumer dollar.

In large part, these merchants have a "captive" market because their customers do not meet the economic requirements of consumers in the larger, bureaucratic marketplace. But also, they can sell inferior goods at high prices because, in their own words, the customers are not "price and quality conscious." Interviews found that the merchants perceive their customers as unsophisticated shoppers. One merchant rather cynically explained that the amount of goods sold a customer depends not on the customer but on the merchant's willingness to extend him credit. If the merchant is willing to accept great risk, he can sell the customer almost as much as he cares to. Another merchant, commenting on the buying habits of the customer, said, "People do not shop in this area. Each person who comes into the store wants to buy something and is a potential customer. It is just up to who catches him."

The notion of "who catches him" is rather important in this economy. Merchants compete not so much in price or quality, but in getting customers to the store on other grounds. (Some of these gathering techniques will shortly be described.)

Another merchant commented rather grudgingly that the Negroes were beginning to show signs of greater sophistication by "shopping around." Presumably this practice is not followed by the newer migrants to the area.

But although the merchants are ready to exploit the naivete of their traditionalistic customers, it is important to point out that they also cater to the customer's traditionalism. As a result of the heavy influx of Puerto Ricans into the area, many of these stores now employ Puerto Rican salesmen. The customers who enter these stores need not be concerned about possible embarrassment because of their broken English or their poor dress. On the contrary, these merchants are adept at making the customer feel at ease, as a personal experience will testify.

Visiting the area and stopping occasionally to read the ads in the windows, I happened to pause before an appliance store. A salesman promptly emerged and said, "I know, I bet you're looking for a nice TV set. Come inside. We've got lots of nice ones." Finding myself thrust into the role of customer, I followed him into the store and listened to his sales-pitch. Part way through his talk, he asked my name. I hesitated a moment and then provided him with a fictitious last name, at which point he said, "No, no—no last names. What's your first name? . . . Ah, Dave; I'm Irv. We only care about first names here." When I was ready to leave after making some excuse about having to think things over, he handed me his card. Like most business cards of employees, this one had the name and address of the enterprise in large type and in small type the name of the salesman. But instead of his full name, there appeared only the amiable, "Irv."

As this episode indicates, the merchants in this low-income area are ready to personalize their services. To consumers from a more traditional society, unaccustomed to the impersonality of the bureaucratic market, this may be no small matter.

So far, we have reviewed the elements of the system of exchange that comprise the low-income market. For the consumer, these are the availability of merchandise, the "easy" installments, and the reassurance of dealing with merchants who make them feel at home. In return, the merchant reserves for himself the right to sell low-quality merchandise at exorbitant prices.

But the high markup on goods does not insure that the business will be profitable. No matter what he charges, the merchant can remain in business only if customers actually pay. In this market, the customer's intention and ability to pay—the assumptions underlying any credit system—cannot be taken for granted. Techniques for insuring continuity of payments are a fundamental part of this distinctive economy.

FORMAL CONTROLS

When the merchant uses an installment contract, he has recourse to legal controls over his customers. But as we shall see, legal controls are not sufficient to cope with the merchant's problem and they are seldom used.

Repossession.—The merchant who offers credit can always repossess his merchandise should the customer default on payments. But repossession, according to the merchants, is rare. They claim that the merchandise receives such heavy use as to become practically worthless in a short time. And no doubt the shoddy merchandise will not stand much use, heavy or light. One merchant said that he will occasionally repossess an item, not to regain his equity, but to punish a customer he feels is trying to cheat him.

Liens Against Property and Wages.—The merchant can, of course, sue the defaulting customer. By winning a court judgment, he can have the customer's property attached. Should this fail to satisfy the debt, he can take the further step of having the customer's salary garnisheed.[7] But these devices are not fully adequate for several reasons. Not all customers have property of value or regular jobs. Furthermore, their employers will not hesitate to fire them rather than submit to the nuisance of a garnishment. But since the customer knows he may lose his job if he is garnisheed, the mere threat of garnishment is sometimes enough to insure regularity of payments.[8] The main limitation with legal controls, however, is that the merchant who uses them repeatedly runs the risk of forfeiting good will in the neighborhood.

---

7. It is of some interest that the low-income families we interviewed were all familiar with the word "garnishee." This may well be one word in the language that the poorly educated are more likely to know than the better educated.

8. Welfare families cannot, of course, be garnisheed, and more than half the merchants reported that they sell to them. But the merchants can threaten to disclose the credit purchase to the welfare authorities. Since recipients of welfare funds are not supposed to buy on credit, this threat exerts powerful pressure on the family.

Discounting Paper.—The concern with good will places a limitation on the use of another legal practice open to merchants for minimizing their risk: the sale of their contracts to a credit agency at a discount. By selling his contracts to one of the licensed finance companies, the merchant can realize an immediate return on his investment. The problem with this technique is that the merchant loses control over his customer. As an impersonal, bureaucratic organization, the credit agency has recourse only to legal controls. Should the customer miss a payment, the credit agency will take the matter to court. But in the customer's mind, his contract exists with the merchant, not with the credit agency. Consequently, the legal actions taken against him reflect upon the merchant, and so good will is not preserved after all.

For this reason, the merchant is reluctant to "sell his paper," particularly if he has reason to believe that the customer will miss some payments. When he does sell some of his contracts at a discount, his motive is not to reduce risk, but rather to obtain working capital. Since so much of his capital is tied up in credit transactions, he frequently finds it necessary to make such sales. Oddly enough, he is apt to sell his better "paper," that is, the contracts of customers who pay regularly, for he wants to avoid incurring the ill will of customers. This practice also has its drawbacks for the merchant. Competitors can find out from the credit agencies which customers pay regularly and then try to lure them away from the original merchant. Some merchants reported that in order to retain control over their customers, they will buy back contracts from credit agencies they suspect are giving information to competitors.[9]

Credit Association Ratings.—All credit merchants report

9. Not all merchants are particularly concerned with good will. A few specialize in extending credit to the worst risks, customers turned away by most other merchants. These men will try to collect as much as they can on their accounts during the year and then will sell all their outstanding accounts to a finance company. As a result, the most inadequate consumers are apt to meet with the bureaucratic controls employed by the finance company. For a description of how bill collectors operate, see Hillel Black, *Buy Now, Pay Later* (New York: William Morrow and Co., 1961), chap. 4.

their bad debtors to the credit association to which they belong. The merchants interviewed said that they always consult the "skip lists" of their association before extending credit to a new customer.[10] In this way they can avoid at least the customers known to be bad risks. This form of control tends to be effective in the long run because the customers find that they are unable to obtain credit until they have made good on their past debts. During the interviews with them, some consumers mentioned this need to restore their credit rating as the reason why they were paying off debts in spite of their belief that they had been cheated.

But these various formal techniques of control are not sufficient to cope with the merchant's problem of risk. He also depends heavily on informal and personal techniques of control.

INFORMAL CONTROLS

The merchant starts from the premise that most of his customers are honest people who intend to pay but have difficulty managing their money. Missed payments are seen as more often due to poor management and to emergencies than to dishonesty. The merchants anticipate that their customers will miss some payments and they rely on informal controls to insure that payments are eventually made.

All the merchants described their credit business as operating on a "fifteen-month year." This means that they expect the customer to miss about one of every four payments and they compute the markup accordingly. Unlike the credit companies, which insist upon regular payments and add service charges for late payments, the neighborhood merchant is prepared to extend "flexible" credit. Should the customer miss an occasional payment or should he be short on another, the merchant considers this a normal part of his business.

---

10. See *Ibid.*, chap. 3, for a description of the world's largest credit association, the one serving most of the stores in the New York City area.

To insure the close personal control necessary for this system of credit, the merchant frequently draws up a contract calling for weekly payments which the customer usually brings to the store. This serves several functions for the merchant. To begin with, the sum of money represented by a weekly payment is relatively small and so helps to create the illusion of "easy credit." Customers are apt to think more of the size of the payments than of the cost of the item or the length of the contract.

More importantly, the frequent contact of a weekly-payment system enables the merchant to get to know his customer. He learns when the customer receives his pay check, when his rent is due, who his friends are, when job layoffs, illnesses, and other emergencies occur—in short, all sorts of information which allow him to interpret the reason for a missed payment. Some merchants reported that when they know the customer has missed a payment for a legitimate reason such as illness or a job layoff, they will send a sympathetic note and offer the customer a gift (an inexpensive lamp or wall picture) when payments are resumed. This procedure, they say, frequently brings the customer back with his missed payments.

The short interval between payments also functions to give the merchant an early warning when something is amiss. His chances of locating the delinquent customer are that much greater. Furthermore, the merchant can keep tabs on a delinquent customer through his knowledge of the latter's friends, relatives, neighbors, and associates, who are also apt to be customers of his. In this way, still another informal device, the existing network of social relations, is utilized by the neighborhood merchant in conducting his business.[11]

The weekly-payment system also provides the merchant

---

11. The merchant's access to these networks of social relations is not entirely independent of economic considerations. Just as merchants who refer customers receive commissions, so customers who recommend others are often given commissions. Frequently, this is why a customer will urge his friends to deal with a particular merchant.

with the opportunity to sell other items to the customer. When the first purchase is almost paid for, the merchant will try to persuade the customer to make another. Having the customer in the store, where he can look at the merchandise, makes the next sale that much easier. This system of successive sales is, of course, an ideal arrangement—for the merchant. As a result, the customer remains continuously in debt to him. The pattern is somewhat reminiscent of the Southern sharecropper's relation to the company store. And since a number of customers grew up in more traditional environments with just such economies, they may find the arrangement acceptable. The practice of buying from peddlers, found to be common in these low-income areas, also involves the principle of continuous indebtedness. The urban low-income economy, then, is in some respects like the sharecropper system; it might almost be called an "urban sharecropper system."[12]

The Customer Peddlers

Characteristic of the comparatively traditional and personal form of the low-income economy is the important role played in it by the door-to-door credit salesman, the customer peddler. The study of merchants found that these peddlers are not necessarily competitors of the store-owners. Almost all merchants make use of peddlers in the great competition for customers. The merchants tend to regard peddlers as necessary evils who add greatly to the final cost of purchases. But they need them because in their view, customers are too ignorant, frightened, or lazy to come to the stores themselves. Thus, the merchants' apparent contempt for ped-

---

12. The local merchants are not the only ones promoting continuous debt. The coupon books issued by banks and finance companies which underwrite installment contracts contain notices in the middle announcing that the consumer can, if he wishes, refinance the loan. The consumer is told, in effect, that he is a good risk because presumably he has regularly paid half the installments and that he need not wait until he has made the last payment before borrowing more money.

dlers does not bar them from employing outdoor salesman (or "canvassers," as they describe the peddlers who work for one store or another). Even the merchants who are themselves reluctant to hire canvassers find they must do so in order to meet the competition. The peddler's main function for the merchant, then, is getting the customer to the store, and if he will not come, getting the store to the customer. But this is not his only function.

Much more than the storekeeper, the peddler operates on the basis of a personal relationship with the customer. By going to the customer's home, he gets to know the entire family; he sees the condition of the home and he comes to know the family's habits and wants. From this vantage point he is better able than the merchant to evaluate the customer as a credit risk. Since many of the merchant's potential customers lack the standard credentials of credit, such as having a permanent job, the merchant needs some other basis for discriminating between good and bad risks. If the peddler, who has come to know the family, is ready to vouch for the customer, the merchant will be ready to make the transaction. In short, the peddler acts as a fiduciary agent, a Dun and Bradstreet for the poor, telling the merchant which family is likely to meet its obligations and which is not.

Not all peddlers are employed by stores. Many are independent enterprisers (who may have started as canvassers for stores).[13] A number of the independent peddlers have accumulated enough capital to supply their customers with major durables. These are the elite peddlers, known as "dealers," who buy appliances and furniture from local merchants at a "wholesale" price, and then sell them on credit to their customers. In these transactions, the peddler either takes the customer to the store or sends the customer to the store with his card on which he has written some

13. A systematic study of local merchants and peddlers would probably find that a typical career pattern is to start as a canvasser, become a self-employed peddler, and finally a storekeeper.

such message as "Please give Mr. Jones a TV set."[14] The merchant then sells the customer the TV set at a price much higher than he would ordinarily charge. The "dealer" is generally given two months to pay the merchant the "wholesale" price, and meanwhile he takes over the responsibility of collecting from his customer. Some "dealers" are so successful that they employ canvassers in their own right.[15] And some merchants do so much business with "dealers" that they come to think of themselves as "wholesalers" even though they are fully prepared to do their own retail business.

Independent peddlers without much capital also have economic relations with local merchants. They act as brokers, directing their customers to neighborhood stores that will extend them credit. And for this service they of course receive a commission. In these transactions, it is the merchant who accepts the risks and assumes the responsibility for collecting payments. The peddler who acts as a broker performs the same function as the merchant in the T.O. system. He knows which merchants will accept great risk and which will not, and directs his customers accordingly.

There are, then, three kinds of customer peddlers operating in these low-income neighborhoods who cooperate with local merchants: the canvassers who are employed

14. According to a former customer peddler, now in the furniture business, the peddlers' message will either read "Please *give* Mr. Jones . . ." or "Please let Mr. Jones *pick out* . . ." In the former case, the customer is given the merchandise right away; in the latter, it is set aside for him until the peddler says that it is all right to let the customer have it. The peddler uses the second form when his customer is already heavily in debt to him and he wants to be certain that the customer will agree to the higher weekly payments that will be necessary.

15. One tiny store in the area, with little merchandise in evidence, is reported to employ over a hundred canvassers. The owner would not consent to an interview, but the student-observers did notice that this apparently small merchant kept some four or five bookkeepers at work in a back room. The owner is obviously a "dealer" whose store is his office. As a "dealer," he has no interest in maintaining stock and displays for street trade.

directly by the stores; the small entrepreneurs who act as brokers; and the more successful entrepreneurs who operate as "dealers." A fourth type of peddler consists of salesmen representing large companies not necessarily located in the neighborhood. These men are, for the most part, canvassers for firms specializing in a particular commodity, e.g., encyclopedias, vacuum cleaners, or pots and pans. They differ from the other peddlers by specializing in what they sell and by depending more on contracts and legal controls. They are also less interested in developing continuous relationships with their customers.

Peddlers thus aid the local merchants by finding customers, evaluating them as credit risks, and helping in the collection of payments. And as the merchants themselves point out, these services add greatly to the cost of the goods. One storekeeper said that peddlers are apt to charge five and six times the amount the store charges for relatively inexpensive purchases. Pointing to a religious picture which he sells for $5, he maintained that peddlers sell it for as much as $30. And he estimated that the peddler adds 30 to 50 per cent to the final sales price of appliances and furniture.

Unethical and Illegal Practices

The interviewers uncovered some evidence that some local merchants engage in the illegal practice of selling reconditioned furniture and appliances as new. Of course, no merchant would admit that he did this himself, but five of them hinted that their competitors engaged in this practice.[16] As we shall see, several of the consumers we interviewed were quite certain that they had been victimized in this way.

---

16. Events are sometimes more telling than words. During an interview with a merchant, the interviewer volunteered to help several men who were carrying bed frames into the store. The owner excitedly told him not to help because he might get paint on his hands.

One unethical, if not illegal, activity widely practiced by stores is "bait" advertising with its concomitant, the "switch sale." In the competition for customers, merchants depend heavily upon advertising displays in their windows which announce furniture or appliances at unusually low prices. The customer may enter the store assuming that the low offer in the window signifies a reasonably low price line. Under severe pressure, the storekeeper may even be prepared to sell the merchandise at the advertised price, for not to do so would be against the law. What most often happens, however, is that the unsuspecting customer is convinced by the salesman that he doesn't really want the goods advertised in the window and is then persuaded to buy a smaller amount of more expensive goods. Generally, not much persuasion is necessary. The most popular "bait ad" is the announcement of three rooms of furniture for "only $149" or "only $199." The customer who inquires about this bargain is shown a bedroom set consisting of two cheap and (sometimes deliberately) chipped bureaus and one bed frame. He learns that the spring and mattress are not included in the advertised price, but can be had for another $75 or $100. The living-room set in these "specials" consists of a fragile-looking sofa and one un-matching chair.[17]

The frequent success of this kind of exploitation, known in the trade as the "switch sale," is reflected in this comment by one merchant: "I don't know how they do it. They advertise three rooms of furniture for $149 and the customers swarm in. *They end up buying a $400 bedroom set for $600 and none of us can believe how easy it is to make these sales.*"

In sum, a fairly intricate system of sales-and-credit has evolved in response to the distinctive situation of the low-income consumer and the local merchant. It is a system heavily slanted in the direction of a traditional economy in which informal, personal ties play a major part in the

17. In one store in which I inspected this special offer, I was told by the salesman that he would find a chair that was a "fairly close match."

transaction. At the same time it is connected to impersonal bureaucratic agencies through the instrument of the installment contract. Should the informal system break down, credit companies, courts of law, and agencies of law enforcement come to play a part.

The system is not only different from the larger, more formal economy; in some respects it is a *deviant* system in which practices that violate prevailing moral standards are commonplace. As Merton has pointed out in his analysis of the political machine, the persistence of deviant social structures can only be understood when their social functions (as well as dysfunctions) are taken into account.[18] The basic function of the low-income marketing system is to provide consumer goods to people who fail to meet the requirements of the more legitimate, bureaucratic market, or who choose to exclude themselves from the larger market because they do not feel comfortable in it. As we have seen, the system is extraordinarily flexible. Almost no one —however great a risk—is turned away. Various mechanisms sift and sort customers according to their credit risk and match them with merchants ready to sell them the goods they want. Even the family on welfare is permitted to maintain its self-respect by consuming in much the same way as do its social peers who happen not to be on welfare. Whether the system, with its patently exploitative features, can be seriously altered without the emergence of more legitimate institutions to perform its functions, is a question to be considered at length in the concluding chapter of this book.

In the following chapters, certain themes running through this account of the low-income market will be systematically examined from the viewpoint of the consumers. It appears, for example, that there are enough consumers of these goods to support the many stores. But

18. Robert K. Merton, *Social Theory and Social Structure,* rev. ed. (New York: The Free Press of Glencoe, 1957), pp. 71-82.

to what extent are low-income families oriented toward major durables? Which types of families are heavy consumers and which are not? What proportions of low-income families buy from neighborhood stores and from peddlers? How do the families with broader shopping horizons differ from those who buy only in the neighborhood? What prices do low-income families pay for their appliances and how do their shopping decisions affect the prices they pay? Since credit is the mainstay of the neighborhood merchant, which types of families make use of credit? And how do the consumers experience the pressures exerted upon them by the merchants? What sales gimmicks have resulted in the purchase of initially unwanted goods, and which families are particularly vulnerable to these gimmicks? What do low-income families do when they get into trouble as consumers? To what extent are they aware of community agencies that can help them with their problems as consumers, and how often do they make use of them? In short, we must still find out how the system of sales-and-credit is experienced by the consumers.

CHAPTER 3

Buying Patterns:
Purchases of
Major Durables

KNOWING NOTHING more of these families than their generally small income, we would understandably suppose that they could not possibly be consumers of many high-cost durables. At most, our reasoning might run that they must turn to the second-hand market for such indispensable possessions as furniture. But as we have begun to see, intricate arrangements of credit have evolved, based largely on networks of social relations, that lessen the risks to local merchants, that allow and even encourage low-income consumers to buy the possessions they have learned to want. How many of these families, then, are consumers of major durables? The answer is that the great majority are and that furthermore, most buy new rather than used goods.

To appreciate the full extent of this consumption of durable goods, we must examine separately their purchases of furniture and of household appliances. Since most families moved into public housing fairly recently—generally within a span of six years before the survey—they had particular need for furniture. Some 86 per cent of the sample moved in within this six-year period; almost half had been living in the project for less than four years, and 20 per cent for less than two years. The record of their purchases of furniture may more nearly reflect the special needs of public housing families rather than a general orientation of the low-income group toward major durables. But the ownership of automobiles is not at all (and of appliances only to a limited extent) linked to residence in public housing or to the matter of moving into new quarters. The frequency of purchases of such goods more nearly reflects the tastes and wants of low-income families rather than those specific to life in public housing.

Purchases of Furniture

The buying of furniture tends to increase when families move. For low-income families moving into public housing this general tendency is apt to be intensified. Some families had no furniture of their own, having lived only with relatives or in furnished rooms before moving to the project. (Almost three in every ten families did not have their own apartment before the move.) And for many, the project apartment so greatly improved upon their previous dwelling that they could not bring themselves to mar their new apartment with old furniture.[1]

Remembering their recent move to the projects, these families could readily recall their furniture problems at the time of the move.[2] Most (78 per cent) had brought some furniture with them from their previous apartment. But almost as many (73 per cent) also bought furniture when they moved into the project. The general practice was to buy sets of furniture rather than isolated pieces. The extent of these purchases is summarized in Table 3.1.

The heavy expenditure for furniture touched off by the

---

1. When asked to compare their project apartment with their previous dwelling, 90 per cent of the interviewed residents said they liked the project apartment better.

2. These questions were not asked of the thirty-five Vladeck families who had been living in the project for more than ten years.

Table 3.1—Amount of Furniture Acquired at Time of Move
(In Per Cent)

None	27
One set	19
Two sets	19
Three, four sets	27
Pieces only	7
Gifts of furniture only	1
Total per cent	100
Total cases	(422)[a]

a. Excluded are the thirty-five long established residents of Vladeck and seven others who did not give this information.

move is evidenced by the 65 per cent who bought at least one set of furniture, and especially by the 27 per cent who bought sets for three or four rooms, presumably furnishing their entire apartment at once. Local merchants are thoroughly aware of this practice; and indeed they help establish it, for they advertise three sets of furniture—for the bedroom, living room, and kitchen—at a single price.

The meaning attached by these families to their *new* apartments is perhaps best symbolized by a substantial 80 per cent who bought new furniture only; another 8 per cent bought furniture that was for the most part new, leaving only 12 per cent who wholly or mostly limited their purchases to used furniture.

The Cost of Furniture

Those who did buy furniture at the time of the move spent an average of about $500. The median figure is $135 for the few families that bought only pieces of furniture, and steadily increases to about $850 for those who bought three or four sets. This can be seen from Table 3.2. (Not all cases are represented in this table because some simply did not know, even approximately, the cost of the furniture.)

It will be noticed that 16 per cent of all the furniture-buyers, and about a third of those buying a full complement of sets, paid $1,000 or more. At times, the expenditures ran to over $1,500. Otherwise put, a few families spent upwards of half of their yearly income equipping their apartment with new furniture. But of course they could seldom pay for it in cash. Later we shall see how most of these families turned to one or another kind of credit in order to furnish their apartments.

Furniture Bought Since the Move

Beyond this great majority who bought furniture at the time of the move, almost half (45 per cent) went on to buy furniture after moving into the projects. A good many of these families had not bought any when they first moved in, but an even larger number had.

Pooling the available information, we find that only a small fraction (12 per cent) did not buy furniture either when they moved or since. Another 43 per cent made purchases only initially, and 16 per cent only since the move. But 29 per cent made furniture purchases at the beginning and afterwards. Although many of these families were replacing old furniture brought from their previous apartment, a number of others were already replacing furniture

Table 3.2—Expenditures for Furniture at Time of Move[a]
(In Per Cent)

Cost	Pieces only	1 Set	2 Sets	3, 4 Sets	Total
Under $100	42	13	3	—	8
$100-$299	46	31	21	5	19
$300-$499	8	36	28	13	23
$500-$699	4	11	23	20	17
$700-$999	—	8	17	28	17
$1,000-$1,499	—	1	8	28	13
$1,500-$1,999	—	—	—	4	2
$2,000 and over	—	—	—	2	1
Total per cent	100	100	100	100	100
Median Expenditure	$135	$335	$490	$850	$500
Total cases	(26)	(75)	(77)	(110)	(288)

a. Time period: 1954-1960.

bought at the time of the move. From the amount of furniture acquired at the two time periods we can roughly estimate the number of families that replaced a *complete set* of furniture bought when they first moved to the projects. For example, fifteen families who had bought three or four sets when they moved have since bought another set; six families who bought at least three sets initially have since bought at least two; and seven families who originally bought two sets have since bought two or more. On this basis we find that at least thirty families, 7 per cent of all the initial furniture-buyers, have replaced sets of furniture which they could not have had for more than six years, and in most instances only three, four, or five years. The speed of replacement suggests either a substandard quality of the new furniture, extraordinarily intensive use, aspirations for new furniture, or a composite of all these.

The tendency to purchase only new furniture is somewhat more marked among those who bought after they had lived in the project for a time. Nine in ten of these purchases involved only new furniture, compared with eight in ten at the time of the move. When it comes to furniture, at least, these low-income families do not patronize the second-hand stores.

As we have noted, the impact of the move is presumably greater in the matter of buying furniture, and so the consumer activity of these families cannot be gauged by this alone. Ownership of household appliances and automobiles can round out this account of the buying of major durables by low-income families.

Appliance Ownership

Respondents were asked to report their ownership of an automobile and five relatively expensive household appliances: a television set, phonograph, sewing machine, vacuum cleaner, and washing machine. These particular appliances were selected after exploratory interviews showed them to be fairly common among families in the projects. Deepfreezers and air conditioners were not considered for a simple enough reason: the management of the projects does not permit families to have them.

Here are some indications of the extent to which these families are consumers of major durables:

> Ninety-five per cent of the families—all but twenty-five of the 464 interviewed—own at least one television set.
>
> Sixty-three per cent have a phonograph—about half owning one separate from their TV set, and another 12 per cent owning a television-phonograph console.
>
> Forty-two per cent own a sewing machine.
>
> Forty-one per cent have an automatic washing machine.
>
> Twenty-eight per cent own a vacuum cleaner.
>
> Fourteen per cent own an automobile.

We all know that television has swiftly become defined as a necessity in the American home. We see now that unlike the merely utilitarian vacuum cleaner, sewing machine, or washer, it is regarded as a prime necessity by these low-income families, practically all of them possessors of television sets. In fact, the 95 per cent of set-owners among these families, which include a substantial proportion in the lower-income range of the working class, is about the same as that found among samples of working-class families in the country at large, these including many skilled workers and home owners.[3] Among the appliances for the everyday life of these low-income families, television alone is ubiquitous; and only second to television is the phonograph, which is found in two thirds of these apartments. As much as any other statistics, these figures reflect the style of life of these young families. There is an accent on entertainment brought into the home by modern technology.

That two out of every five families should own a washing machine may at first be puzzling since each of the

3. See Lee Rainwater *et al.*, *Workingman's Wife* (New York: Oceana Publications Inc., 1959), p. 183.

projects provides communal laundry rooms. But the housewives themselves quickly dispel the puzzlement. Many families are so large that the housewife needs to use a washing
machine practically every day. Some of the buildings do
not have a laundry room and many housewives have to
travel some distance to and from the laundry room, a trip
made more inconvenient by the inordinately slow elevators
in the projects. And since the machines are coin-operated,
the housewife who deposits her dimes and quarters several
times a week soon hits upon the idea that for little more
she can pay the installments on her own machine. Convenience and economy, rather than indulgent overexpendi-
ture, dictate the decision to acquire a washer of their own
rather than to use the public washers.

The consumer activity of these low-income families
can be compared with that of other strata, at least with respect to TV sets and automatic washing machines. A survey
was made in 1957 of 10 thousand households in New York
City and suburbs with an average income considerably
higher than that in our sample. Two thirds of the households had incomes over $5,000; a quarter, over $7,000. Yet
the extent of ownership of television sets and automatic
washing machines differed only a little between our sample
and the general population of the area. The general survey
found that 88 per cent of the families in New York City
owned TV sets in 1957, compared with 95 per cent of our
low-income families in 1960; and that 50 per cent owned
automatic washing machines, compared with 41 per cent
of our sample.[4]

Nationwide surveys of consumers conducted for the Federal Reserve Board found that 14 per cent of all spending
units in the country purchased TV sets in 1960 and 11 per
cent purchased washing machines.[5] In the year preceding

---

4. I am indebted to Mr. Herbert Steele of the New York *Daily News* for
making these data available from the report entitled *Profile of the Millions*,
produced for the *Daily News* by W. R. Simmons and Associates.

5. *Federal Reserve Bulletin*, May, 1961. The figures are based on the
summation of quarterly surveys conducted during 1960.

our interviews, some 18 per cent of the families in our low-rent projects bought TV sets and 13 per cent bought washing machines, thus exceeding the national average.

It is hard to assess the comparative frequency of automobile ownership among the project families. The 14 per cent in our sample who have automobiles is far below the 74 per cent of car-owning families in the United States as a whole.[6] But the proportion of households with automobiles in the five boroughs of New York City is also far below the national figures, running to about 40 per cent. And although statistics are not available for the separate boroughs, Manhattan, of all the boroughs, undoubtedly has the smallest proportion of car owners. Nevertheless, it is evident that, unlike TV sets and perhaps other household appliances, automobiles are considerably less common among these low-income families.

Most of the appliances owned by these families were relatively new. From 17 to 32 per cent of them were only about a year old, and most of the rest had been acquired within the last five years. In part, this may result from the circumstances that many of the families were newly established and that most had moved into the projects within the past five years. Both circumstances would normally intensify the need or desire for appliances. But it is also possible that the relative newness of the appliances reflects a cycle of rapid replacement owing to the poor quality of the goods bought. In any case, a comparison with the metropolitan New York survey shows that a far greater proportion of the project families have relatively new television sets and washing machines than is true for the general population. Seventy-two per cent of the television sets owned by the low-income sample were less than six years old, compared with 51 per cent in the metropolitan survey; the comparable figures for washing machines are 80 per cent and 56 per cent.

Whether old or new, appliances are frequent in the

6. Comparative data were provided by the American Automobile Association.

households of these projects, as can be seen from the summary in Table 3.3. From the first column we learn that

Table 3.3—*Distribution of Families According to Number of Appliances Owned and Number Acquired in Last Five Years*[a]

(In Per Cent)

	Appliances Owned	Appliances Acquired in Last Five Years
None	2	13
One	16	29
Two	28	30
Three	28	18
Four	20	9
Five	6	1
Total per cent	100	100
Total cases	(464)	(464)

a. A combination TV and phonograph is counted as two appliances in this tally.

only 2 per cent of the families (nine out of 464) do not own any of these five household appliances. At the other extreme are 6 per cent (thirty families) owning all five. More than half the families have at least three of the appliances, and about a quarter have at least four. Although 13 per cent did not buy any of these appliances in the last five years, the average family acquired two during this period, and more than a quarter obtained at least three.[7]

As was true of furniture, the great majority of the families purchased their appliances new rather than used. Eighty-three per cent of the TV sets, phonographs, and vacuum cleaners were new; so were 78 per cent of the washing machines and 67 per cent of the sewing machines. Furthermore, the fact that some families owned used appliances does not necessarily mean that they bought them at a second-hand store. As we shall see in the next chapter, some families bought their appliances from friends or relatives or else received them as gifts.

---

7. Automobile ownership is not considered in this count of major durables. The data show, however, that car owners are much more likely than nonowners to have many appliances.

Not only do they strongly prefer new appliances, but they are inclined to buy the more expensive models. Seventy-two per cent of the TV sets, for example, are the more costly consoles rather than table or portable models. Almost two thirds of the phonographs are also the more expensive consoles.

The preference for new and more expensive models points toward something more than a strictly utilitarian interest in these appliances. It has all the earmarks of what we have described as "compensatory consumption." Their usefulness matters of course, but beyond that these appliances evidently express their owners' aspirations for status. We see this motive, for example, at work in the case of a Negro housewife explaining that her very new $500 stereophonic hi-fi console was a "piece of furniture, not just a phonograph." Another bit of evidence points to a pattern of compensatory consumption among these families. Although the interview did not inquire into their having a telephone, the interviewers were instructed to take note of observed telephones and particularly of that new symbol of gracious living, telephones in color. The interviewers observed a telephone in 175 apartments, and in a sizeable 23 per cent of these it was of the colored variety.[8] This is a case of purely nonutilitarian consumption, with the added cost ensuring nothing by way of greater utility.

Plans for Purchases

In assembling the evidence that the families in the projects tend to be active consumers of high-cost durables—as their income would not lead us to expect—we have focused on the major purchases they have already made. But another aspect of "consumer activity" is the extent to which they plan to make major purchases in the future.

With this in mind, interviewers asked whether there

---

8. Undoubtedly many other families owned telephones not visible to the interviewers.

were any things which the families felt they should, but did not, own. Those replying in the affirmative were asked to name the things and whether they planned to buy any of them in the course of the next year. Although the question referred only to things not currently owned, the frequent mention of furniture in the response indicates that many understood it to apply to replacement purchases as well.[9] Three of every four answered the question in the affirmative, mentioning at least one commodity they would like to have. The frequency with which various items were mentioned can be seen in Table 3.4.

Table 3.4—Consumption Aspirations of the Low-Income Families

Category	Number of Mentions	Per Cent of Sample
Furniture (including rugs and linoleum)	214	46
Labor-saving appliances (washing machine, sewing machine, vacuum cleaner)	199	43
Entertainment appliances (television and phonograph)	62	13
House	29	6
Automobile	27	6
Clothing	24	5
Other (e.g., larger apartment, jewelry, encyclopedias, etc.)	22	5
Total per cent		124[a]

a. The percentages add up to more than 100 because each family could name more than one item. It will be remembered that 26 per cent of the families did not express any aspiration for possessions they did not have.

The desire for more furniture looms largest in the consumption plans of the project families, and was mentioned by almost half of them. This category includes linoleum and rugs, as well as more beds—chiefly for children. Nevertheless, many of those who mentioned furniture indicated

9. The question read: "Are there any things that you feel you should own that you don't own now?" The phrase "should own" was deliberately used in order to get at norms of consumption. The wording may of course invite aspirations in fantasy, but the frequency with which furniture and appliances were mentioned suggests that most responded in terms of realistic buying intentions.

that they meant replacements, once again testifying to the felt inadequacies of the furniture on hand.

Labor-saving appliances, especially washing machines, were almost as popular as furniture. (Presumably television sets and phonographs were mentioned less often because most families already owned these.)

Although three of four families have these consumer aspirations, they did not necessarily plan to realize them in the near future. The twenty-nine families who mentioned a house of their own, for example, were probably referring to long-range aspirations rather than to immediate plans. Some indication of the time perspective underlying these aspirations is obtained from the second part of the question. When asked whether they intended to buy any of the things to which they aspired within the next year, about a third of the families answered in the affirmative; another 17 per cent were not sure that it would be that soon; 22 per cent more were quite certain that it would be more than a year; and 26 per cent did not expect to buy major durables in the foreseeable future.

This considerable interest in further purchases at once raises the question: Is consumer activity in the past related to activity expected in the future? It is easy enough to conjure up opposite possibilities. On the one hand, we might suppose that the people who do not feel there is anything more they should own are those who already have most of the major household appliances. On the other hand, some people are presumably more consumption-minded than others, having many possessions and wanting still more. The facts of the matter, shown in Table 3.5, suggest that both tendencies may be working at cross purposes, for there is little relationship between consumption in the past as measured by appliance ownership and plans for the future.

It is true that the families most inclined to say they need nothing else are those who already own at least four major appliances. But those who own as many as three are *most* likely to want more, even beyond those who have

**Table 3.5—Consumption Plans According to Number
of Appliances Owned**

(In Per Cent)

Number of Objects They "Should Own"	Number of Appliances Owned			
	0-1	2	3	4-5
None	22	26	17	31
Mentions one	35	35	47	35
Mentions two or more	43	39	36	34
Total per cent	100	100	100	100
Total cases	(82)	(130)	(130)	(122)

hardly any appliances. The tendency to want two or more
additional commodities decreases somewhat with the number of appliances owned, but this tendency is slight. The
fact is that the future consumers are distributed in roughly
the same proportion throughout the range of current ownership of appliances.

So far, we have seen that most of the families are active
consumers of major durables. They do not limit their high-
cost purchases to the time of the move when furniture needs
are particularly great. Many of them continue to buy furniture and household appliances and, as we have just seen,
most of them expect to make major purchases in the future
—many within the next year.

At the same time, it is evident that not all of the families
are equally active as consumers of major durables. Some
own hardly any appliances and some own four or five. In
short, within the broad category of low-income families,
consumer activity varies widely. This leads directly to the
question: What kinds of families tend to be active consumers?

The Active Consumers

In order to characterize the families actively engaged
in buying durable goods, it is convenient to have a single
measure of consumer activity. One such index was developed by combining the number of appliances owned with

data on consumer aspirations. Families were first scored as low, medium, or high on appliance ownership and were then given one of three scores according to the immediacy of their purchasing plans. Those without any plans were placed in the category of "low," those definitely planning a major purchase within the year in the category of "high," and those who were indefinite about when they would buy what they want, or knew that it would not be for at least a year, were placed in the "medium" category. These two sets of categories combined give the following distribution of consumer activity among these families:

Consumer Activity	Number of Cases	Per Cent of Sample
Very high	43	9
High	131	28
Medium	182	40
Low	90	19
Very low	18	4
Totals	464	100

The highly active consumers may be thought of as the 37 per cent who have a high or very high score on this index.[10] As Table 3.6 shows, they tend to be the large families, the young families, the higher-income families, and the nonwhite families.

Most of these characteristics are, in turn, related to each other. For example, the nonwhite families tend to be younger and larger in size than the whites. In fact, when either age of head or family size is taken into account, nonwhites are not consistently more active consumers than the whites. Among families where the head is under 40, the white families are slightly more active, and among the older families, the Negroes are more active consumers than the whites and Puerto Ricans.

Family size and age of the head are closely associated, and it is the younger households that have most of the

10. Although based only on appliance ownership and consumer plans, this index is highly related to other indicators of consumer activity—for example furniture purchases since the move and automobile ownership.

Table 3.6—Characteristics of Active Consumers
(Per Cent Highly Active)

Family Size	Per Cent	Number	Age of Head	Per Cent	Number
1-2 persons	8	(63)	20-29	46	(93)
3 persons	36	(86)	30-39	49	(158)
4 persons	42	(127)	40-49	35	(112)
5 or more	45	(188)	50 and over	15	(101)

Income	Per Cent	Number	Race	Per Cent	Number
Under $2,500	23	(101)	White	27	(115)
$2,500-$3,499	37	(151)	Negro	44	(133)
$3,500-$4,499	44	(124)	Puerto Rican	40	(216)
$4,500 and over	46	(88)			

young children. Taken together, these characteristics indicate that the active consumers tend to be in the early stages of the family life-cycle. Many of them are still in the process of establishing households so that their interest in consumer goods and need for them is understandably marked.

It is hardly surprising that size of income and consumer activity are also related. If family size indicates a need for consumption, income indicates the means for consumption. How then, do both of these in conjunction—income and family size—relate to consumer activity?[11] When we classify families jointly on both characteristics we are, of course, approximating a measure of per capita income. Small families with relatively large incomes are presumably in better financial positions than large families with the same income. Thus, if income alone determines the extent of consumption, the most active consumers would be the small, relatively high-income families; and the least active, the large, relatively low-income families. The extent to which this reasoning applies to the empirical data can be seen from Table 3.7 which shows the joint association of income and family size on consumption.

The findings in Table 3.7 do not support the expectation that per capita family income primarily affects the

---

11. Because of the rules of the housing projects which take family size into account when determining income ceilings, income and family size are closely related.

**Table 3.7—Joint Association of Income and Family Size
with Consumer Activity**[a]

(Per Cent Highly Active)

INCOME	FAMILY SIZE					
	1-3 Persons		4 Persons		5 or more Persons	
Under $3,000	19	(79)	41	(46)	43	(49)
$3,000—$3,999	26	(46)	36	(42)	49	(53)
$4,000 and over	38	(24)	49	(39)	44	(82)

a. A word of explanation about this kind of table is in order. Unlike the earlier tables, three variables are represented here: family size, income, and consumer activity. The percentages refer to highly active consumers in each income and family-size group. The number of cases on which the percentages are based appear in parentheses. In this kind of table the indicated percentages do not, of course, add to 100. The proportion of less active consumers in each group can be determined by subtracting each percentage from 100.

extent of consumption. Only among the smallest families do we find consumer activity increasing with income. Among the medium-sized and relatively large families, increased income does not consistently lead to greater consumption. Moreover, the rows in Table 3.7 show that on each income level it is the larger rather than the smaller families who are the more active consumers. It is clear then, that within this band of "low-income families," *need,* as indicated by family size, affects the extent of consumption, independently of income.[12] This is not as self-evident as it might at first seem. Need must somehow be translated into consumption for this pattern to hold. How then are these families able to realize their needs for major durables when they lack the necessary income? They cannot easily ignore the basic necessities of food, rent, and clothing, which are all the greater because of their size. Bridging the gap between current income and extensive needs and aspirations is the institution of credit, the institution which, in its local version, we examined in Chapter 2 from the viewpoint of the

12. It will be remembered that the index of consumer activity consists of both appliance ownership and consumption plans. One objection might be that the large but poor families appear as active consumers because of their consumption *plans* rather than because of goods they have already bought. But when appliance ownership alone is considered, the same patterns are found. The large families actually own more appliances than the small families of the same income.

merchant's role in it. Were this a cash economy only, different patterns would probably have been uncovered in Table 3.7.

Overriding all else in this chapter is the fact that the low-income families in our sample turn out to be active consumers of major durables. In large part this is so because they are in the stages of the family life-cycle where consumer needs are great. As we have just seen, need, independent of income, markedly affects the extent of such consumption. We have found, too, that contrary to what their economic position might seem to imply, these families are strongly oriented toward new, rather than used, furniture and appliances, and tend to prefer the more expensive models. This suggests that their consumer activity is not only a matter of need but also one of embellishing their status by consumers' goods. In place of actual movement up the social ladder, they turn to symbols of status in a pattern of "compensatory consumption." It is almost as though consumption compensates for status deprivations they have experienced in other spheres of life.

CHAPTER 4

Shopping Patterns I:
Scope of Shopping

IN THIS CHAPTER we look at the places where low-income families buy their durable goods. What is the geographical scope of their shopping, their use of stores in the neighborhood and "downtown"? How many shop in the neighborhood, and how many frequent the more bureaucratic stores outside? What kinds of stores do they go to when they leave the neighborhood? Finally, how do the people with broader scope for their shopping differ from those who shop mainly in the neighborhood?[1]

---

1. The idea of scope of shopping investigated in this chapter was first discussed by Jahoda, Lazarsfeld, and Zeisel in their classic study of the unemployed of Marienthal. They noticed that lower-class families tended to limit their shopping to stores within a narrow radius.. This, they concluded, was part of a more general tendency toward a restricted "life-space" or "effective scope" that characterizes lower-class people.

The poor consumer is less psychologically mobile, less active, more inhibited in his behavior than the well-to-do consumer. The radius of stores he considers for possible purchases is always smaller. The poorer people more often buy at the same store. . . . Their food habits are more rigid and less subject to seasonal variations. . . . It is part of this reduction in effective scope that the interest in other than essential details is lost; the requirements in regard to quality, appearance and other features of merchandise are the less specific and frequent the more we deal with consumers from lower social strata. [Marie Jahoda, Paul F. Lazarsfeld, and Hans Zeisel, *Die Arbeitslosen von Marienthal* ("The Unemployed of Marienthal") (Allensback und Bonn, Germany: Verlag für Demoskopie, 1960).

The Sources of Durables

A number of families reported that they either received appliances as a gift or else bought them from friends or relatives. Depending upon the kind of appliance, this group ranges from about 15 to 25 per cent of the owners. Low-income families possibly rely on these personal sources for their appliances to a greater extent than higher-income families. Nevertheless, pretest interviews found that the report of these as "gift" is not always true. Welfare families are apt to claim that their appliances are gifts in order to circumvent the rules forbidding such purchases. In any case, our data show that welfare families are more likely than others to report that their new appliances were gifts.

Table 4.1 shows the proportion buying their appliances from a commercial source, or receiving them as gifts or through purchases from friends.

Table 4.1—Commercial Versus Personal Sources of Appliances
(In Per Cent)

	TV Set	Phonograph	Sewing Machine	Vacuum Cleaner	Washing Machine
Commercial source	73	65	56	61	71
Personal sources	16	22	26	19	23
No information	11	13	18	20	6
Total Per Cent	100	100	100	100	100
Total cases	(440)	(239)	(193)	(129)	(187)

The exact proportion relying on commercial sources cannot be determined because information is missing for a sizable number of cases.[2] But it is quite likely that the pro-

2. There are two reasons for this gap in information. During the early stages of field work, interviewers were instructed not to obtain detailed information on appliances that were more than five years old. This rule was changed after about a quarter of the interviews had been completed. Furthermore, in even more cases, the respondent, frequently the wife, simply did not know where the appliance was obtained. In most of these cases it can be assumed that the respondent did not know the name of the store, not whether it was obtained from a commercial source. If the family owned the appliance, the interviewee was asked, "Where did you get it?" The

portion obtaining their appliances from commercial sources is somewhat greater than these data suggest. This is all the more so since some of the alleged gifts were really bought in a store.

Families were asked to name the store where the appliance was bought and whether it was located in the neighborhood. The distribution of families according to their own definition of whether they shopped in or out of the neighborhood is shown in Table 4.2.

Table 4.2—Frequency of "In Neighborhood" and "Out of Neighborhood" Purchases of Appliances

(In Per Cent)

Respondent's Definition of Location	APPLIANCE				
	TV Set	Phonograph	Sewing Machine	Vacuum Cleaner	Washing Machine
"In neighborhood"	47	44	34	61	41
"Out of neighborhood"	53	56	66	39	59
Total per cent	100	100	100	100	100
Total cases[a]	(303)	(144)	(101)	(70)	(126)

a. "Don't knows" and no answers are excluded from the table.

Table 4.2 shows a slight tendency for these families to purchase appliances outside of the neighborhood. But these figures, too, must be treated with caution, for there is reason to assume that the "out of neighborhood" proportions are exaggerated. First, some of the families purchased the appliance in their old neighborhood before moving into the project or else returned to their old neighborhood to make the purchase.[3] Second, some of the fami-

---

intent of the question was to find out the name of the store in which the purchase was made. It was at this point that some disclosed that their appliance was a gift or had been purchased from a friend.

3. The high proportion of "out of neighborhood" responses for the sewing machines is probably due to the fact that almost half of the machines are more than five years old and were probably bought in the old neighborhood. The high percentage of "in neighborhood" responses for the vacuum cleaner is a result of the common practice of buying this item from door-to-door salesmen.

lies in East Harlem consider the 125th Street stores to be out of their neighborhood; this is particularly the case for those living in Washington Houses which is located between 97th and 104th Streets. It would be a mistake, then, to interpret "out of neighborhood" as referring only to the large down-town stores. Yet even with this liberal definition, we find that 47 per cent of the television sets, for example, were purchased in the neighborhood.

Since most families own more than one appliance, the proportion who have bought at least one of these outside the neighborhood can not be read in Table 4.2. This figure was found to be 52 per cent of the entire sample. Thus, even under the respondents' extended conception of "out of the neighborhood," almost half the families acquired all the appliances they owned within the neighborhood.

A more precise picture of the scope of sources is obtained when we consider the type of store in which appliances are bought. The sources mentioned by respondents were classified as department stores, discount houses, chain stores, independent neighborhood dealers, or peddlers. The category of department store includes not only large ones like Macy's, Gimbels, and Bloomingdales, but a number of somewhat smaller ones. Discount houses include several small stores as well as the two largest in the city, Korvette and Masters. "Chain store" refers to Vim, Davega, and similar appliance chains that do a large credit business and advertise "easy-payment" plans. Table 4.3 shows the frequency of these types of sources for each appliance.

Quite clearly, department stores and discount houses are not major sources of appliances for these families. When they do not buy in neighborhood stores or from peddlers they tend to go to chain stores. The ubiquitous salesman of vacuum cleaners, moving from door to door, shows up amply in the category of peddler, accounting, it will be noted, for more than half of these appliances.

Comparative data from the 1957 *Daily News* Survey point up a striking difference between the shopping patterns of these low-income families and the population-at-

Table 4.3—Source of Appliances[a]
(In Per Cent)

Source	TV Set	Phonograph	Sewing Machine	Vacuum Cleaner	Washing Machine
Department store	9	11	16	11	16
Discount house	4	6	—	—	9
Chain store	36	33	35	19	35
Independent neighborhood dealer[b]	45	42	34	11	33
Peddler	6	8	15	59	7
Total per cent	100	100	100	100	100
Total cases	(273)	(132)	(86)	(63)	(114)

a. This table is based on fewer cases than Table 4.2 since a number of interviewees could not name the store, although they did know whether or not it was in the neighborhood.

b. Independent dealers are all stores which are not department stores, chain stores, or discount houses. They are almost always neighborhood stores, and we will frequently refer to them as such.

large in New York City. About the same proportion in both samples buy appliances from neighborhood dealers. But when low-income families leave the neighborhood for shopping they go to chain stores, unlike the general population which goes to discount houses. The comparisons are shown in Table 4.4. (Peddler purchases by our families have been grouped under independent dealer in this table since the 1957 survey did not have an equivalent category.)

Perhaps low-income families do not know about discount houses. But a more important reason for their distinctive buying pattern, we believe, is the matter of credit.

Table 4.4—Low-Income Sources of Appliances Compared With All of New York Area Population
(In Per Cent)

Source	TELEVISION SET		WASHING MACHINE	
	Daily News Survey	Low-Income Sample	Daily News Survey	Low-Income Sample
Department store	12	9	19	16
Discount house	33	4	31	9
Chain store	6	36	6	35
Independent neighborhood dealer and Peddlers	49	51	44	40
Total per cent	100	100	100	100

The chain stores offer "easy" credit to low-income families, unlike the discount houses which, until recently, did only a cash business.[4]

Social Variations in Shopping Scope

We have seen that about half the families, according to their own conception of "neighborhood," bought at least one appliance outside their neighborhood. This reported practice has been combined with a reported preference and shopping pattern to provide a crude measure of the geographical scope of each family's shopping. Asked whether they preferred to shop in neighborhood stores or in big "downtown" stores, about two in every five expressed a preference for neighborhood stores, roughly the same proportion choosing downtown stores, with the others giving a qualified answer. The third item used in the index of scope is where the wife or mother ordinarily buys her clothes. Roughly half the women said they bought their clothes in downtown stores, for the most part in one or another of the large department stores.[5] These three items of practice and attitude are closely associated. Families who have bought at least one appliance outside the neighborhood also tend to prefer downtown stores for purchasing in general, and the women in these households tend to shop for clothes in these stores. By combining these items, we can roughly assess the shopping scope of these families:

Index of Shopping Scope[a]	Per Cent	Number
Marked in-neighborhood orientation	20	94
Moderate in-neighborhood orientation	22	99
Moderate out-of-neighborhood orientation	30	140
Marked out-of-neighborhood orientation	28	131
Totals	100	464

a. Families were first scored 0 or 1 on each of the three items, the final index being the sum of these scores.

---

4. Discount houses, including the largest ones, have recently entered the credit field. Most of them have arrangements with banks, which take over the responsibility for the installment contract. To be eligible, the credit customer must, of course, satisfy the bank's rather stringent credit requirements.

5. The source of the woman's clothes was used rather than the man's because husbands are missing in a fair number of these families.

Various characteristics of families are associated with the breadth of their shopping scope: family income, age of household head, the extent of his education, the length of time the family has lived in New York City, and race. The higher the family income, the greater the education of the head, and the younger his age, the greater the tendency of the family to shop out of the neighborhood. Families that have been living in New York City for a long time, or where the head grew up in a city, also have wider shopping horizons. Puerto Rican families restrict their shopping to neighborhood stores more frequently than either white or Negro families; Negroes in the sample, since they tend to be younger than whites, are oriented most of all to the stores outside the neighborhood. These relationships are summarized in Table 4.5.

As we examine these characteristics related to broad shopping scope we gain the impression that sophistication in the ways of urban society is a major determinant. This is variously implied by the strong effect of education, by the length of time in the city, by the size of community

Table 4.5—Characteristics of Families Related to Shopping Scope

(Per Cent Intermediate or Broad Shopping Scope)

Income	Per Cent	Number	Education	Per Cent	Number
Under $2,500	49	(101)	Grade school	45	(220)
$2,500-$3,500	53	(151)	Some high school	68	(155)
$3,500-$4,500	62	(124)	High school graduate	71	(61)
$4,500 and over	74	(88)	Beyond high school	94	(18)

Age of Head	Per Cent	Number	Length of Time in New York City	Per Cent	Number
20-29	66	(93)	Under ten years	50	(114)
30-39	70	(158)	More than ten years	59	(278)
40-49	63	(112)	Born in New York City	68	(77)
50 and over	45	(101)			

Community of Origin	Per Cent	Number	Race	Per Cent	Number
Small town or farm	51	(215)	White	60	(115)
City	66	(238)	Negro	76	(133)
			Puerto Rican	47	(216)

of origin, and by the difference between the more recent migrants—the Puerto Ricans and other ethnic and racial groups. In further support of this interpretation is the bearing of proficiency in the English language on shopping scope. Among families in which the housewife's command of English was rated as good by the interviewer, 73 per cent were oriented to non-neighborhood stores, compared with only 40 per cent of the families in which English was substandard.[6]

Apart from the matter of assimilation to the city's culture, the findings of Table 4.5 suggest that the extent of consumer activity also affects shopping scope. The comparatively small proportion of the older families oriented outside the neighborhood probably reflects the lower level of consumer activity among older families. (The sheer inconvenience of extended shopping trips may of course be another factor.) The marked association of income levels and shopping scope also suggests that consumer activity is a factor, for we already know that income is associated with the extent of consumption. These intimations are borne out by Table 4.6, which shows a positive relationship between consumer activity and shopping scope.

In large part, the association between consumer activity and shopping scope is due to the greater sophistication and economic resources of the more active consumers, coupled with the restriction in wants and physical activity of the less active older families. But this finding may indicate that a learning process is at work. The more that families buy the more familiar they can become with alternatives to neighborhood merchants.[7]

---

6. Ratings of the housewife's, rather than the husband's, English were used because the interviewers had more opportunity to judge the housewife. This rating is even more closely associated with the places where the housewife shops for clothes, one of the three items used in the index. Some 70 per cent of the women who speak English well do their shopping in non-neighborhood stores, compared with 31 per cent of the women who have difficulty with the language.

7. Consumer activity may interact with shopping scope, both as cause and consequence. Families familiar with the downtown stores and the goods they display may be stimulated to increase their consumer activity.

Table 4.6—Shopping Scope According to Consumer Activity
(In Per Cent)

	CONSUMER ACTIVITY		
SHOPPING SCOPE	Low	Medium	High
Narrow (within neighborhood)	53	46	30
Broad (out of neighborhood)	47	54	70
Total per cent	100	100	100
Total cases	(108)	(182)	(174)

The index of scope of shopping is primarily based on the sources of durable goods. As we have seen, this orientation seems to be largely an expression of urban sophistication. The orientation is fairly general, manifesting itself *within* the neighborhood when it comes to shopping for nondurables, namely food. The families who are inclined to shop in the more bureaucratic non-neighborhood stores for their durables are more likely than the others to buy their food in supermarkets rather than in the small independent groceries. About one in five families in the sample said that they bought food in small groceries, and only 37 per cent of them have a broad shopping scope; in contrast, 65 per cent of the families who shop in supermarkets are generally oriented to stores outside the neighborhood. This is further confirmation of the traditional element underlying shopping preferences. However, interpretation in terms of adaptive rationality cannot be ignored. Families who buy food at small groceries may do so in part because they feel more at home with the storekeeper; but it is also true that they can get credit there which is not available at the supermarket. And the same pervasive need for credit may explain why some shop for durables only in the neighborhood. In the end, traditionalistic practices and the basic requirement for credit work in the same direction: they limit the scope of alternative places in which to buy the necessities of life. And, as will become evident, this limitation of scope is related to other patterns of consumption behavior.

CHAPTER 5

Shopping Patterns II:
The Peddler Economy

DURING the early decades of this century, customer peddlers thrived among urban immigrants —and they still do. Peddling has been revitalized by the recent migrations to New York from the rural South and Puerto Rico. The slum-clearance programs in our cities may have inadvertently stimulated peddling. Today's peddler need no longer climb the rickety stairs of dilapidated tenements, but can ride in state to every floor of the new low-income housing projects, where he will find large concentrations of potential customers.

Having noted in Chapter 2 the kinds of relationships that exist between peddlers and local storekeepers, we turn now to peddlers as they are seen by the consumers. How prevalent is this method of buying? What is bought from the peddler, who buys, and what are their motives for buying?

From the consumer's perspective, we can distinguish two kinds of peddlers, one offering traditional credit, the other offering bureaucratic credit. The more traditional type of peddler depends upon personal rather than legal controls over his customers. Although he sells credit, he operates outside the law since he does not use installment contracts. He makes periodic visits to his customers, both to collect payments (which are noted in the customer's "book") and to sell more merchandise. His credit is flexible; he will allow his customers to miss occasional payments or pay less than the specified amount on a particular visit. Often, he has customers of many years standing who have come to regard him almost as a friend of the family. He provides what may fairly be described as "traditional credit."

In contrast to the traditional peddler is the company representative who specializes in selling high-cost items, such as encyclopedias, pots and pans, wrist watches, vacuum cleaners, or some other appliance. Experts in high-pressure selling, these men use installment contracts and depend upon legal controls to insure payments. Once the customer signs the contract, he is given a coupon book and is instructed to mail monthly payments, often to a finance company which has underwritten the contract. This is what we intend by the term "bureaucratic credit."

As we shall see in Chapter 10, these door-to-door credit merchants, particularly the company-representative type, are responsible for some of the more outrageous incidents of exploitation reported by the families.

According to the local merchants, many of whom employ peddlers, this method of buying is highly inefficient since the peddler adds greatly to the cost of the merchandise. Nevertheless, buying from peddlers is fairly widespread. Half of the 464 families interviewed said that they had made a purchase from a door-to-door credit salesman *since* they had been living in public housing. Another 10 per cent had bought from peddlers where they last lived, but not since moving into the housing project. The actual proportion who have dealt with peddlers is probably higher, since some respondents may not have known that their spouse made such a purchase and some may have been reluctant to admit that they trade with these men.[1]

---

1. Later in the interview, people were asked about the source of their appliances. Some who claimed they did not buy from peddlers turned out to have bought appliances with their aid. Another reason for believing that the true proportion buying from peddlers is probably higher than reported

A checklist of the kinds of items likely to be bought from peddlers was included in the questionnaire. Table 5.1

Table 5.1—Kinds of Merchandise Purchased from Peddlers Since Move to Public Housing

Category of Merchandise	Number of Mentions	Per Cent of Sample
Lamps or mirrors	99	21
Sink attachment	98	21
Sheets, blankets, bedspreads	82	18
Slip-covers or linoleum	73	16
Major appliances	57	12
Encyclopedias	19	4
Bibles and other religious articles	19	4
Clothing for children	13	3
Clothing for husband, wife	11	2
All other items	79	17

shows the frequency of various purchases made by those who had bought from peddlers since moving into public housing. The seventy-nine respondents in the last line of Table 5.1 reported a numerous variety of such items as electric fans, wrist watches, curtains, shower attachments, and pots and pans.[2]

The single most popular item purchased from peddlers is the "sink attachment," a pseudo-cabinet that hooks onto the sink and hides the water pipes beneath. (Unlike true cabinets, these are panels having neither doors nor bot-

---

is that some families may not have understood the question. We had considerable difficulty wording the question about peddlers. During the pretests, we initially asked about buying from door-to-door salesmen. One family we talked with said they never bought from those "pests" that came around. Later, when we asked where they shopped for clothes, they said they bought most of their clothes from "Charley." Further probes revealed that Charley was a peddler they had been dealing with for many years. To them, Charley was not at all like the anonymous salesmen who kept turning up at the door. To capture the "Charleys," we finally asked: "Have you ever bought on credit from someone who brings the things to your apartment?" But even this wording may not have covered all the nuances of relationships between customers and peddlers.

2. Since these items were not anticipated when the questionnaire was constructed, categories were not provided for them. Some, such as curtains and pots and pans, were mentioned more frequently than clothing.

tom.) Some families were tricked into buying the panel by salesmen posing as maintenance men employed by the Housing Authority. These travelling enterprisers would show up soon after the family had moved in, take up their guise of maintenance men, install the sink panel, and then demand a payment from the occasionally unsuspecting family. Nevertheless, most who bought these panels knew they were dealing with salesmen. In some cases, they first saw the device in the apartment of a neighbor and asked the neighbor to send the salesman around.

Almost as popular as the sink attachment is the mirror. We found that peddlers were having great success selling two types, the "shadow-box" mirror recessed in a wooden frame, the lower edge of which serves as a shelf for knick-knacks, and the "flamingo" mirror, so named because flamingo birds are painted on it. The presence of these in an apartment almost invariably meant that the family had dealt with a peddler.

The proportion actually buying major appliances from peddlers is probably higher than the 12 per cent shown in Table 5.1. Canvassers for stores are apt to take their customers to the store to pick out the appliance they want, and in some such instances the buyer may feel he has bought the appliance from the store, thus failing to mention the role of the peddler. A comment by a young Negro husband interviewed during the pretest brings out the complexity of pinning down the sources of appliances. He explained that he bought his television set from a "friend who owned an appliance store." Further questioning revealed that he was referring to a peddler who had dealt with his family for many years. We later learned that this particular neighborhood store employs a number of canvassers, and it is doubtful that his "friend" owned the store as the respondent assumed.[3]

---

3. The "peddler" category in Table 4.3 is based on a more stringent criterion with respect to the sources of appliances. This coding revealed that 16 per cent of the sample purchased at least one appliance from a peddler, in contrast with the 12 per cent shown in Table 5.1. One reason

As the sink-panel racket suggests, not all families who bought from peddlers may have intended to do so, nor had they any degree of continued association with them. A more revealing statistic, therefore, is the number who have made repeated purchases from peddlers. With the data on hand, we can give only a most conservative estimate of the size of this group, for we only know about *categories* of purchases, not *specific* purchases. For example, since slip covers and linoleum were grouped in the same category, the family that bought both items cannot be distinguished from the family that bought only one. Again, some families may have made repeated purchases of linen or clothing but are counted only once in each category, as is the family that bought more than one major appliance from peddlers. Thus, our measure of repeated buying is extremely crude and must underestimate the extent of buying from peddlers. It refers only to the number of categories (shown in Table 5.1) in which purchases were made.

As can be seen from Table 5.2, at least one third of these

Table 5.2—Distribution of Families According to Number of Different Kinds of Purchases from Peddlers

	Number	Per Cent
Did not buy since move	233	50
Bought in one category only	80	17
Bought in two categories	63	14
Bought in three categories	45	10
Bought in four or more categories	43	9
	464	100

low-income families made more than one purchase from peddlers. Among those who had dealt with peddlers at all, the great majority did so repeatedly. This shows that the typical customer does not basically regret this method of buying, for he goes on to make additional purchases.

---

for the discrepancy is that Table 5.1 is based on purchases made *since* the move to public housing. Some families may have purchased appliances from peddlers before coming to public housing. Also, the 16 per cent includes instances in which the peddler served as an intermediary in the transaction.

The Peddler's Customer

It might seem self-evident that the peddler's customers must be the most underprivileged members of the low-income group, the families who lack credit even in the neighborhood store. Yet the high proportion of sales involving accessories rather than necessities—the decorated mirrors, sink panels, and slip covers—suggests an alternative hypothesis. The people who buy this way may be those who are particularly interested in consumption and unable to resist the impulse to buy when subjected to the peddler's sales pressure and the bait of "easy payments."

Still a third reason for this mode of buying might be that the more informal relationship offered by the peddler is welcomed by those accustomed to a more traditional economy. According to this view, people buy from peddlers not so much out of economic necessity or because they have little sales resistance, but because they feel more comfortable dealing with these men. In reviewing the characteristics of the people who buy from peddlers, we shall be alerted to each of the three possibilities. We begin by considering the role of consumer interest and impulse buying.

THE ROLE OF IMPULSE BUYING
AND CONSUMER ACTIVITY

The first clue that buying from peddlers is associated with a general interest in consumption is probably the fact that it is related to the index of consumer activity. Some 57 per cent of the most active consumers (those with many appliances and more immediate shopping plans) have purchased from peddlers, as compared with 31 per cent of the least active consumers. The most active consumers are also more likely to be "repeat buyers," 38 per cent compared with 16 per cent of the least active.[4] In short, if these low-

4. These and all subsequent statistics on the peddler's customers refer to purchases made since moving to public housing. Those who only bought before the move are grouped with the nonbuyers.

income families buy often, they more often buy from peddlers.

To a large extent, the practice of buying from peddlers
is a manifestation of what has come to be called "impulse
buying"—i.e., purchases made on the spur of opportunity,
not of prior intent. The families who have bought from
peddlers at least once, and especially those who have made
repeated purchases from them, are much more likely to
have behaved in ways indicative of impulse-buying. Early
in the interview, all respondents were asked whether salesmen had ever "talked them into" buying things they did
not want. About one in every five reported that this had
happened to them, and they turn out to have been much
more involved with peddlers altogether. As many as 78 per
cent of them had bought from peddlers, compared with
42 per cent of those who claimed they were never talked
into buying things they didn't want. Moreover, these people
were more often repeat buyers, 58 per cent compared with
26 per cent.

In response to another question bearing on impulse
buying, sixty-four families in the sample said that they
occasionally bought things they didn't really need. These
families, too, often dealt with peddlers. Sixty-nine per cent
of them had bought at least one item, and more than half
had been repeat buyers. Among those who reported never
buying things they didn't need, only 46 per cent had bought
from peddlers and less than a third had made repeated
purchases. Families were also asked whether they were inclined to "shop around" before buying, or whether they
"decided quickly." The "quick deciders" have also been
more involved with peddlers than those who "shop around."
(Fifty-nine per cent of the former compared with 47 per
cent of the latter.)

Another pattern of shopping, indicative of both interest in consumption and impulse buying, is closely related
to buying from peddlers. This is the "demonstration party,"
commonly called a "Stanley Party" after the company that
is most active in organizing them. The demonstration party

is held in the home of a housewife who invites her friends and neighbors to attend. A salesman for the sponsoring company helps create a party atmosphere by organizing games, and in the course of this he demonstrates a variety of household items. The hostess's aid is enlisted in this congenial enterprise by promises of various premiums, and this exerts further pressure on her friends to buy.[5] The demonstration party is as popular among low-income families as the practice of buying from peddlers. Half the respondents had attended such parties, and one in every three had attended several. As Table 5.3 shows, the people

Table 5.3—Experience with Peddlers According to Attendance at Demonstration Parties
(In Per Cent)

	DEMONSTRATION-PARTY ATTENDANCE		
Experience[a]	None	One	Two or More
Ever bought	39	54	63
Repeat buyers	25	32	44
Total cases	(231)	(81)	(152)

a. The format of this table requires some explanation. The top row refers to those who have bought at least once from peddlers and thus includes the cases in the second row. These percentages of course do not total 100. The full table, of which this is a condensation, consists of three entries, those who never bought since the move, those who bought only once, and those who bought more than once. The percentage who never bought from peddlers can be determined by subtracting the top row from 100. Similarly, the per cent who bought only once can be found by subtracting the second row from the first.

who go to demonstration parties tend to be the same people who buy from peddlers.

Not only is attendance at demonstration parties related to having bought from peddlers at one time or another, but as the second row of Table 5.3 shows, the people who go to these parties are much more apt to have made repeated purchases from peddlers. In both methods of shop-

---

5. The entire affair is exotically like the "smallpox parties," popular before Jenner's discovery of smallpox vaccine, in which people would be brought together with a victim of the dreaded disease so that after exposure to a mild case they could become immune. The "demonstration parties" are designed for contagion of another sort: under the skilled guidance of a genial salesman, the itch to buy presumably spreads by example and mutual stimulation.

ping we detect the workings of the consumer's network of social relations. This is at once evident in the demonstration party, which, after all, depends entirely upon the sponsoring housewife's set of friends. But to some extent it is also true of the practice of buying from peddlers. As we shall see, a number of people meet the peddler through friends, relatives, or neighbors.

The various reported behaviors dealing with impulse buying, including the practice of attending demonstration parties, can be combined into a single index. The general effect of impulse buying upon dealing with peddlers is shown by the marked correlation in Table 5.4.

Table 5.4—Relation of Impulse Buying to Experience with Peddlers

(In Per Cent)

| | IMPULSE-BUYING | | | |
EXPERIENCE	Low	Medium-Low	Medium-High	High
Ever bought	29	52	57	75
Repeat buyers	16	31	39	56
Total cases	(149)	(110)	(122)	(83)

It is no surprise that the people most vulnerable to sales pressure and most given to impulse buying tend to trade with peddlers. By calling on the housewife, frequently when the husband is not home, the peddler is able to break down many of the usual constraints upon consumption. He requires only a small down-payment; so lack of funds is no deterrent. The housewife with limited cash on hand, need not say "come back later when my husband is home." And so the controls implicit in consulting her husband do not operate. By bringing his goods to the door and offering easy credit, the peddler, in effect, elevates the housewife to the role of the major consumer, activating whatever impulses she may have to buy.

All this assumes that the wife rather than the husband usually buys from the peddler. There is evidence to support this. The families currently in debt to peddlers were asked which member of the family ordinarily bought from them. Responses to this question contrast instructively with those given to a question about the family member who bought the most recent major appliance. These results are shown in Table 5.5.

Table 5.5—The Family Member Who Buys from Peddlers and Who Bought the Most Recent Major Appliance
(In Per Cent)

Family Member	Buyer from Peddler	Appliance Buyer
Wife	67	28
Husband	20	38
Both	13	34
Total per cent	100	100
Total cases[a]	(81)	(372)

a. The question pertaining to the peddler was asked only of those families who were in debt to peddlers at the time of the interview. Ten of these failed to answer the question and are excluded. About 14 per cent of the sample did not purchase a major appliance within the past five years. These cases have also been excluded as well as a few instances in which the buyer was someone other than the husband or wife.

We have not taken into account the fact that husbands are missing in some families since complete families are as likely to deal with peddlers as broken ones.

Table 5.5 shows clearly that it is primarily the wife who buys from peddlers.[6] When it comes to a major appliance, apt to involve more money than the typical purchase from a peddler and more planning by the family, the husband takes a much more active part.

Since consumer activity in general is associated with buying from peddlers, it is only to be expected that the two characteristics indicative of consumer needs (and activity) —stage in the life-cycle and family size—are closely related to buying from peddlers. Table 5.6 shows the relation between the age of the family head and the use of peddlers.

Families headed by persons over 40 are far less inclined to trade with peddlers than families headed by younger persons. Apart from their more pressing needs which make

6. Had this question been asked of former customers of peddlers, the proportion of wives who had done the buying would probably be greater. Some housewives explained that their husbands made them stop buying from peddlers once they learned of such purchases.

Table 5.6—Experience with Peddlers According to Age of Family Head

(In Per Cent)

EXPERIENCE	AGE OF HEAD			
	20-29	30-39	40-49	50 and Over
Ever bought	65	63	40	26
Repeat buyers	39	43	26	18
Total cases	(93)	(158)	(112)	(101)

them interested in the peddler's wares, it may be that the younger families are less experienced as consumers and so more vulnerable to the peddler's sales pressure. That factors other than consumer interest are at work is suggested by the fact that when the degree of consumer activity is held constant, the young families are still more likely to buy from peddlers. This can be seen by reading down the columns of Table 5.7. To simplify the matter, data are

Table 5.7—The Joint Association of Consumer Activity and Age of Household Head With Experience With Peddlers

(Per Cent Repeat Buyers)

AGE OF HEAD	CONSUMER ACTIVITY					
	Low		Medium		High	
Under 40	23	(30)	44	(101)	43	(120)
Over 40	13	(77)	25	(79)	28	(53)

shown for the repeat buyers only, those who presumably have been most deeply involved with peddlers.[7]

The relative inexperience of the younger families as consumers is suggested by their disproportionately large representation among the impulse buyers. (Fifty-one per cent of the younger families compared with 36 per cent of the older ones score high on the index.) But just as consumer activity by itself does not explain the relationship between age and buying from peddlers, neither does impulse buying. As Table 5.8 shows, age and impulse buy-

---

7. This format will be followed in subsequent tables involving three variables.

Table 5.8—The Joint Association of Impulse Buying and Age of Household Head With Experience With Peddlers

(Per Cent Repeat Buyers)

AGE OF	IMPULSE BUYING			
HEAD	Low		High	
Under 40	32	(123)	50	(128)
Over 40	13	(134)	37	(75)

ing are independently associated with buying from peddlers.

Putting together the results of Tables 5.7 and 5.8, we see the likelihood that great consumer activity and tendencies toward impulse buying combine to dispose the younger families to trade with peddlers.

The effect of family size on dealing with peddlers can be seen from Table 5.9.

Table 5.9—Experience With Peddlers in Families of Different Size

(In Per Cent)

	SIZE OF HOUSEHOLD			
	1-2	3	4	5 or More
EXPERIENCE	Persons	Persons	Persons	Persons
Ever bought	29	43	50	59
Repeat buyers	16	18	23	44
Total cases	(63)	(86)	(127)	(188)

Both the proportion of families who ever bought and the proportion of repeat buyers increases with the size of the household. Nor is this pattern a result of the fact that the younger families tend to be larger in size. As Table 5.10

Table 5.10—The Joint Effect of Family Size and Age of Household Head on Experience With Peddlers

(Per Cent Repeat Buyers)[a]

AGE OF	SIZE OF HOUSEHOLD					
	1-3		4		5 or More	
HEAD	Persons		Persons		Persons	
Under 40	33	(42)	34	(86)	49	(120)
Over 40	11	(107)	31	(39)	34	(62)

a. The patterns shown here are more irregular for the proportion who ever bought from peddlers. Many of the very small young families made only one purchase from peddlers. Hence size of family makes little difference in whether younger families ever bought from peddlers.

shows, size of family and age of head are independently related to buying from peddlers.

Like the young families, the large ones have many pressing consumer needs, and may therefore be more active in dealing with all kinds of merchants. (Whether their penchant for buying from peddlers stems from marked economic deprivation will be considered shortly.) But the significance of family size may also lie in another direction. The housewife in the large family may have too many commitments to the household to leave her apartment to shop. She has more children to attend to; some of the children will be young enough to need close supervision; she must work more and clean more. Even if she has the income to shop for the things she wants, she may not have the time. Family size then, may not only indicate need, but also the constraints upon the housewife which increase her vulnerability to peddlers. One housewife offered an opinion, based on her own experiences, that relates this aspect of family size to the propensity to buy from peddlers. In her view, the busy housewife who has to contend with spirited children all day sees the peddler's appearance at the door as a welcome relief from the strains of life as mother.

THE ROLE OF ECONOMIC DEPRIVATION

If it were poverty alone that made families resort to peddlers, we should find that such families consisted almost entirely of those dependent upon welfare or at a very low income level. After all, such families have few other sources of credit. Nevertheless, the data suggest that strict economic necessity alone does not dispose families to deal with peddlers. The families who receive welfare assistance differ little in this respect from those who derive their income entirely from earnings, just as the very low-income families differ little from those with higher income.

As Table 5.11 shows, welfare families are no more likely to buy from peddlers than are wage earners. In contrast

Table 5.11—Experience With Peddlers According to Source of Income

(In Per Cent)

| | | SOURCE | |
EXPERIENCE	Earnings Only	Welfare (Whole or Part)	Social Security and Other Pensions
Ever bought	52	51	36
Repeat buyers	33	37	27
Total cases	(333)	(72)	(59)

to both these groups, the families on social security are much less involved with peddlers. These are, of course, older families, and we already know that older families are less apt to buy this way.

The lowest and the highest income groups (Table 5.12) have a slightly lesser tendency than those in the middle groups to have bought from peddlers at any time, but the

Table 5.12—Experience With Peddlers According to Family Income

(In Per Cent)

| | INCOME | | | |
EXPERIENCE	Under $2,500	$2,500- $3,500	$3,500- $4,499	Over $4,500
Ever bought	42	55	53	46
Repeat buyers	34	32	31	33
Total cases	(101)	(151)	(124)	(88)

proportion of repeat buyers is approximately the same on each income level. It may be that the poorest families do not consume very much altogether and so tend not to buy from peddlers as well. This possibility can be checked by taking into account consumer activity as well as income. The relation of income to buying from peddlers at each level of consumer activity is shown in Table 5.13.

Reading down each column of the table we see that income has very little connection with peddler experience, even when consumer activity is taken into account. Among those showing little consumer activity, the poorest families rely slightly more on peddlers than do those of higher

Table 5.13—Joint Effect of Income and Consumer Activity on Experience With Peddlers
(Per Cent Repeat Buyers)

	CONSUMER ACTIVITY					
INCOME	Low		Medium		High	
Under $3,000	19	(53)	36	(67)	42	(55)
$3,000-$3,999	12	(34)	39	(54)	38	(53)
$4,000 and over	14	(21)	37	(61)	36	(66)

income, and among those with high consumer activity there is a slight tendency for poorer people to deal with peddlers. But these are small differences, and among the moderately active consumers there is no relationship at all.

Before leaving the matter of income we must consider its connection with family size. We have learned that large families more often buy from peddlers. Perhaps they do so because they are more pressed for money than smaller families with the same income. They must stretch their dollars more thinly. Table 5.14 shows us how things actually stand.

Table 5.14—The Joint Effect of Income and Family Size on Experience With Peddlers
(Per Cent Repeat Buyers)

	SIZE OF HOUSEHOLD					
INCOME	1-3 Persons		4 Persons		5 Persons	
Under $3,000	20	(79)	35	(46)	51	(49)
$3,000-$3,999	17	(46)	36	(42)	41	(53)
$4,000 and over	8	(24)	28	(39)	42	(82)

Reading down each column, we see that the relation of income to size of family does influence decisions about buying from peddlers. For each size of family, those with the lowest income are in general more often repeat buyers than those of higher income. The differences are not large (not nearly as large as the differences shown in the rows of Table 5.14) but they do suggest that economic necessity plays some part in this method of buying. That the poverty of families is not unimportant in the appeal of peddlers is suggested further by what was reported in the interviews. A 31-year-old Negro mother of two children living on welfare expresses a fairly typical opinion: "It's not that I don't have sales resistance. People come to the door every day . . . *but by buying from these fellows I get some of the things I have to have sooner.*"

At first she was reluctant to admit how much she owed to peddlers because, as she put it, "I'm scared it will get back to welfare." Later, she admitted to a debt of over $275 to one peddler and of $20 to another. This sizeable debt included the remaining payments for a TV set she had bought over a year ago. Asked whether she would buy from the peddler if she could get credit at a store, she said: "Yes, I would, because he's a good guy. Many stores won't give credit to welfare families . . . I guess if I was working, I would pay less carrying charges both to door-to-door salesmen and to stores."

Well aware that she is a "poor credit risk," and of the higher charges she pays, she, like other families in her position, finds the peddler the only available source of what she wants to buy.

THE ROLE OF CULTURAL FACTORS—TRADITIONALISM

The practice of buying from peddlers appears to be more closely related to cultural differences between these families, rather than to economic differences. To begin with, this is suggested by the far smaller tendency of white families to deal with peddlers than either Negroes or Puerto Ricans, as can be seen from Table 5.15. Negroes are somewhat more apt than Puerto Ricans to make at least one

Table 5.15—Experience With Peddlers According to Race
(In Per Cent)

EXPERIENCE	Whites	RACE Negroes	Puerto Ricans
Ever bought	33	66	56
Repeat buyers	11	41	39
Total cases	(115)	(133)	(216)

purchase from peddlers, but the proportion of repeat buyers, approximately two out of every five, is about the same in the two groups.

It is true that nonwhite families are younger and larger in size than the white families, but this does not account for the differences shown in Table 5.15. For each size of family and for each age group, nonwhites are far more likely than whites to trade with peddlers.

It might be assumed that nonwhites more often deal with peddlers because many of them are migrants from more traditionalistic areas and are presumably more accustomed to this kind of relationship. If this were so, the more recent migrants within each racial group would be most involved with peddlers. But as Table 5.16 shows, this is not the case.

Table 5.16—Experience With Peddlers According to Length of Time in City for Each Racial Group

(Per Cent Repeat Buyers)

	LENGTH OF TIME IN NEW YORK CITY		
RACE	10 Years or Less[a]	Over 10 Years	Born in N.Y.C.
White	[b] (2)	9 (65)	13 (46)
Negro	42 (31)	39 (82)	53 (17)
Puerto Rican	41 (82)	36 (129)	[b] (3)

a. All but 13 per cent of the 115 families in this category have been in New York City at least five years.
b. Too few cases for percentages.

Peddler involvement does not decrease appreciably with length of time in the city. (Although the earlier Puerto Rican migrants are somewhat less likely to be repeat buyers, they are just as apt as the newer arrivals to have bought at least once since moving to public housing.) In fact, among Negroes (and to some extent among whites as well), those born in New York City are *more* likely to be repeat buyers than the migrants. Being raised in New York City does not, apparently, provide immunity from the more traditional economic relationships.[8] Indeed, some families in our sample had "inherited" peddlers from their parents and this would indicate that indoctrination into more traditional relationships continues in the low-income sections of even this large city.

Since length of time in the city does not alone affect the extent to which the dominant urban culture is assimilated, the data of Table 5.16 are not enough to disprove any connection between the persistence of peddling and the traditionalism of the consumer. The degree to which families are oriented to the more bureaucratic stores outside the neighborhood is perhaps a better indication of the assimilation of urban culture. The question to be considered, then, is whether shopping scope is related to buying from peddlers. If traditionalism does play some part, then people with narrow shopping scopes should trade more often with peddlers. The patterns in each racial group appear in Table 5.17.

Table 5.17—Experience With Peddlers According to Shopping Scope for Each Racial Group

(Per Cent Repeat Buyers)

	SHOPPING SCOPE		
RACE	Narrow	Intermediate	Broad
White	9 (46)	6 (36)	18 (33)
Negro	53 (32)	46 (41)	32 (60)
Puerto Rican	42 (115)	46 (63)	18 (38)

The expected relationship does not occur among the whites, but does occur among both the Negroes and Puerto Ricans. Among these, the families with a broad shopping scope trade far less often with peddlers than the others. Among whites, there is a slight tendency toward the opposite pattern. Perhaps this is explained by the fact that the more traditional whites in our sample tend to be elderly

---

8. See Herbert Gans, *The Urban Villagers* (New York: The Free Press of Glencoe, 1962), for a description of the continuity of the ethnic subculture within a major urban culture.

Jews, who are not only relatively inactive consumers but, as we shall see in a later chapter, have a strong aversion to credit buying from any source.

Formal education might be thought to be an antidote to traditionalism. Yet among these families the level of education is not at all related to involvement with peddlers. High school graduates have bought from them just as often as elementary school graduates. Even the few families in which the head has had some college education tend to buy at least once from a peddler, although they are not given to repeated buying.

The results shown in Table 5.18 might have been con-

Table 5.18—Experience With Peddlers According to Education of Head of Household

(In Per Cent)

	EDUCATION			
EXPERIENCE	Elementary School	Some High School	High School Graduate	Some College
Ever bought	45	55	51	50
Repeat buyers	32	36	30	13
Total cases	(220)	(155)	(61)	(18)

founded by the factor of age, since the older heads of families are not as well educated as the younger ones. But when age is held roughly constant, no relationship develops between level of education and peddler involvement. When we take race into account, however, the picture changes, as can be seen from Table 5.19.

Table 5.19—Experience With Peddlers According to Education for Each Racial Group

(Per Cent Repeat Buyers)

	EDUCATION					
RACE	Elementary School		Some High School		High School Graduates and College	
White	12	(51)	6	(36)	16	(25)
Negro	49	(35)	42	(60)	32	(34)
Puerto Rican	36	(134)	49	(59)	30	(20)

The higher the level of education among Negroes, the less often they trade with peddlers. Among Puerto Ricans, the pattern is more irregular. Those with some high school education are most inclined to buy this way, but those who have completed high school are least so. Among whites, education plays no part in this pattern of buying.

To summarize, we have found that families who buy from peddlers are more active consumers and have strong tendencies toward buying on impulse. Family size and age, both of which are associated with consumer needs, are closely related to this mode of buying. These characteristics may also be related to others that increase the family's vulnerability to the peddlers: youth, with relatively little experience with shopping, and family size, with the constraints the large family imposes upon the housewife. The peddler's customers are by no means only the most economically deprived families, but there is some indication that a low per-capita income makes for trading with peddlers. A background of traditionalized culture also seems to be important. Puerto Ricans and Negroes trade with peddlers far more often than do whites, but this decreases as their educational levels get progressively higher and as they develop broader scope for shopping.

We turn now to the families who were involved with peddlers at the time of the interview, the minority who were still in debt to them. These families have given us more extensive information on their attitudes toward peddlers.

Attitudes Toward Peddlers

At the time of the interviews, ninety-one families, about one in every five, were in debt to peddlers. The typical family among them owed between $25 and $50; twenty-three owed more than $100, and nine owed more than $200.

Of the 140 families who had bought from peddlers since the move to the housing project but who were *not* in debt to them when interviewed, the great majority—more than 75 per cent—claimed they would not buy from peddlers again. The others said either that they would, or at least might do so. The families who reportedly stopped buying from peddlers gave as their chief reasons the excessive cost and the poor quality of goods. But since many of these families had made repeated purchases in the past, it is questionable whether all of them will be able to resist the temptation of the peddler's "easy payments" in the future.

The ninety-one families currently in debt were asked a variety of questions about this system of buying. It could not be assumed at the outset that all the families who had purchased from peddlers would feel that they had been exploited. The exploratory interviews had disclosed that some families actually prefer to buy this way. They appreciate the personal relationship they have with the peddler and the flexibility of the system of payments. In some cases, it will be remembered, families were trading with the same peddler who had served their parents. In the unfriendly, impersonal metropolis, the peddler was for them someone they could trust.

The evidence provided in the interviews suggests that a minority of families—at the least, one in every ten in the sample—have what they consider to be a satisfactory relationship with a peddler. About half the families owing money to a peddler told us that they planned to go on dealing with him. Most of these satisfied customers reported that he was a "nicer person" to deal with than the typical salesman in a store, and that they would continue to deal with him even if they could obtain credit in a store.

Of those who owed money to a peddler, more than 75 per cent were satisfied with the quality of his goods and only 11 per cent thought him dishonest. The flexibility of the system of payments is in effect reported by the 87 per cent who said the peddler did not add a service charge when they missed a payment. (The others were probably dealing with company representatives who used installment contracts.)

Interestingly enough, most of those in debt to peddlers, (some 63 per cent) reported that the peddler's prices were higher than those charged in stores. Apparently they were willing to exchange the "easy payments" and other conveniences for the added cost—or perhaps they felt that they were ineligible for store credit.

That dealing with a peddler can be more than business, that it can develop into a personal relationship, is suggested by the more than a third of the ninety-one families who reported spending time in small talk with the peddler. The deepening of a personal relationship is also implied by its extended duration. More than half of those in debt to peddlers had been dealing with the same man for more than a year; about a third, for more than two years; and eleven families, for over five years.

The peddler operates within the social networks of his customers, as shown by the fact that more than 70 per cent of these families know other people who buy from their own peddler. Through these networks of social ties, the peddler can exercise a measure of control over his customers, for when trying to collect from a recalcitrant customer, he can apply pressure to friends, neighbors, and relatives. He can shame the delinquent customer into paying by complaining to his friends or relatives, or he can threaten to withhold service from the friends until they persuade the delinquent customer to make good his debt.

There is evidence also that this penetration of the family's social networks helps the peddler to retain his customers. Ex-customers, those who bought after moving to the project but no longer owed money, were more likely to have met the peddler in an impersonal way than those still in debt. Only 31 per cent of former customers met the peddler through someone they knew, compared with 47 per cent of those still in debt. In both groups the most frequent mode of contact was through the peddler's appearing at their door on his own.

An unusually close relationship between peddler and customer is illustrated by the case of a middle-aged widow with three children. As summarized by the interviewer:

Mrs. W's cousin introduced her to Mr. Ben about 15 years ago. He came to show Mrs. W. some curtains which she bought. Eventually Mr. Ben opened a store and whenever she needed something he did not have, he would give her his card and the address of the store where she could buy it. The bill would be sent to Mr. Ben and he would add it on to her balance. She has been paying him $15 each month for some time. She sends her pension check directly to him along with her book. He deducts the $15 and sends her the balance due her from the check. . . . Several years ago she tried to get a bank loan of $50 for Christmas shopping and gave his name as a reference. When the bank notified him, he called her and told her he would lend her the $50 without interest.

This widow went on to say that she would continue to buy from Mr. Ben even if she could get credit at other stores, because "he makes it easier for me and he trusts me." Yet even this close relationship was based on the need for credit; when asked whether she would still buy from Mr. Ben if she could pay cash the emphatic reply was: "No, then I'd buy somewhere else because it would be cheaper."

Some families, then, have achieved relatively satisfying relationships with door-to-door salesmen. For them, the "benevolent" peddler is more than a figment. But as we shall see in Chapter 10, many more families reported their outrage at the exploitative practices of door-to-door sales-men. And whether for better or worse, the peddler remains an integral part of the consumption patterns of these low-income families.

CHAPTER 6

Price Patterns: Costs of Major Durables

As was noted in Chapter 2, the poor credit potential of most low-income families combined with their lack of shopping sophistication often results in the irony that they pay much more for a given quality of durables than do consumers in higher income brackets. This does not mean that they spend more, although even this may sometimes be the case, but that they obtain considerably less value for their dollar.

As we look at the prices the families reported paying for their appliances, we shall see that they are generally quite high, some almost unbelievably so. And we shall find that such matters as family income, where the goods are purchased, the method of payment, and, significantly, race are associated with variability in cost.

The analysis focuses on the three appliances for which the largest number of cost estimates was obtained: the television set, phonograph, and washing machine. For some purposes, we examine only the cost of television sets, since there are not enough cases of the other items to permit detailed analysis.

The Cost of Appliances

In many cases, it was not possible to obtain precise information about the amount paid for appliances. Occasionally, families simply did not remember how much they had paid. And when they did quote prices, it was often unclear whether these included credit charges, delivery, and installation fees. The problem is further complicated in transactions involving trade-ins. Nevertheless, the families' estimates of what their appliances cost are of an order of magnitude related to the actual costs, and these will suffice for the rough comparisons we shall be making. Moreover, these estimates tell us what the families *think* their appliances cost and presumably what they are willing to pay. If there is any systematic error in the reported costs, it is in the direction of underestimating them, since the cash price was occasionally mistaken for the final credit price.[1]

As Table 6.1 shows, the prices for these appliances range up to $900. It must be said, however, that this extraordinary price was paid by only one family for an elaborate "combination model" of a television set and phonograph. Another family reported paying over $800 for a television set, and two, over $700. Phonograph costs ran as high as $800 for one family and over $700 for another. The upper limit on washing-machine prices is considerably lower, with only two families reporting having paid as much as $400. As

---

1. There is another reason for assuming that the data give a conservative picture of the prices paid. A number of wives did not know how much their husbands had paid for an appliance or even where it had been bought. We suspect that these families generally paid more than the average. Such "don't-know" responses are more frequent among Puerto Rican wives and, as we shall see, this group tends to pay more for appliances. Furthermore, the "don't-know" response often reflects tension between the spouses, and where this is the case, higher prices may well have been paid; for interviewers found that marital tensions are sometimes produced by one spouse making what the other considers to be an extravagant purchase. Also, when marital tensions exist, consultation before buying is less apt to occur, and so there is less wisdom in shopping. To the extent that these processes operate, they make for the underreporting of higher prices.

the median prices indicate, the television set is the most expensive appliance, followed by the washing machine and then the phonograph.

The variability of prices paid for television sets and phonographs is far greater than for washing machines, presumably because of the greater variation in models. For every family paying under $200 for a television set, almost two paid over $300, and 4 per cent of the sample, fourteen families, paid more than $500.

Table 6.1—The Prices of Appliances
(In Per Cent)

Price Range	Television	Phonograph	Washing Machine
Under $100	4	23	4
$100-$199	19	30	32
$200-$299	37	22	45
$300-$399	27	14	18
$400-$499	9	8	1
$500-$900	4	3	—
Total per cent	100	100	100
Median price	$275	$190	$231
Total cases[a]	(313)	(146)	(130)

a. The numbers are considerably smaller than the number of owners, due to the exclusion of those who received their appliances as gifts or bought them from noncommercial sources and to the large number who could not estimate costs.

Correlates of Varying Cost

For greater comparability, this analysis will be limited to new appliances purchased from a commercial source. And since the cost of combination models of TV sets is generally greater than the others, a "high" price for a combination model will be defined as $400 or more; for the console and table models, as $300 or more.[2] Since we shall be concerned with the factors related to paying a "high" price, this definition should be kept in mind throughout.

2. Somewhat surprisingly, almost as many table models cost over $300 as console models; we therefore did not distinguish between them.

FAMILY INCOME AND COST

The hypothesis that higher-income families pay less for appliances can be tested within the range of families in this study by comparing the poorest with those that are somewhat better off. The evidence of Table 6.2 bears this

Table 6.2—The Cost of Appliances Among Families of Different Income

Appliance	Under $3,500		Over $3,500	
Television: per cent high price	46	(141)	37	(145)
Phonograph: per cent over $300	29	(69)	21	(71)
Washing machine: per cent over $230[a]	49	(49)	35	(69)

a. This odd figure comes closest to the median price paid for a washing machine by these families.

out. For each appliance, a larger percentage of the families earning under $3,500 paid a high price.

In Chapter 4 it was shown that higher-income families have broader scopes of shopping. This would suggest that they generally receive higher-quality merchandise than lower-income families who depend primarily on local sources. If so, the pattern in Table 6.2 becomes all the more significant; the poorer families tend to pay more even though they may be getting lower-quality merchandise.

SHOPPING SCOPE AND COST

More important than family income in affecting prices paid for appliances, is the matter of where the family shops. Using their own definitions of whether the appliance was bought in the neighborhood or outside, we find that those who buy outside pay less. This is especially marked in the purchase of television sets, less so for phonographs, and shows up only for those washing machines costing the unusually high price of $300 or more.

Table 6.3—Cost of Appliances According to Reported Locus of Purchase

Appliance	"In Neighborhood"		"Outside Neighborhood"	
Television:				
Per cent high price	51	(121)	34	(148)
Phonograph:				
Per cent over $200	52	(56)	43	(74)
Washing Machine:				
Per cent over $230	37	(42)	39	(66)
Per cent over $300	31	(42)	15	(66)

This finding, based on aggregated reports of the families, supports the observation independently advanced in Chapter 2 that neighborhood merchants will compensate for extending credit to poor risks by high markups. The "traditional" credit economy of the local merchants may be more convenient than the "bureaucratic" one outside, but the convenience is at a price.

The effect of shopping scope on cost is even more apparent when we look at the type of store in which families buy their appliances, irrespective of whether they consider the store to be in or out of the neighborhood. (Two sets of figures are presented for the washing machine because the patterns differ somewhat when different definitions of "high price" are used.)

Some of the percentages are based on too few cases to be reliable. But the general pattern is fairly clear, particularly for television sets where the percentages are based on the largest number of cases. The few families shopping in

Table 6.4—Cost of Appliances According to Type of Source

APPLIANCE	BUREAUCRATIC SOURCES						TRADITIONAL SOURCES			
	Discount House		Department Store		Chain Store		Neighborhood Dealer		Peddler	
Television:										
Per cent high price	8	(12)	22	(24)	31	(88)	53	(103)	67	(15)
Phonograph:										
Per cent over $200	14	(7)	46	(13)	51	(39)	51	(47)	55	(11)
Washing machine:										
Per cent over $230	30	(10)	50	(14)	29	(38)	54	(28)	87	(8)
Per cent over $300	10	(10)	14	(14)	8	(38)	36	(28)	87	(8)

discount houses pay the least for their appliances; those shopping in department stores and chain stores pay more, but they are nevertheless better off than the families patronizing neighborhood dealers and peddlers. In every instance, the families buying from peddlers pay the highest prices.

These findings might lead us to assume that income is related to cost only because the higher-income families tend to shop in stores outside the neighborhood. But in fact, both income and shopping scope independently affect cost, as can be seen from Tables 6.5 and 6.6.

Table 6.5—The Joint Association of Income and Reported Locus of Purchase With Cost of Television Set[a]

(Per Cent Paying "High" Price)

Income	"In Neighborhood"		"Outside Neighborhood"	
Under $3,500	54	(68)	40	(62)
Over $3,500	47	(53)	30	(86)

a. Since we are examining several variables simultaneously, we deal only with the television set because of the larger number of cases. This procedure is followed throughout.

Whether we use the family's own definition of "out of neighborhood" or consider the type of store matters little, for the patterns are similar in both cases. Wherever television sets are bought, the higher-income families tend to pay less. At the same time, on each income level, the non-

Table 6.6—The Joint Association of Income and Type of Store With Cost of Television Set

(Per Cent Paying "High" Price)

Income	Traditional Sources (Neighborhood Dealers and Peddlers)		"Bureaucratic" Sources (Department, Discount, Chain)	
Under $3,500	60	(63)	31	(51)
Over $3,500	49	(55)	24	(68)

neighborhood shoppers are apt to pay less. The highest prices are paid by the very poor families who shop in the neighborhood and the lowest prices by the better-off families who shop outside. To them that hath not, less is given. But it is of some interest that the lower-income families that shop outside tend to pay less than the higher-income families who buy in the neighborhood.

The implications of these findings for a program designed to help these families might be that low-income consumers can be helped by encouraging them to shop out of the neighborhood, particularly at discount houses. But the problem is by no means this simple. Basic to the findings on income and shopping scope is an important fact: the dependence of families upon credit. As we shall now see, the cost of appliances is affected most by the method of payment, and the families who need credit are most dependent upon neighborhood merchants and peddlers.

CREDIT AND COST

Buying on credit turns out to be quite expensive as can be seen from Table 6.7.

Table 6.7—Cost of Appliances by Method of Payment

Appliance	Cash		Credit	
Television: per cent high price	15	(79)	52	(205)
Phonograph: per cent over $200	34	(45)	56	(93)
Washing machine: per cent over $230	19	(37)	51	(79)

For each appliance, the proportion paying a high price is considerably smaller among the minority who paid cash. The differences are much larger than those found when we considered income and shopping scope. The implications for a program of action are now somewhat different: if these families are to utilize their income most effectively, they must come to avoid the temptation of the installment plan. Clearly, this task of consumer education is not an easy one.

Credit has such a great effect on cost that we must ask whether income and the place of purchase have any impact other than that due to credit. Higher-income families and those who shop out of the neighborhood may be more likely to pay cash, and this alone may account for their observed tendency to pay lower prices for appliances.

The fact is, however, that the higher- and lower-income families do not differ much in using credit to buy television sets. Credit was used by most in both strata—70 per cent of those with an income over $3,500 and 74 per cent of those with an income under that amount used credit. Apparently the income differential within the sample is not great enough to make income alone a major determinant of the method of payment. But if they do not differ in their use of credit, they do seem to differ in what they pay for credit. The higher-income families tend to pay somewhat less for credit, if we may judge from the results summarized in Table 6.8.

Table 6.8—The Joint Association of Income and Method of Payment With Cost of Television Set

(Per Cent Paying "High" Price)

Method of Payment	Under $3,500		Over $3,500	
Cash	17	(36)	14	(43)
Credit	56	(103)	47	(102)

Among the cash payers, there is a difference of only three percentage points between the two income strata; among the credit users, the difference amounts to nine percentage points. These differences are small, but they may reflect the dissimilarity between credit positions of the poorer families and of those better off. This may result in part from merchants putting higher markups on the goods they sell on credit to poorer families in order to compensate for their greater risk, and in part from the dependence of poor families on the more costly, because longer, payment plans.

Although the use of credit has little to do with income it is closely related to where families shop. Of those who paid cash for their television sets, 70 per cent reported that they bought them outside the neighborhood, compared with the 50 per cent of those who used credit. Table 6.9 shows that the use of credit is also related to the type of store in which appliances are bought.

Table 6.9—Method of Payment for Appliances According to Source[a]

(In Per Cent)

METHOD OF PAYMENT	SOURCE				
	Discount House	Department Store	Chain Store	Independent Dealer	Peddler
Cash	61	34	31	21	—
Credit	39	66	69	79	100
Total per cent	100	100	100	100	100
Total cases	(28)	(50)	(164)	(178)	(34)

a. Based on aggregate of three appliances: TV, phonograph, and washing machine.

Contrary to popular belief, the discount houses do offer credit. Some of the smaller ones have done so for some time and even the two largest in the city now have arrangements with banks that are prepared to extend credit to the consumer. But as the data show, most of the purchases at discount houses were for cash. The proportion of credit purchases jumps markedly in the department and chain stores; it is even higher in the neighborhood stores; and all the appliances purchased from peddlers were, as we have come to expect, bought on credit.

Given the decision to use credit, does it make any difference where the family shops for its appliances? The data on hand indicate that it does. Looking first at the distinction between sources in and out of the neighborhood, we find that television sets cost less when bought outside, even when method of payment is taken into account. Far more of those who use credit pay a high price wherever they shop, but shopping scope still makes a difference, as can be seen by reading the columns in Table 6.10.

As demonstrated in Table 6.11, these patterns become

Table 6.10—Joint Effect of Reported Locus of Purchase and Method of Payment on Cost of Television Set

(Per Cent Paying "High" Price)

Where Purchased	Cash		Credit	
"In neighborhood"	29	(21)	56	(99)
"Outside neighborhood"	10	(50)	47	(98)

still more evident when we consider the type of store. (Because of the small number of cases, we have grouped department and discount store.)

Table 6.11—Joint Effect of Type of Store and Method of Payment on Cost of Television Set

(Per Cent Paying "High" Price)

Where Purchased[a]	Cash		Credit	
Department and discount stores	—	(13)	27	(22)
Chain store	7	(27)	41	(61)
Independent neighborhood dealer	29	(21)	60	(82)

a. TV sets purchased from peddlers are omitted from this table since they were only bought on credit.

Both the cash and credit prices are substantially higher when the sets are bought from the neighborhood dealers. None of the thirteen families who paid cash in a department or discount store paid a high price, but 29 per cent of the cash payers who went to neighborhood dealers did. Among the credit users, the difference is even greater. Clearly, even the families that depend upon credit have much to gain by extending their shopping horizons to the large, nonneighborhood stores.

RACE AND COST

So far, we have found a series of relationships which are in keeping with an economic model. People must of course pay for the privilege of credit and the cost of credit must take into account the element of risk. That small independent stores charge more is to be expected from their smaller volume of business and less efficient operating procedures. Since it is presumably more convenient to shop in the neighborhood, some people may be willing to pay for this convenience. We now consider a factor affecting cost which has no place in a strictly economic model: the race of the consumer.

The amount paid for appliances differs greatly among the racial groups. Whites pay the least, Puerto Ricans the most, with Negroes in between. This can be seen from Table 6.12.

Table 6.12—Cost of Appliances According to Race

Appliance	White		Negro		Puerto Rican	
Television:						
Per cent high price	26	(61)	43	(83)	47	(142)
Phonograph:						
Per cent over $200	17	(18)	48	(52)	56	(70)
Washing machine:						
Per cent over $230	18	(27)	33	(27)	53	(64)

In large part, the close connection between race and cost reflects the varying tendencies of the three racial groups to rely on credit. As we shall see in the next chapter, whites use credit far less often than the others. But the use of credit does not account for all the differences in cost shown in Table 6.12. For when method of payment is taken into account, it turns out that nonwhites who use cash do *not* pay more than whites for television sets. In fact, among the cash users, the nonwhites tend to pay somewhat lower prices. But among the credit users, the association between race and cost remains intact, as can be seen from the second row of Table 6.13.

Table 6.13—The Joint Effect of Method of Payment and Race on Cost of Television Set
(Per Cent Paying "High" Price)

Method of Payment	White		Negro		Puerto Rican	
Cash	20	(35)	9	(11)	12	(33)
Credit	32	(25)	49	(71)	58	(109)

We have seen that credit costs more in neighborhood stores than in non-neighborhood stores. A possible interpretation of this finding, then, is that Negro and Puerto Rican families, who more often need credit, turn to neighborhood sources more often than the whites. This indeed turns out to be the case. Among Puerto Ricans who used credit to buy a TV set, 62 per cent dealt with independent neighborhood dealers or peddlers, compared with 45 per cent of the Negroes and 40 per cent of the whites. Their source of credit in conjunction with their greater use of it accounts in large part for the fact that nonwhites pay much higher prices than do whites. But these factors do not fully explain the racial differences in cost. For note how things stand when we distinguish between families who obtained credit at large "bureaucratic" stores and those who turned to neighborhood dealers or peddlers for credit. In the large stores, nonwhites, if anything, pay less than whites when buying on credit. But among those who turn to the more traditional sources for credit, it is the nonwhites who are much more likely to pay high prices.

Table 6.14—The Relationship Between Race and Cost of Television Set for Credit Purchases According to Source

(Per Cent of Credit Users Paying "High" Price)

Source	White		Negro		Puerto Rican	
Bureaucratic (department, discount, and chain)	46	(13)	36	(33)	36	(39)
Traditional (neighborhood dealer, peddler)	13	(8)	56	(27)	69	(61)

The percentages for the whites, shown in Table 6.14, are based on very few cases and therefore are not very reliable. But these patterns are at least suggestive. In the large, bureaucratic stores where prices are standardized, the race of the customer does not affect the price. The neighborhood merchants and peddlers, on the other hand, are specialists in a more personal system of credit and apparently do take the race of the customer into account. The pattern may reflect a tendency among neighborhood merchants to exploit the new migrants whom they consider to be naive shoppers. Their relative unfamiliarity with "comparative shopping" may also be reinforced by their pattern of compensatory consumption. Both characteristics would make it easier for the merchants to persuade the newer migrants to buy more expensive models. And finally, the neighborhood merchants may consider the newer migrants to be poorer credit risks and so charge them higher prices. Whatever the explanation for the pattern disclosed in the second row of Table 6.14, neighborhood merchants do evidently make discriminations along racial lines, the basis for which may lie in exploitation, sales pressure, or distrust.

In sum, the price patterns examined in this chapter corroborate quite closely the picture of the "traditional" marketing system presented in Chapter 2 on the basis of the interviews with local merchants. As we have seen, merchandise costs more in this market than in the larger, "bureaucratic" market, even though it is of generally poorer quality. The data have also borne out the merchants' claim that buying from peddlers is particularly costly. And since many low-income families have a restricted scope of shopping—either by choice or because they are excluded from the larger market—they tend to pay dearly for their appliances. In the next chapter, we examine more closely an important element in this economy, one which has been shown to have a marked effect on cost—credit.

CHAPTER 7

Credit Patterns: Sources and Users of Credit

IMPLICIT in the preceding chapters has been the prime importance of consumer credit for the low-income families we interviewed. Most of them buy major durables in spite of their limited income; they shop in neighborhood stores or chain stores which advertise "easy credit" rather than in department stores or discount houses; and as we have just seen, the use of credit significantly affects the prices they pay.

We now consider the materials bearing directly on this use of credit. How many families depend upon credit when buying major durables? How many use credit for less expensive purchases such as clothing and food? And which types of families pass up credit and pay only cash for their goods? How large is this group, and how does it differ from those which rely heavily on credit?

Method of Payment for Major Durables

Early in the interview, families were asked the following question: "Do you think it is a good idea or a bad idea to buy things on credit?"

On the basis of the expressed *attitude* toward consumer credit, we might assume that credit was inconsequential in their lives, for only 15 per cent said that buying on credit was a good idea; 26 per cent gave a qualified answer—e.g., "it depends"—and the remaining 59 per cent (virtually three in every five) said it was a bad idea.

When asked to explain their opinion, more than half spontaneously mentioned the high cost of credit, saying "it costs too much," or "you pay too much in carrying charges." Some referred specifically to the pressures of keeping up payments; others mentioned their fears of repossession; and still others pointed to the long period of time over which payments are made, often beyond the life of the merchandise. But even some of those who felt that buying on time was a bad idea went on to say that this is "the only way poor people could buy." Some reported that they found it easier to buy on time than to try to save the money and pay cash. In all, 40 per cent made some reference to the need for credit if people like them were to get the goods they needed or wanted.[1]

But attitudes and behavior need not coincide. Their expressions of negative attitude toward this method of buying notwithstanding, we know that most of the families do use credit when buying major durables. More than two-

---

1. These findings on attitudes toward installment buying differ sharply from those reported by George Katona on the basis of his nationwide surveys of consumers. In November, 1959, for example, Katona found that a majority of consumers on all income levels considered installment buying a "good idea"; only about a third viewed it as a "bad idea." Katona's data show that very low-income families, those earning under $3,000, are less favorably disposed toward installment buying than those of somewhat higher income, but even in this group some 55 per cent considered it favorably. Some of the apparent differences between our findings and those of Katona may be an artifact of coding decisions. Katona apparently considers the qualification, "can't buy without borrowing," as a favorable attitude. But even if we reclassify those who said that "credit is the only way poor people can buy" as holding a positive attitude, we still find a substantially smaller proportion in our sample viewing credit buying favorably. See George Katona's statement in *Consumer Credit Labeling Bill, op. cit.,* pp. 810-812, esp. Tables 2 and 5. See also, George Katona, *The Powerful Consumer* (New York: McGraw-Hill Book Co., Inc., 1960), p. 100.

thirds of those who bought furniture at the time of the move bought it on credit, and close to the same proportion used credit to pay for their major appliances. Almost all who used credit turned to stores or peddlers for it; the others, ranging from 3 to 8 per cent, borrowed the money from banks or finance companies. These figures are shown in Table 7.1.

Table 7.1—Method of Payment for Major Durables
(In Per Cent)

Method of Payment	Furniture at Move	Furniture Since Move	TV	Phono-graph	Sewing Machine	Vacuum Cleaner	Washing Machine
Store and peddler credit	66	53	64	59	59	61	55
Cash borrowed	3	5	4	4	3	4	8
Cash savings	31	42	32	37	38	35	37
Total per cent	100	100	100	100	100	100	100
Total cases[a]	(297)	(203)	(322)	(155)	(108)	(79)	(132)

a. Those who did not buy appliances from a commercial source or who did not answer the question on method of payment are excluded from the table.

As it happens, these low-income families do not differ greatly from the population at large in their use of credit. A survey conducted for the Federal Reserve Board disclosed that 55 per cent of the nation's consumers who purchased furniture or major household appliances in 1958 used credit. Among the nation's low-income consumers—those earning under $6,000—the proportion who used credit for these purchases ranged from 58 to 65 per cent, figures similar to those found in our sample.[2]

By aggregating the various purchases shown in Table 7.1, we can determine the number of families who have ever used credit when buying major durables. When this is done, we find that 44 per cent have used only credit for these purchases; 35 per cent have used cash for some and credit for others, and only 21 per cent have always paid cash.

We find that the families who only pay cash are not as

2. "1959 Survey of Consumer Finances: The Financial Position of Consumers," *Federal Reserve Bulletin* (July, 1959), 719, Supplementary Table 15.

active consumers as those who use credit. They less often own three or more appliances as can be seen from Table 7.2.

Table 7.2—Method of Payment for Major Durables by Appliance Ownership
(In Per Cent)

Number of Appliances	Credit Only	Mixed	Cash Only
0-2 (low)	49	29	58
3-5 (high)	51	71	42
Total per cent	100	100	100
Total cases[a]	(197)	(155)	(91)

a. Excluded are about 5 per cent of the sample who either did not purchase any of these durables from a commercial source or else did not make known the method of payment used.

Families using both cash and credit are most apt to own many appliances, but those who always buy on credit still manage to own more than those who pay only in cash. This finding may reflect in part what we know to be the greater consumer needs of the families who depend most on credit. But it also suggests that credit facilitates the acquisition of major durables by low-income families. This may seem paradoxical, for, as we have found, credit is expensive. The cash customer could conceivably buy three appliances for the same amount that the credit customer pays for two. What probably underlies this apparent paradox is the psychology of the low-income consumer rather than the logic of economically rational decisions. We have noted before that some family heads felt that it was *easier* to buy on credit than to save and pay cash. They made it plain that they were referring to the discipline required for advance saving. This they found difficult to achieve. Faced with many day-to-day demands upon their resources, they found it hard to build up substantial reserves. For them credit provided a system of enforced savings with the discipline imposed from without.[3] At a price, it enables them to accumulate more durable

3. A felt need for the external discipline imposed by installment buying is not confined to the low-income consumer. In a study of the appeal of credit buying for young, middle-class families, William H. Whyte suggests that the monthly installment fits neatly into their efforts to budget their

goods than they otherwise would, and probably it seduces them into buying more expensive models, the costs of which are perceived in terms of small payments rather than as a lump sum.

One consequence of relying exclusively on credit for major durables is the narrowing of the family's shopping scope. Families who use credit only depend more on neighborhood merchants than those who sometimes or always pay cash. This can be seen from Table 7.3, which shows the association between method of payment and orientation to nonneighborhood stores.

Table 7.3—Method of Payment by Shopping Scope
(In Per Cent)

Shopping Scope	Credit Only	Mixed	Cash Only
Narrow	50	34	34
Broad	50	66	66
Total per cent	100	100	100
Total cases	(197)	(155)	(91)

This finding emphasizes an obstacle to any educational program aimed at extending the family's shopping scope. Although some families may buy from neighborhood merchants out of ignorance of alternatives, others may do so because they fail to meet the credit requirements of the more "reliable" stores. In part, the low-income family is caught up in the choice of doing without or relying on credit and therefore paying more.

Credit for Food and Clothing

As we shift from major durables to commodities of smaller unit cost, we find, of course, far fewer families resorting to credit. A little more than one in every five use

income. His study of some eighty middle-class families indicates that they too are more apt to think of the monthly payment rather than the cost of the merchandise or the cost of credit. See William H. Whyte, Jr., "Budgetism: Opiate of the Middle Class," *Fortune*, May, 1956.

credit to buy clothing. Most of these—fifty-nine out of ninety eight—maintain revolving credit accounts at well-known department stores or clothing stores. These families tend to be younger, better educated, and with higher income than the rest, who do not have revolving credit accounts. Negroes are more likely than either whites or Puerto Ricans to be in this group.

Even fewer families (12 per cent) buy food on credit. The proportion relying on credit for at least *some* of their food needs is actually greater, for almost one in every five (18 per cent) have their milk delivered by a milk company. As some explained, this arrangement provided needed credit. We can assume that others in this group also depend upon credit extended by the milkman, but since this established pattern is so familiar, they did not think to mention it as a form of credit. Those who buy groceries on credit do so, of course, at the small independent stores, rather than at the supermarkets or city markets, once again emphasizing the role of credit in restricting shopping alternatives.

Commercial Loans

We have seen that some families financed their major purchases by borrowing money from a commercial source. Others found it necessary to borrow money to pay off their consumer debts or to meet emergencies. Our survey shows that 40 per cent of the families have at some time or another borrowed from a lending institution. At the time of the survey, 22 per cent still owed money on such loans. Those who borrowed went in roughly equal numbers to commercial banks and finance companies, and a few made use of credit unions. (Of the borrowers, 46 per cent took out bank loans, 44 per cent went to finance companies, and 10 per cent borrowed from credit unions.)

Borrowing money from a lending institution depends on the family's credit standing as well as on its needs. Higher-income families and those whose income is based exclusively on earnings are more apt to have obtained such loans. Fifty-two per cent of the families earning over $3,500 have had such loans, compared with 38 per cent of those earning under $3,500; the same is true for 48 per cent of the wage earners, compared with 14 per cent of the families on welfare.

The youngest families (where the head is under 30 years of age) and the oldest (where the head is over 50) borrowed money less often than those of middle age. Families headed by persons between 30 and 39 years of age have most often taken out loans.[4] This age pattern suggests that through the life cycle debts are shifted from stores to banks and finance companies. The youngest families are apt to turn to stores for installment credit; as their debts mount and the payments become increasingly more difficult to meet, they are apt to obtain loans to pay off their other debts. In this way they obtain relief in the form of smaller monthly payments at the cost of a longer period of indebtedness.

Income affects the source of the loan as well as the ability to get one. The proportion of borrowers who go to banks rather than to finance companies increases steadily with income. Only 15 per cent of the poorest families who obtained loans went to banks or credit unions, compared with 85 per cent of the families in the highest (over $4,500) income group. White families borrow less often than either Negroes or Puerto Ricans, but when they do, they almost always turn to banks rather than to finance companies. In contrast, twice as many Negroes borrow from finance companies as from banks. Among Puerto Ricans who borrow, bank loans are slightly more frequent than finance company loans.

The Families Who Use Consumer Credit

It will be remembered that 75 per cent of the families used credit for at least some of their major purchases. When

---

4. Thirty-one per cent of the family heads in their twenties, 48 per cent of those in their thirties, 41 per cent in their forties, and only 21 per cent over fifty have borrowed from a commercial source.

we consider the use of credit for clothing, buying from peddlers, and outstanding personal loans, the proportion making use of consumer credit rises to 81 per cent.[5]

The great majority (60 per cent of the entire sample) had consumer debts at the time of the interview. This refers to installment debts only, not to debts to grocers, physicians, or relatives.[6] This proportion with consumer debt is about the same as that found for all consumers in the United States in 1959.[7] In whatever respects this low-income sample differs from the population at large, it is *not* in the extent of having debts. (The next chapter considers this comparative material in more detail to see whether our families have larger debts than comparable groups in the population.)

In examining the characteristics of those who use credit, we shall distinguish the families in debt from the others. In this way, we can roughly identify the families who no longer rely on credit. This is a crude measure at best, since families who once used credit but have no outstanding debts may resort to credit again for their future purchases. However, there is some merit to the distinction, for the family that accepts credit as a way of life is likely to be continuously in debt. We deal then with three groups: those for whom there is no indication of credit usage (about 20 per cent of the sample); those who have used credit but are not now in debt (another 20 per cent); and those who still have consumer debts (60 per cent).

Since we know who the active consumers are, and who buys from peddlers, we already know a great deal about the

---

5. We do not include here the families that have milk delivered or who buy food on credit. If these families did not use credit for durables and did not owe money on loans, they were excluded from this count. Since the reasons for past loans are unknown, some sixteen families who said they once borrowed from a bank or finance company, but now have no debt and who gave no other signs of relying on credit, are excluded from the count. Were they included, the proportion using credit would reach 84 per cent.

6. There are twenty-eight families—6 per cent of the sample—whose only debt is of this kind. These debts are counted along with installment· debts in Chapter 8. The proportion with *any* debt comes to 66 per cent of the sample.

7. "1959 Survey of Consumer Finances," *op. cit.*

families who rely on credit. In brief, they are the larger, younger, and nonwhite families. The education of the household head has little bearing on the use of credit. Variations in income are relevant only in that the poorest families least often use credit, as can be seen from Table 7.4.

Table 7.4—Reliance on Credit According to Income

(In Per Cent)

	INCOME			
RELIANCE ON CREDIT	Under $2,500	$2,500-$3,499	$3,500-$4,499	$4,500 and Over
Did not use credit	36	14	12	18
Used credit—no debts	21	21	20	17
Debts outstanding	43	65	68	65
Total per cent	100	100	100	100
Total cases	(101)	(151)	(124)	(88)

The families in the lowest-income group are smaller and older than the others. The fact that as many as 36 per cent do not use credit reflects their lack of consumer interest as well as their failure to meet the minimal requirements of obtaining credit. In the highest-income group, where presumably families are in a better position to pay cash, somewhat fewer resort to credit.

Several studies, including the Survey of Consumer Finances[8] of the Federal Reserve Board, show that consumer activity and indebtedness are closely related to the family life-cycle. Younger families have more pressing consumer needs (and less accumulated savings), and therefore greater debts. This pattern shows up clearly in our data when the age of the family head is used to indicate the stage in the life cycle.

The marked relationship shown in Table 7.5 is quite striking. Practically all of the youngest families have used credit, and most of them are still in debt. In contrast, almost half of the oldest group have not used credit for the goods they now own and fewer than a third have consumer debts.[9]

8. *Ibid.*

9. These figures are close to those found in the 1959 national survey. In that study, among families headed by persons between 25 and 34, 80 per

Table 7.5—Reliance on Credit According to Age of Family Head

(In Per Cent)

| | AGE OF HEAD | | | |
RELIANCE ON CREDIT	20-29	30-39	40-49	50 and Over
Did not use credit	2	8	21	50
Used credit—no debts	14	20	25	21
Debts outstanding	84	72	54	29
Total per cent	100	100	100	100
Total cases	(93)	(158)	(112)	(101)

This pattern does not correspond completely with variations in consumer activity through the life cycle. As we saw
in Chapter 3, the most active consumers are in the 30–39-
year age group. The discrepancy probably results from the
fact that although consumer needs are great in the early
stages of the family life cycle when households are getting
established, peak earnings are generally not reached until
later. The figures in Table 7.5 illustrate the tendency of
younger families to mortgage future income to meet current consumer wants.[10]

Family size, which is closely related to consumer activity,
is also related to dependence upon credit, as can be seen
from Table 7.6. Larger families not only use consumer credit

Table 7.6—Reliance on Credit According to Family Size

(In Per Cent)

| | SIZE OF HOUSEHOLD | | |
RELIANCE ON CREDIT	1-2 persons	3-4 persons	5 or more
Did not use credit	52	14	14
Used credit—no debts	24	23	15
Debts outstanding	24	63	71
Total per cent	100	100	100
Total cases	(63)	(213)	(188)

cent had personal debt compared with about 33 per cent of the families
headed by persons over 55. "1959 Survey of Consumer Finances." *Ibid.*

10. Since the older families show up as non-credit users rather than as
credit-users without debts, it is tempting to interpret the table as a reflec-
tion of the secular trend toward consumer credit in our society. Although
this may be so, it must be remembered that the older families belong to
different ethnic groups than the younger ones. Furthermore, the data on use
of credit refers to current possessions; the older families may have used

much more than smaller ones, but they find it much harder to get out of debt. They move from one debt to another on the installment plan.

The marked differences between whites and nonwhites with respect to the use of credit appear in Table 7.7.

Table 7.7—Reliance on Credit According to Race
(In Per Cent)

		RACE	
RELIANCE ON CREDIT	White	Negro	Puerto Rican
Did not use credit	51	6	10
Used credit—no debts	18	17	23
Debts outstanding	31	77	67
Total per cent	100	100	100
Total cases	(115)	(133)	(216)

Even though race is related to family size, age of household head, and consumer activity, this difference between the races persists when these other factors are taken into account. Thus, quite apart from considerations of need, there are socially based attitudes toward credit buying associated with race. The importance of ethnicity becomes apparent when the whites are differentiated still further into Jews and non-Jews. Only 39 per cent of the Jewish families, compared with 58 per cent of the other white families, have used credit.

As all these data make plain, credit is a mainstay of low-income consumption just as it is for somewhat higher-income groups.[11] The temptation to resort to credit and the need for it is particularly strong among the nonwhites, and among the younger and the larger families. In the next five chapters, we will examine some consequences of this method of buying.

credit to buy the goods they needed when they were in the early stages of the family life-cycle.

11. Katona has found that installment-buying is more frequent in middle-income groups than in the very low-income groups. George Katona, *The Powerful Consumer, op. cit.,* p. 100.

CHAPTER 8

Family Finances:
Debts and Assets

WE HAVE SEEN that most of the families
are in debt. But how much do they owe? Do these families
in public housing have more or less debt than families of
comparable income living elsewhere? What do they have
in savings and how many carry life and health insurance?
When the answers to these questions have been worked
·out, we shall make use of them to identify the marginal
families, those on the brink of insolvency and consequently
vulnerable to unanticipated financial demands.

Debts

The families were asked questions about specific debts.
The ones who dealt with peddlers or did not pay cash for
their furniture, appliances, automobiles, clothing or food,
were asked if they still owed money and how much. The
same information was obtained from those who had borrowed from banks, finance companies, and other lending
institutions. All families were asked about medical and
dental bills, about debts to friends and relatives, and even
about debts to loan sharks.[1] After these questions about

1. All families were asked whether they had ever borrowed from a "loan
shark," a phrase which they had no difficulty understanding. Sixteen ad-

specific debts, they were asked, in summary, to estimate the full amount of their outstanding debts. By totaling the specific debts we arrive at a figure which we call the "objective" debt total as distinct from the individual's own summary estimate of his total indebtedness. A small number did not know how much they still owed on particular purchases. In these cases we were forced to estimate the debt from the cost and age of the appliance and the size of the monthly payments. For six families, information on debts was so incomplete that it was difficult to estimate the total, and twenty-five families were unable to estimate their total debt. The distribution of families according to the "objective" total and their own estimate of their debt is shown in Table 8.1.

Table 8.1—Distribution of Families According to Size of Debt
(In Per Cent)

	Total of Specific Debts ("Objective")	Total Estimated by Interviewee
None	35	35
$1-$99	18	14
$100-$199	11	10
$200-$499	19	17
$500-$999	13	14
$1000 and over	3	5
Has debt, specific amount unknown	1	5
Total per cent	100	100
Total cases	(464)	(464)

The discrepancies between the two estimates are negligible. They both show the proportion with no debt to be the same—a little more than a third of the sample. On their own estimates, 19 per cent had debts in excess of $500, compared with the 16 per cent when specific debts covered by the questionnaire were tallied.[2] It will be noted that debts in excess of $1,000 are not unknown in this low-

mitted to having dealt with a loan shark, and six still owed money on such a loan at the time of the interview. Others probably had dealt with these illegitimate lenders but were unwilling to admit it.

2. Some may have responded to the summary question by including debts that we deliberately excluded—rent and telephone bills, or the next insur-

income sample. The 3 per cent in the first column represents fifteen families, and the 5 per cent in the second represents twenty-five.

To assess the significance of these figures requires comparative data. Are these unusually large debts, contracted for equipment bought when they moved into public housing? Has the move touched off a "consumer explosion" which has increased their debt over that of comparable groups in the population? Fortunately, comparable data are provided by the Federal Reserve Board survey of consumer finances.[3] In that study, personal debt is defined as "all short and intermediate term consumer debts other than charge accounts and exclusive of mortgage and business debt." This definition is somewhat narrower than ours since we include money owed to friends and relatives as well as grocery and medical bills, which are not ordinarily counted as consumer debts.

In comparing our sample with the general population, we shall classify families by whichever of the two estimates of debt is greater, the "objective" total or the respondent's own estimate. This, of course, maximizes the estimated amount owed. Nevertheless, the families in our sample do *not* have greater debts than families of comparable income throughout the country. The comparisons are shown in Table 8.2.

The two top rows of Table 8.2 show how our sample compares with a sample of the consumer population at large. The national survey includes spending units with incomes below $1,000 and in excess of $10,000, and in both these extreme groups proportionately fewer families have debts. This partly explains the somewhat greater propor-

---

ance premium—and some had consumer debts which escaped through the sieve of our specific questions. A few explained that they owed money for their children's tuition at parochial schools, and one family even owed for college tuition; some were in debt for purchases that we did not ask about, such as jewelry, and some probably had in mind debts on appliances that they no longer owned.

3. "1959 Survey of Consumer Finances," *op. cit.* The survey was made at the end of 1958, almost two years before our study. This reduces somewhat the strict comparability of the data.

Table 8.2—Debts of Local Sample (1960) Compared With National Sample (1958) According to Family Income

(In Per Cent)

	None	$1-$99	$100-$199	AMOUNT OF DEBT $200-$499	$500-$999	$1000 Plus	Total Per Cent
TOTAL							
Local Sample (458)	34	15	11	18	16	6	(100)
National sample— all income groups	40	10	7	14	11	18	(100)
FAMILY INCOME							
$1,000-$1,999							
Local sample (47)	66	11	11	4	8	—	(100)
National sample	57	14	10	12	4	4	(101)
$2,000-$2,999							
Local sample (127)	30	18	14	17	17	4	(100)
National sample	44	12	11	17	10	6	(100)
$3,000-$3,999							
Local sample (139)	32	14	12	22	13	7	(100)
National sample	36	11	7	16	14	16	(100)
$4,000-$4,999							
Local sample (94)	30	14	8	20	21	7	(100)
National sample	32	14	6	14	16	17	(99)
$5,000-$5,999a							
Local sample (51)	28	18	6	18	20	10	(100)
National sample	30	9	8	16	14	23	(100)

a. We have included seventeen families with incomes between $6,000 and $6,600 in this group. Since the Federal Reserve classifies families with incomes between $6,000 and $7,500 together, we are prevented from comparing these seventeen families with comparable families in the national sample.

tion of our sample having at least some debt. Another reason is our broader definition of debt, which includes noninstallment debts to friends, relatives, and for groceries.[4] But these tend to be small. And, in fact, our sample tends to have smaller debts than the population at large. On every income level, a smaller percentage of families in our sample have debts in excess of $1,000, and in all but one of the comparisons, proportionately fewer have debts in excess of $500. The one exception occurs in the $2,000–$2,999 income range.

A clue to the greater frequency of large debts in the general population is provided by the few families in our sample who owe more than $1,000. This debt is often due to the purchase of an automobile. Since automobile ownership in our sample is well below that of the national average, this helps explain the difference in large debts.

In both our sample and the national sample, debts increase with income. The national survey finds this pattern continuing until income reaches $10,000, at which point the proportion with any debt drops sharply, although those in debt tend to owe a good deal.

The comparative data indicate that living in public housing does not materially affect the amount of debt owed by families. At least those in our sample are no more in debt than families of comparable income in a sample of the general population. But this does not necessarily mean that they are no worse off financially than other low-income groups. An important aspect of consumer finances has yet to be considered: savings. The families in our sample *are* worse off, not because they have greater debts, but because they have fewer assets.

Savings

The families in the projects were asked several questions about their savings: whether husband or wife had

---

4. In Chapter 7 we saw that 60 per cent of the sample had installment debts, the same proportion as in the population at large.

savings accounts, checking accounts, money invested in Christmas Clubs; whether they owned government savings bonds, belonged to credit unions, or had money saved in any other place. These questions about the location of savings were followed by one about the amount saved. All families were asked whether they had at least $500 in savings and if not, whether they had at least $100. The question was asked in this way because the pretest interviews had shown that they were reluctant to answer a direct question about the exact amount of their savings.[5]

The proportion of families with savings in various forms is as follows:

	Per Cent
Savings account in bank	26
Checking account	5
U.S. Savings Bonds	6
Credit union	3
Christmas Club	13
Money saved elsewhere	3

As for the amount of savings, 13 per cent of the families have at least $500, and another 14 per cent have at least $100; the remaining 73 per cent either have less than $100 or nothing at all. The families without any savings can be seperated from those with less than $100 simply by taking note of answers about the various locations of savings. Families that reported having money in one or more of these forms, but less than $100, make up only 5 per cent of the sample.[6] The rest, then, must be the families without *any* savings, constituting 68 per cent of the sample (73 per cent reporting "less than $100," minus the 5 per cent stating where they had savings).

How the savings of these families compare with those

---

5. Reluctance to answer questions about savings is probably not unique to this group. The Federal Reserve Board (*Op. cit.,* p. 704 n.) notes that their survey technique tends to underestimate savings. The amount of savings based on surveys is substantially smaller than the amount indicated by the Federal Reserve Board's flow-of-funds accounts.

6. This estimate excludes Christmas Club members since the rules of these "clubs" do not allow them to withdraw their investment at will.

of others with the same income throughout the country can be seen from Table 8.3.[7]

Table 8.3—Savings of Local Sample (1960) Compared With National Sample (1958)

(In Per Cent)

	None	AMOUNT OF SAVINGS Up to $499	$500 and Over	Total Per Cent
TOTAL				
Local sample	68	19	13	(100)
National sample (all income groups)	25	31	44	(100)
FAMILY INCOME $1,000-$1,999				
Local sample	79	6	15	(100)
National sample	50	24	26	(100)
$2,000-$2,999				
Local sample	84	12	4	(100)
National sample	44	24	32	(100)
$3,000-$3,999				
Local sample	63	25	12	(100)
National sample	28	36	36	(100)
$4,000-$4,999				
Local sample	56	24	20	(100)
·National sample	21	45	35	(100)
$5,000-$5,999				
Local sample	50	23	27	(100)
National sample	14	43	43	(100)

Although debts of the families in our sample approximate those of families of comparable income in the nation at large, their savings are far below. Far more of them are without any savings, and far fewer have substantial savings; unlike most of the nation's consumers on the same levels of income, their consumer debts are not backed up by savings. Whether this finding is related to their living in public housing must be a matter of speculation, for we

---

7. The definition of liquid assets in the 1959 Survey of Consumer Finances corresponds closely to ours. It refers to "United States savings bonds, checking accounts, savings accounts in banks and shares in savings and loan associations and credit unions." Currency is not counted. The national survey uses different categories for classifying savings under $500. Hence, Table 8.3 groups together all those with savings under $500.

do not have comparable figures for low-income families in New York City who are not living in public housing. Since they tend to be much younger than the general consumer population, many probably never had any savings. But it is also possible that whatever savings they had were used up in the process of getting settled in their new apartments.

Insurance

At any rate, our low-income families are poorly equipped to cope with such emergencies as unemployment, sickness, or death. But savings are not the only resource in an emergency. Insurance can provide some protection. Although they have little or no savings, most of the families—three out of every five—do have some form of life insurance. More than one in four have policies including twenty-year endowments for the children. They may be choosing to save through these policies to a greater extent than does the general population. But this is a precarious method of saving. The families often find it a heavy burden to meet the monthly payment. A few told us that they were unable to keep up payments, and so lost the money they had invested. One housewife volunteered the information that she had tried to close out her insurance policy and have her money returned, but without success. Nevertheless, the families that do have insurance policies of whatever kind, are presumably better protected against emergencies than those without them.

Apart from life insurance, almost half the families (48 per cent) had some form of health insurance, usually obtained through their place of employment and usually covering the entire family.

By combining the information on savings and insurance we can classify families according to their assets. In making up this index, we assigned the highest rank to families with at least $100 in savings. Those who did not have this amount in savings, but had either life insurance or health insurance, were assigned to the middle rank; those without insurance or savings were assigned to the lowest.[8] This results in the following distribution of families on the index of resources:

		Cases	Per Cent
(High)	Families with $100 or more in savings	128	28
(Medium)	Families with insurance but less than $100 in savings	226	48
(Low)	Families without insurance or $100 in savings	110	24
Totals		464	100

Measuring Family Solvency

From the beginning, we wanted to learn as much as possible about the families who, because of consumer debts, are on the verge of insolvency. These marginal families are described in detail in the next chapter. Here we consider only how this group of families is defined.

To measure solvency, we classify families not by the absolute amount of debt but rather by the ratio of debt to income, as set forth in Table 8.4.

Table 8.4—The Debt-Income Ratio of the Low-Income Families

Debt as Percentage of Annual Income	Cases	Per Cent of Sample
Less than one per cent	169	36
1-4 per cent	91	20
5-9 per cent	71	15
10-19 per cent	76	17
20-39 per cent	42	9
40-101 per cent	15	3
Totals	464[a]	100

a. Although we could not compute a debt estimate for six of the families because of incomplete information, we were able to make reasonable guesses about their debt-income ratio. For example, we may not know whether a family owes $300 or $500, but in either case it may owe between 10 and 20 per cent of its income.

---

8. Almost all the families with at least $100 in savings also have insurance; insurance was therefore not included in the definition of the "high" asset group. Families with life insurance also tend to have health insurance, but those with only one kind are also included in the middle group.

More than a third of the families owe less than one per cent of their yearly income. (This includes, of course, the families without any debts.) At the other extreme are fifteen families whose debts come to more than two fifths of their income, one family actually owing more than its annual income. Almost a third (29 per cent) owe more than 10 per cent of their income.

The concept of family solvency could be defined by these debt-income ratios alone, but it is more reasonable to include other assets besides income. The family with a high debt-income ratio that also has savings is obviously better off than the family of the same ratio without savings. Conversely, a family without any consumer debt may still be vulnerable to emergencies because it has neither savings nor insurance. True, savings of $100 or so will not go very far in an emergency, but the fact that a family has saved this amount indicates an attitude of some prudence in managing family finances. This is another reason for taking savings and insurance as well as debts and income into account. In this way we can treat the debt-income ratio as one component of solvency and the savings-insurance index as the other.

In order to measure family solvency, we distinguish three groups of roughly equal size on the debt-income ratio: families with debts that come to less than one per cent of income, those in the 1–9 per cent range, and those with debts amounting to 10 per cent or more of income. Table 8.5 shows how these are related to assets, the other component of solvency.

Table 8.5—Debt-Income Ratios and Assets

	DEBT-INCOME RATIO		
ASSETS	0-.9 Per Cent (Low)	1-9 Per Cent (Medium)	10 Per Cent plus (High)
Savings (High)	37	27	16
Insurance (Medium)	38	50	61
Neither (Low)	25	23	23
Total per cent	100	100	100
Total cases	(169)	(162)	(133)

In the top row of Table 8.5, we see that the proportion having savings decreases as the debt-income ratio increases. But the last row shows no relationship between the absence of assets and the ratio of debt to income. Families without savings or insurance are found as often among those with relatively few debts as among those with many. This comes as no surprise, in view of some earlier findings. It will be remembered that a minority of families are relatively inactive consumers and do not accumulate installment debts. These tend to be the poorest families, presumably too poor to have savings or insurance.[9] In other words, families that are not particularly solvent can nevertheless have a low debt-income ratio. This points up the advantage of including the assets index in the measure of solvency.

The more solvent families are those at the upper left of Table 8.5—those with savings and few debts relative to income—and the least solvent, at the lower right. By combining the two ratings we obtain the following distribution of families on the index of solvency:

Solvency Ratings	Cases	Per Cent	
Very High	63	14	} 37
High	108	23	
Medium	144	31	
Low	118	25	} 32
Very Low	31	7	
Totals	464	100	

The families scoring low or very low on this index (about one third of the sample) border on insolvency. None of them have savings. A little more than half have high debt-income ratios and insurance. About a fourth are rated medium on the debt-income ratio but have no assets at all, and almost one quarter are without any assets and have high debt-income ratios.

Having identified these marginal families, we have now to examine their major characteristics.

---

9. As can be seen from the second row of Table 8.5, the likelihood of having insurance increases with debts.

CHAPTER 9

The Marginal Families: Consumption and Insolvency

A PORTRAIT of the marginal families will direct us toward those attributes that cause insolvency and toward certain consequences of this marginal condition. As we shall see, the marginal families have distinctive consumer habits, are found most frequently in particular social groups or categories, and manifest symptoms of instability and maladjustment in their daily lives.

Consumer Practices of Marginal Families

There is a marked association between insolvency and certain self-evidently ineffective consumer practices. The families who rely exclusively on credit for purchases of major durables are much more often insolvent than those who sometimes or always pay cash; the families shopping primarily in the neighborhood and dealing with peddlers are also more given to insolvency. All this is summed up in Table 9.1.

It is clear that inept consumer practices are associated with insolvency, and it is probable that these are mutually reinforcing. To shop where prices are high and quality of products often poor and to pay the costs of credit are good ways of exhausting limited resources. Conversely, families perennially close to the limits of their resources and still wanting what they consider the necessities of life have fewer alternatives for shopping realistically open to them. Breaking this vicious cycle would require that these consumers be re-educated and provided with less costly alternatives to their current practices.

Table 9.1—Consumer Practices and Insolvency
(Per Cent Insolvent)

	Cash Only		Mixed		Credit Only	
Method of payment for major durables	8	(91)	30	(155)	48	(197)
	Broad		Intermediate		Narrow	
Shopping scope	22	(131)	31	(140)	39	(193)
	Never Bought		Bought Once		Repeat Buyers	
Experience with peddlers	21	(233)	28	(80)	51	(151)

Although certain procedures for buying commodities are related to insolvency, the *amount* of commodities owned is not. Marginal families are no more likely to own many appliances than the more solvent ones. But, by the same token, their precarious economic position has evidently not lessened consumption since they do not own *fewer* appliances.

Insolvency, is however, related to the second component of consumer activity: purchasing plans. Families intending to make major purchases are more often insolvent than families without such intent, and those intending to buy within the year are more often insolvent than those planning to postpone buying for a longer period. These results are shown in Table 9.2.

The fact that families who intend to buy soon are most often insolvent, significantly more than those who intend to wait at least a year, largely reflects the more pressing needs

Table 9.2—Insolvency According to Immediacy of Purchasing Plans

(Per Cent Insolvent)

Will Buy Within Year		Uncertain		Will Not Buy in Year		No Intent to Purchase	
43	(163)	29	(89)	29	(100)	21	(112)

of the less solvent families. As we shall soon see, insolvent families are more frequently in groups with pressing needs. But this finding also suggests that insolvent families are less willing than others to defer gratifications. Their time perspectives may be shorter. Concerned with the present rather than the future, they may be more willing to incur great debt in order to satisfy their wants sooner. They more often live by the slogan of the American credit economy, "buy now, pay later." In short, apart from need, the absence of cultural values that call for the discipline of postponing gratifications may contribute to insolvency.

Social Characteristics of Marginal Families

Previous chapters have repeatedly shown that consumer practices vary with three basic characteristics of families: race, age of household head, and family size. The same characteristics are closely related to insolvency. As can be seen from Table 9.3, nonwhites, particularly Puerto Ricans, young families, and large families, are much more frequently insolvent.

That age of household head and family size should be associated with insolvency is to be expected, for both are

Table 9.3—Dominant Social Characteristics of Insolvent Families

(Per Cent Insolvent)

Race			Age of Head			Family Size		
White	11	(115)	20-29	47	(93)	1-2 persons	11	(63)
Negro	35	(133)	30-39	37	(158)	3 persons	24	(86)
Puerto Rican	41	(216)	40-49	27	(112)	4 persons	36	(127)
			50 plus	16	(101)	5 or more	40	(188)

indicative of pressing consumer needs, difficult to meet in the face of limited resources. As we have noted, families in the early stages of the life cycle have the greater needs, whereas their peak earnings are generally not reached until later. So, too, the large family in our sample is apt to have a smaller per-capita income, and indeed it is the large families in the lower-income range that are most often insolvent. Forty-four per cent of the large families with incomes under $3,500 are marginal, compared with 34 per cent of the large families with a higher income. Among small families, income makes little difference. On both income levels only about 18 per cent of the small families are marginal.

More puzzling is the pronounced effect of race on solvency. What accounts for the marked difference between whites and nonwhites? Is it the result of culturally related values affecting consumer behavior, or the result of differences in need and financial resources between the three racial groups? The rest of this section will deal with possible interpretations of this finding. Identifying the characteristics of the marginal families may help explain the association between race and solvency, as well as tell us more about the three racial groups.[1]

The racial pattern might merely be an artifact of differences in age of family head or in family size. To test the first possibility, Table 9.4 examines the joint association of race and age of family head with insolvency. In each broad age-group, whites continue to be less often insolvent than nonwhites. Comparison of the columns and rows in Table 9.4

Table 9.4—Insolvency According to Race and Age of Household Head

(Per Cent Insolvent)

Age of Head	White		Negro		Puerto Rican	
Under 40	14	(21)	40	(88)	46	(142)
Over 40	10	(94)	27	(45)	33	(74)

1. Race is emphasized in this analysis because it is such an important factor in the social organization of the community. The social groups now existing in these projects tend to follow racial lines, and the proposed program of action will probably have to work through these groups.

will show, in fact, that race is the more important factor. Age actually makes little difference among the whites, younger white families avoiding insolvency almost as often as the older ones. It is the young Puerto Rican and Negro families who are most subject to financial troubles.

The joint association of race and family size with insolvency can be seen in Table 9.5. These figures show that

Table 9.5—Insolvency According to Race and Family Size
(Per Cent Insolvent)

Family Size	White		Negro		Puerto Rican	
1-2 persons	—	(35)	13	(15)	38	(13)
3-4 persons	15	(53)	29	(65)	41	(95)
5 or more persons	19	(27)	49	(53)	42	(108)

race continues to be a major factor when family size is taken into account. Among families of every size, the whites are least often marginal. A striking difference emerges when we read the columns in Table 9.5. The economic condition of both whites and Negroes is strongly affected by family size, but this is not true for Puerto Ricans. The sources of insolvency among the Puerto Ricans must lie elsewhere.

RACE, CONSUMER PRACTICES, AND INSOLVENCY

We know from previous chapters that the consumer practices related to insolvency also vary with race. Whites more often pay cash when purchasing major durables. Negroes are most oriented to stores outside the neighborhood, and Puerto Ricans are least so. To what extent then are the differing tendencies toward insolvency among these racial groups related to consumer habits? Table 9.6 shows how

Table 9.6—Insolvency According to Race and Method of Payment for Major Durables
(Per Cent Insolvent)

Method of Payment	White		Negro		Puerto Rican	
Cash only	—	(51)	27	(11)	14	(29)
Mixed	8	(24)	33	(55)	36	(76)
Credit only	38	(26)	41	(64)	54	(107)

method of payment for major durables affects insolvency within each racial group.

By reading down each column of percentages, we see that reliance on credit is closely related to insolvency among the whites and Puerto Ricans, but somewhat less so among the Negroes. White families who rely exclusively on credit for their major purchases are almost as often insolvent as their nonwhite counterparts. But the fact is that whites do not use credit as much as the others, and are therefore more likely to be solvent.

The connection between shopping scope and insolvency within each racial group is shown in Table 9.7.

Table 9.7—Insolvency According to Race and Shopping Scope
(Per Cent Insolvent)

Shopping Scope	White		Negro		Puerto Rican	
Broad	12	(33)	25	(60)	26	(38)
Intermediate	6	(36)	41	(41)	40	(63)
Narrow	15	(46)	47	(32)	47	(115)

Shopping scope has no consistent relation to the financial situation of white families. This is in keeping with an earlier finding (see Table 6.14 in Chapter 6), showing that whites pay less than nonwhites when buying on credit at neighborhood stores. But shopping scope has a pronounced effect among Negroes and Puerto Ricans. Among both, the proportion of marginal families declines sharply as the families leave the neighborhood to shop. This suggests that educational efforts designed to widen the shopping horizons of families should be directed mainly at the nonwhites, for they have most to gain from shopping outside the neighborhood.

Socioeconomic Condition of Marginal Families

We have seen that racial differences in solvency can not be explained solely on the basis of consumer needs as indicated by family size and stage in the family life cycle. But the difference in the use of credit between whites and nonwhites suggests that culturally determined attitudes toward indebtedness may be involved. Perhaps nonwhites incur debts more often because they want to defer gratifications less often.[2]

But before concluding that such a value-orientation contributes to insolvency, we must examine other alternatives. The nonwhites, particularly the Puerto Ricans, are relatively recent migrants to the city, and their more marginal position may reflect the hardships associated with a period of cultural transition.

Apart from adjusting to life in the city, they must come to terms with life in public housing. The white families, many of whom live in Vladeck, tend to be "old-timers" in the projects. And since moving puts a strain on family finances, we must consider the effect of length of residence in the projects. Also to be considered is the fact that newer migrants tend to be at a disadvantage in the job market, and so their income and occupational position may be substantially lower than those of whites.

Consider first the connection between migration and family solvency set out in Table 9.8. The top row would seem to indicate that length of time in the city is associated with insolvency. But this is due entirely to the differing times of arrival of the three racial groups. Within each racial group, the duration of stay in the city has no effect on insolvency. This is surprising, for it seems to contradict the widely held belief that the economic position of migrants improves in time. The explanation of this discrepancy may lie in the fact that this sample is restricted to low-income families, the older migrants may be a negatively selected group which consists largely of those who have not advanced economically during their stay in the city. Those

2. Nonwhites with purchasing plans more often say they will buy within the year than whites. Somewhat more than half the nonwhites and less than a third of the whites did so. This may reflect a difference in values as well as need.

Table 9.8—Insolvency According to Length of Time in New York City

(Per Cent Insolvent)

	TIME IN NEW YORK CITY					
	10 Years or Less		11 Years or More		Born in N.Y.C.	
Entire Sample	39	(115)	31	(276)	23	(66)
Whites	a	(2)	9	(65)	15	(46)
Negroes	35	(31)	34	(82)	35	(17)
Puerto Ricans	41	(82)	40	(129)	a	(3)

a. Too few cases for determining percentages.

who have are presumably not eligible to live in low-income housing, and are therefore not represented in the sample.

The connection between length of residence in the project and insolvency is shown in Table 9.9. The top row shows that insolvency decreases with length of residence, and this may reflect, in part, the financial strains associated with the move. But this is by no means a uniform pattern within each racial group. The most recent white residents are not the most insolvent ones; instead, insolvency increases only among the oldest. Among Negroes, insolvency decreases through the first five years only to increase again among the oldest residents. Only among Puerto Ricans does insolvency decline steadily with length of residence. The reason for the upward trend among whites and Negroes longest in residence is not clear. Perhaps the fact that these families still live in low-income housing reflects their enduring inability to achieve a financially stable position. But if this were a general characteristic of project "oldtimers" we should find the same pattern among the Puerto Ricans as well.

Table 9.9—Insolvency According to Length of Time in Project

(Per Cent Insolvent)

	LENGTH OF TIME IN PROJECT							
	Under 2 Years		3 Years		4-5 Years		6 or More Years	
Entire sample	40	(93)	36	(126)	28	(141)	25	(104)
Whites	6	(17)	7	(15)	8	(36)	17	(47)
Negroes	43	(28)	36	(42)	28	(43)	40	(20)
Puerto Ricans	50	(48)	44	(69)	40	(62)	27	(37)

Table 9.9 also shows that the greater solvency of white families is not due to longer residence in the projects, for whatever the term of residence, whites are more likely to be solvent than nonwhites.

One sign of the strains of adjustment experienced by the more recent migrants is the fact that the nonwhites are more likely to have received welfare assistance. Roughly half the Puerto Rican families have been or still are on welfare, compared with one third of the Negroes and only about one quarter of the whites. As might be supposed, our measure of insolvency based on current debts and assets is related to both past and present welfare assistance.

This is shown in Table 9.10 which also shows the pattern

Table 9.10—Insolvency According to Public Welfare Assistance
(Per Cent Insolvent)

	Now on Welfare		Formerly on Welfare		Never on Welfare	
Entire sample	42	(72)	46	(105)	27	(264)
White	33	(9)	22	(18)	10	(73)
Negro	50	(22)	52	(23)	28	(81)
Puerto Rican	39	(41)	50	(64)	37	(110)

for each racial group. If the facts were not classified by race, the first row would lead us to suppose that those formerly receiving welfare assistance are most often insolvent. But as we see from the rest of Table 9.10, this is not consistently the case. The pattern is particularly marked only among the Puerto Ricans, negligible among the Negroes, and absent among the whites. The Puerto Ricans currently receiving welfare are no more given to insolvency than those who never received such aid.

The third column of the table shows that even among families that have entirely avoided public assistance, race is still related to insolvency. This might reflect possible differences in income between white and nonwhite families. For the entire sample, which includes many nonwage-earning families, there is no association between race and income. Among wage earners, the differences are striking: 67 per cent of the whites, 61 per cent of the Negroes, and only 41 per cent of the Puerto Ricans earn over $3,500. Therefore, in examining the relationship between family income and insolvency in Table 9.11, we first consider the

Table 9.11—Insolvency According to Family Income
(Per Cent Insolvent)

Entire Sample	Under $2,500		$2,500-$3,499		$3,500-$4,499		$4,500 and Over	
Whites	6	(33)	8	(24)	27	(30)	4	(28)
Negroes	44	(25)	23	(39)	36	(42)	44	(27)
Puerto Ricans	49	(43)	44	(88)	44	(52)	18	(33)
Total	34	(101)	33	(151)	37	(124)	22	(88)
Wage Earners Only								
Whites	14	(7)	6	(18)	28	(25)	4	(26)
Negroes	50	(12)	19	(26)	34	(38)	43	(21)
Puerto Ricans	62	(16)	44	(68)	45	(47)	17	(29)
Total	49	(35)	32	(112)	37	(110)	20	(76)

results for all families (including welfare and pension families), and then for wage-earning families only.

The top half of Table 9.11 shows that for the entire sample, the proportion of insolvent families remains fairly constant until income reaches $4,500, whereupon it declines sharply. But there are considerable differences among the racial groups. For example, unlike whites and Puerto Ricans, the insolvency of Negroes *increases* in the highest income group.

Among families dependent upon earnings alone, income is more closely related to insolvency. The lowest paid wage-earners are especially apt to be insolvent, much more so than those in the highest income bracket. This pattern is most characteristic of the Puerto Rican wage earners. Among both whites and Negroes, the pattern is irregular. Again we find that insolvency increases among the Negroes in the highest income bracket.

We have only to read down each column in Table 9.11 to see that variations in income do not explain the racial differences in insolvency; for on each level of income, whites are less often insolvent than nonwhites.

It will be remembered that insolvency is measured by

both debts and assets. How, then, are these components separately related to income within each racial group? The connection between income and debts is shown in Table 9.12. On each income level, whites are much less likely

Table 9.12—Relation of Income to the Debt-Income Ratio Within Each Racial Group

(Per Cent Owing 10 Per Cent or More of Their Income)

Income	Whites		Negroes		Puerto Ricans	
Under $2,500	—	(33)	44	(25)	19	(43)
$2,500-$3,499	8	(24)	26	(39)	39	(88)
$3,500-$4,499	30	(30)	43	(42)	35	(52)
Over $4,500	18	(28)	44	(27)	18	(33)

than Negroes to have large debts, but their debt patterns differ from those of Puerto Ricans only when family income is below $3,500. Once Puerto Ricans earn as much as $3,500, their level of debt approximates that of the white families.

Reading down each column, we see that for both whites and Puerto Ricans the debt-income ratio is curvilinearly related to the amount of income. Both the lowest and highest income groups have relatively fewer debts than have those in the middle. Among Negroes, however, the pattern is quite different. Their debts tend to increase with income, the result being that Negroes in the highest income group experience as much pressure from debt as do those of less income.

Turning now to the second component of insolvency, assets, we find in Table 9.13 that whites and nonwhites have quite different patterns of savings. On each income level, white families are much more likely to save. The poorest

Table 9.13—Relation of Income to Savings Within Each Racial Group

(Per Cent Having at Least $100 in Savings)

Income	Whites		Negroes		Puerto Ricans	
Under $2,500	33	(33)	12	(25)	7	(43)
$2,500-$3,499	42	(24)	36	(39)	10	(88)
$3,500-$4,499	50	(30)	38	(42)	15	(52)
Over $4,500	75	(28)	26	(27)	33	(33)

white families have savings as often as the highest-income nonwhites.

The relation of income to savings differs between the three groups. Among whites, the proportion with savings increases markedly as income increases. The same pattern, but less pronounced, is found for Puerto Ricans. But among Negroes, the relationship is curvilinear. Somewhat fewer Negroes in the highest income group have savings than do those in the middle groups. Just as they were more prone than whites and Puerto Ricans to debt, so, too, the higher-income Negroes are less prone to saving.

The striking differences in debts and savings between whites and nonwhites (particularly the Negroes) is no doubt related to the larger size of the nonwhite families, who must spend a greater proportion of their income on the necessities of life. But these findings also suggest racial differences in compensatory consumption. Nonwhite low-income families, particularly Negroes, are doubly disadvantaged; their poverty is compounded by racial discrimination, and they have comparatively few opportunities to improve their social standing in the community. Since the sphere of consumption is one of the few that is open to them—even Southern racists respect the Negro's dollar—they turn to it with the result that greater income leads to greater consumption, rather than greater savings. Such families may see little point in deferring gratifications.[3]

If there is any merit to the thesis that social status bears on consumption and family solvency, we should expect the

---

3. Starting from a "keeping-up-with-the-Joneses" theory of consumption, James S. Duesenberry (*Income, Saving, and the Theory of Consumer Behavior* [Cambridge, Mass.: Harvard University Press, 1949], especially pp. 50-52) argues that Negroes will spend less and save more than whites of comparable income. He assumes that Negroes compare themselves with other Negroes, and since proportionately fewer Negroes are to be found in the higher income groups, they will as a whole experience less pressure than whites to spend their money. However, our data do not support his thesis. Perhaps the relative prosperity of the postwar era, combined with high-pressured advertising through mass media, have extended Negroes' reference groups; and perhaps the pressure toward compensatory consumption has increased.

occupational status of the wage earner to be related to debts and assets. Those who have managed to achieve a relatively higher status in the occupational sphere should presumably have less need for compensatory consumption. Of course, it is not easy to make such distinctions of status in our sample, owing to its narrow range of occupations. But we can at least distinguish between unskilled and more skilled workers, and some are white-collar workers and a few are semi-professionals (technicians, musicians, etc.) and independent businessmen (e.g., cab owners and storekeepers).

When families are classified by their occupational status, we find that the expected patterns emerge among the Negroes and Puerto Ricans. This can be seen from Table 9.14. The

Table 9.14—Insolvency According to Occupational Status of Wage Earners

(Per Cent Insolvent)

| | OCCUPATIONAL STATUS | | |
	Unskilled	Semi-Skilled and Skilled	White-Collar and Business
Entire sample	48 (150)	28 (160)	20 (55)
Whites	— (16)	16 (45)	17 (24)
Negroes	42 (53)	29 (42)	25 (16)
Puerto Ricans	51 (81)	36 (73)	20 (15)

aggregate pattern (top row) is not due to the pronounced tendency for the white families to have higher occupational status than the others. In fact, among whites, the relationship tends to be reversed. None of the relatively few unskilled white wage earners are insolvent, whereas some of those in higher occupations are. The general finding holds, as we assumed, for the nonwhites. As Table 9.14 shows, a very close relationship between race and insolvency among the unskilled workers lessens among the skilled and semi-skilled, and virtually disappears in the higher occupational groups. Of course, the income of these families is related to their occupational status, but this probably does not explain the findings of Table 9.14. (It will be remembered that Negroes in the highest income group were especially prone to insolvency.) It is more likely that motives and values associated with occupational status account for these results. When members of minority groups move even a short distance up the occupational ladder, they may be less given to the almost exclusive emphasis on consumption. They are readier to take on the values of the middle class, values which, though they are stretched to allow for installment buying, frown upon heavy indebtedness and which encourage savings and the postponement of gratifications.

Social Adjustment of Marginal Families

Insolvency presumably has its economic and social costs. To what extent is the functioning of the family impaired by its marginal position? Do marginal families find themselves doing without certain necessities, such as food, clothing, and medical care, more frequently than other families? Are they more often delinquent in their rent and apt to create other problems for the housing management? To what extent do they take part in the social life of the community?

STRAINS ON THE FAMILY BUDGET

Families were asked about possible difficulties in meeting certain necessities of life. The question dealing with the food budget was the most difficult to phrase. Pretest interviews soon made it apparent that any implication of skimping on food needs aroused resentment. This ruled out any direct question such as "are you having trouble getting enough food for your family?" As a best approximation, this question hinting at the problem was devised: "Compared with last year, do you have more money now to spend on food, less money now, or about the same?"

Indirection created its own problems. Some misinterpreted the question as asking whether the cost of food was greater or less than a year ago. And, of course, since the question calls for a comparison with the previous year it does not deal directly with the issue at hand. With all its recognized faults, the question nevertheless elicited a tendency for the marginal families to report having less money for food now than before. The relationship between these responses and insolvency are shown in Table 9.15, which also

Table 9.15—*Extent of Difficulty in Meeting Food, Clothing and Health Needs, According to Family Solvency*[a]

Item	Relatively Solvent	Somewhat Solvent	Relatively Insolvent
1. Compared with last year, do you have more money now for food, less, or about the same?			
Per cent "less"	22	23	29
2. During the past year, have you been able to get all the clothes you need for yourself and your family?			
Per cent "no"	32	45	53
3. Have you had to put off medical care that you or your family need?			
Per cent "yes"	8	8	19
4. Have you had to put off dental care that you or your family need?			
Per cent "yes"	28	28	40
Total cases	(171)	(144)	(149)

a. The "solvent" category comprises the 37 per cent who were rated "very high" and "high" on the solvency index; the next category is the 31 per cent that scored "medium"; and the "insolvent" category takes in the 32 per cent who scored "low" and "very low."

shows how the more and the less solvent families responded to questions about meeting their clothing and health needs.

In every instance, the relatively insolvent families (those with large consumer debts relative to assets) are the ones who most often report difficulty in coping with the necessities of life. For example, the proportion of families who have had to put off medical care is generally quite small, but still is more than twice as large in the insolvent group.

Data bearing on the adjustment of families were obtained from the housing managers at two of the four projects.[4] They rated the families in the sample on their record of

---

4. The managers of the other two projects refused to give us the information. It need hardly be said that the managers who rated the families did not know how they ranked on our index of insolvency.

paying rent and on whether they were "problem families" in the sense of committing infractions of the project rules. The managers were thoroughly persuaded that rent delinquency is often the result of a family's consumer debts, and the actual data support this impression. The more nearly insolvent the family, the more it was apt to be delinquent in paying rent. Chronic rent delinquents are over seven times as frequent in the insolvent as in the solvent group.

Table 9.16—Rent Delinquency According to Family Solvency
(In Per Cent)

Rent Payment Record	Relatively Solvent	Somewhat Solvent	Relatively Insolvent
Pays on time	90	72	62
Some lateness	8	17	23
Chronic lateness	2	11	15
Total per cent	100	100	100
Total cases[a]	(84)	(70)	(94)

a. Families in the two projects for which rankings could be obtained.

SOCIAL PARTICIPATION

These findings dealing with budgetary matters only confirm obvious expectations. But insolvency has wider ramifications in the life of families. For example, marginal families more often have difficulty living up to the rules of the housing projects. The rules cover such matters as upkeep of the apartment, relations between tenants, the reporting of changes in income and in family composition, and, of course, abiding by the law.

When the managers' ratings of individual families are aggregated and the families classified in terms of the insolvency index, it turns out, as can be seen from Table 9.17, that insolvency is related to designation as a "problem family."

Almost all the relatively solvent families abide by the rules of the housing management. The somewhat solvent families create limited problems more often than the insol-

Table 9.17—Adjustment to Housing Rules According to Family Solvency

(In Per Cent)

Adjustment to Rules	Relatively Solvent	Somewhat Solvent	Relatively Insolvent
No problems	90	74	77
Some problems	8	19	10
Many problems	2	7	13
Total per cent	100	100	100
Total cases	(84)	(70)	(94)

vent ones, but the insolvent families are most apt to present many problems. But in the judgment of the managers, the great majority, even in this group, obey the rules.

Families were asked about their informal and formal participation in the life of the community. They were asked how many of their project neighbors they knew by name, whether they belonged to any organizations inside and outside the project, and whether they had voted in any of the recent elections.

Judging from these indicators, the marginal families participate much less in the formally organized aspects of community life, but whether they are isolated from their neighbors depends upon the racial group to which they belong. This can be seen from Table 9.18 which shows the proportion who know more than an average number of their neighbors in the project.

Among whites, insolvency is closely associated with knowing many neighbors. Were this the pattern in the other

Table 9.18—Knowing Project Neighbors According to Family Solvency

(Per Cent Knowing at Least Five Neighbors)

	Relatively Solvent		Somewhat Solvent		Relatively Insolvent	
Entire sample	53	(171)	60	(144)	47	(149)
Whites	57	(71)	71	(31)	84	(13)
Negroes	54	(42)	64	(44)	60	(47)
Puerto Ricans	46	(58)	52	(69)	34	(89)

racial groups as well, a strong case would be made for the power of the peer group to stimulate consumption and indebtedness. But among Negroes, no distinctive pattern appears, and among Puerto Ricans the insolvent families are the most socially isolated.

Table 9.19 shows the relationship between insolvency and membership in voluntary associations, inside or outside the projects. Since nonwhites, especially Puerto Ricans, belong less often than do whites, the results are again presented separately for each group.

Table 9.19—Membership in Organizations According to Family Solvency

(Per Cent Members)

	Relatively Solvent		Somewhat Solvent		Relatively Insolvent	
Entire sample	36	(171)	26	(144)	16	(149)
Whites	48	(71)	52	(31)	32	(13)
Negroes	48	(42)	34	(44)	21	(47)
Puerto Ricans	12	(58)	10	(69)	9	(89)

For the sample as a whole, and within each racial group, the more solvent families more often belong to voluntary associations. This is particularly true of Negro families.

The association between family solvency and voting in recent elections can be seen in Table 9.20.

Again we find a distinct tendency for solvency to be related to participation in community affairs. Among whites there is little difference, but among Negroes and Puerto

Table 9.20—Voting Participation According to Family Solvency[a]

(Per Cent Voters)

	Relatively Solvent		Somewhat Solvent		Relatively Insolvent	
Entire sample	74	(143)	62	(105)	46	(115)
Whites	84	(61)	90	(20)	82	(11)
Negroes	69	(32)	68	(31)	46	(35)
Puerto Ricans	66	(50)	48	(54)	41	(69)

a. These results are based on the voting participation of the male family head. Families without a male head are excluded.

Ricans the insolvent families vote less frequently than the more solvent ones.

Numerous studies have shown that membership in voluntary associations and voting are closely associated with social class, the lower class being much less given to joining and voting. These findings suggest that this pattern occurs within the lower class as well; the less the financial stability of the low-income family, the less its participation in the life of the broader community.

The Perception of Insolvency

Some of the previous findings may have left the impression that insolvent families go their way, almost as though they were thoroughly unaware of their perilous financial state. This is, of course, possible. In more societies than one, people in chronically difficult circumstances come to take their problems for granted, and in a significant sense do not *know* that they are in trouble.[5] Is this the case here? Are the insolvent families unconcerned in the sense that they fatalistically take their condition as inevitable or irremediable? A clue to their perception of insolvency is provided by answers to the following question, asked at the very end of the interview: "Every family seems to have problems these days. What would you say are the main problems facing your family right now?"

The responses were quite varied. Some families mentioned health problems, others were worried about their children. Some mentioned marital troubles, some were worried about the deterioration of the neighborhood. But many spontaneously singled out financial worries. It is of no small interest, as we see from Table 9.21, that the more objec-

---

5. The distinction between the objective aspects of a problem and its perception as such by people in society is developed by Merton in his essay, "Social Problems and Sociological Theory," in Robert K. Merton and Robert A. Nisbet (eds.), *Contemporary Social Problems* (New York: Harcourt, Brace and World, 1961), pp. 708-715.

Table 9.21—Financial Worries According to Family Solvency
(In Per Cent)

	Relatively Solvent	Somewhat Solvent	Relatively Insolvent
Financial	24	38	69
Other	51	45	36
None	33	24	15
Total per cent[a]	108	107	120
Total cases	(171)	(144)	(149)

a. Percentages add up to more than 100 because many families mentioned more than one problem.

tively difficult their financial state, the more often they worry about it. Evidently they are not resigned to their condition. And this expressed state of concern can provide a basis for organized remedial action among those who need it most.

With this evidence of realistic concern, we bring to a close this review of marginal families, the one third in the sample bordering on financial insolvency. We have seen that they turn to the less effective consumer practices, such as buying on credit, shopping at neighborhood stores, and dealing with peddlers. Their more immediate shopping plans suggest that they are less willing than the more solvent families to defer gratifications.

The insolvent families tend to have heavy consumer needs: they more often have many members, and are in the early stages of the family life cycle. Race turns out to be important in that Negroes and Puerto Ricans are more frequently insolvent than whites, a difference not wholly explained by their also having more of the larger and younger families. The racial pattern results from differences in income, sources of income, and shopping patterns, but above all, from differences in occupation. When nonwhites achieve as high an occupational status as whites do, they tend to show the same degree of financial stability. In the long view, solvency among nonwhites would therefore seem contingent upon their opportunity to rise in the occupational structure. As their occupational status (not just their income) increases, they are apt to turn less to consumption as compensation for status, and tend to develop the attitudes and consumer habits that make for a more stable financial position.

Insolvent families more often do without basic necessities and take a much less active part in community affairs, as indicated by their less frequent membership in organizations and their relatively poor voting record. Also, they are more likely to confront the management of the housing projects with problems created by their departure from the rules of the project. Altogether, insolvency seems to ramify into varied departments of everyday life.

The next two chapters describe the consumer difficulties of these families—difficulties that in some cases have contributed to their marginality.

CHAPTER 10

Consumer Problems I: Shady Sales Practices

ON SEVERAL OCCASIONS during the interview, families were given the opportunity to report whatever consumer problems they may have had, and how they felt about certain purchases they had made. These materials tellingly portray the difficulties encountered by low-income consumers. The main task of this and the following chapters will be to describe and illustrate the various troubles these consumers have—the kinds of exploitative schemes they encounter and the strains they experience as a result of their credit obligations. As a prelude to this, we first present statistical data showing the frequency of these problems and the kinds of families who are apt to have them.

Frequency of Consumer Complaints and Difficulties

In response to a question about whether they were ever cheated by a merchant, more than two in every five answered that they had been. Some complained about the poor quality of the merchandise or its high price without further elaboration. However, many—about a third of the entire sample—described in detail some incident in which they felt they had been cheated. In response to another question asking about difficulties with storekeepers, some 12 per cent cited additional incidents.

Furniture purchased at the time of the move to public housing was a source of dissatisfaction for a number of families. About one in five complained about the quality of the furniture they had bought.

Still another statistic bearing on the consumer complaints of these families concerns their opinion of their most recently purchased appliance. More than a third of the families had some regrets. Significantly, the most frequent complaint had to do with buying on credit. More than half of those who regretted the purchase said they would not buy it on credit if they had it to do over again. As this indicates, and as their reports will bear out, most of the consumer problems of these families stem from buying on credit. Either the families did not anticipate the difficulty of keeping up payments, or else they discovered that the merchandise sold under "easy-payment" plans was of extremely poor quality.

In view of the high level of credit buying among these families, we might expect that many have experienced the legal sanctions of repossession and garnishment. But, it will be remembered, the local merchants told us that they were reluctant to apply legal sanctions and did so only when more personal efforts at control had failed. The statistical data bear this out. Only twenty-seven families (6 per cent of the sample) had something bought on credit repossessed. Somewhat more (8 per cent) had been garnisheed. The use of persuasion and threats rather than legal controls is illustrated by the fact that another 10 per cent had been threatened with a garnishment although it was not actually carried out. In all, one in every five families had encountered the penalties of repossession, garnishment, and threat of garnishment.

The items dealing with cheating, complaints about purchases, and legal difficulties have been combined into a single tabulation of consumer problems and difficulties. The idea of "consumer problems," as summed up here, consists of two aspects: instances in which merchants failed to live up to their obligations and those in which consumers failed to live up to theirs. The former refers to high-pressure tactics, overcharging, fraud, and misrepresentation; the latter, to the legal difficulties and threats resulting from missed payments.[1] The distribution of families according to this measure is shown in Table 10.1.

Table 10.1—Distribution of Families According to Severity of Consumer Problems

	Cases	Per Cent
No apparent difficulties	186	40
Complaint about price or quality only—no details	79	17
Accounts of exploitation not involving legal controls	105	23
Complications resulting in repossession, garnishment, or threat of garnishment	94	20
Totals	464	100

Forty per cent of the 464 families did not report any difficulties as consumers. They were satisfied with their recent purchases, they did not feel that merchants had cheated them, and they never had goods repossessed nor were they ever garnisheed. Another 17 per cent complained about the price or quality of some purchases without furnishing any details. These are rather ambiguous cases. Some in this group may have been merely voicing a general suspicion of merchants. Others may have experienced as much exploitation as those in the next group but were less articulate in communicating their problem. Because of this ambiguity we have not grouped them with the families who were more explicit in detailing their complaints of exploitation (almost a fourth of the sample). And finally, 20 per cent had such severe difficulties that they encountered legal pressures. These were not only cases of consumers

1. These dimensions are not wholly independent of each other. As we shall see, some families stop payments when they discover they have been cheated.

defaulting on payments; for as we shall see, many in this group were also exploited. If we make the conservative assumption that only the last two categories refer to serious consumer problems, we find that this description applies to more than two in every five families.

TROUBLE-PRONE CONSUMERS

Accounts of consumer difficulties were much more frequent among the families who had bought on credit. Only 34 per cent of those who always paid cash for their major purchases had consumer complaints, compared with 70 per cent of those who always or sometimes used credit. And of those who had bought from peddlers, 75 per cent reported some consumer difficulty, compared with 44 per cent of the families who never bought from them.

It is of course not surprising that the insolvent families reported such problems much more frequently than the others. This can be seen from Table 10.2. The third row

Table 10.2—Consumer Difficulties According to Family Solvency
(In Per Cent)

Difficulties	Relatively Solvent	Somewhat Solvent	Relatively Insolvent
None	53	43	23
Price or quality complaints— no details	19	16	15
Accounts of exploitation	17	26	26
Legal complications	11	15	36
Total per cent	100	100	100
Total cases	(171)	(144)	(149)

shows that the solvent families were somewhat more successful in avoiding serious exploitation. The more significant pattern, however, appears in the fourth row. Insolvent families were much more prone than the others to troubles stemming from missed payments.

In view of these relationships, we already know a good deal about the families who had consumer problems. Like the credit users and the insolvent families, they tend to be young, large, and nonwhite. The relationship with age is particularly striking. Eighty-five per cent of the youngest families reported consumer problems, compared with 37 per cent of the oldest. Such troubles were reported by 68 per cent of the Negroes, 65 per cent of the Puerto Ricans, and 42 per cent of the whites.

We now turn to a closer examination of the problems themselves. It should be kept in mind that the difficulties to be described were experienced by less than half of the families we interviewed. Moreover, we have deliberately selected the more detailed and complicated incidents for illustrative purposes.

Types of Exploitation

The numerous accounts of exploitation fall under several general headings. Some reveal the high-pressure sales techniques to which these families are subjected. Others relate to the misrepresentation of the price of goods. And still others refer to the substitution of inferior goods for those ordered. Included here are accounts of the sale of reconditioned goods as new.

The repetitiveness of the incidents is quite striking. Some families were victimized by unethical television repairmen, a few by the same company. Another group were victims of the pots-and-pans salesmen; encyclopedia salesmen show up in several of the accounts, as do the peddlers selling sink attachments.

As we shall see, the incidents touch upon a number of themes. These include the role of the mass media in setting off the chain of events with alluring ads; the anonymity of many of the credit transactions to the point where the consumer is not sure who the merchant is; the bewilderment of the consumer in the face of powerful forces brought into play by the merchant; and the hopelessness, frustration, and resignation of many in the face of exploitation.

BAIT ADVERTISING AND THE SWITCH SALE

A sizable number of the families had been victimized by "bait" advertising. Responding to advertisements for sewing machines, phonographs, washing machines, and other items offered at unusually low prices, they succumbed to the salesmen's "switch-sale" technique by buying a much more expensive model.

The technique is illustrated by the story of a 26-year-old Negro housewife:

> *I saw a TV ad for a $29 sewing machine,* so I wrote to the company and they sent down a salesman who demonstrated it for me. It shook the whole house, but I wanted to buy it anyway. But he kept saying it would disturb all the neighbors by being so noisy, and *went out to the hall and brought in another model costing $185. . . .*
> I actually had to pay $220. He promised if I paid within a certain amount of time I would get $35 back. *But since my husband was out of work, we couldn't pay within the time period,* so I didn't get the refund. . . . *I was taken in by the high-pressure sales talk.*

A middle-aged Puerto Rican husband was victimized by a variant of this racket. Instead of responding to an ad, he received a call from a salesman saying that his wife had won a sewing machine:

> He brought the machine to the house. It was worth $25, and we ended up buying another one for $186. A friend of mine bought a similar machine, maybe better than mine, for $90. *They tricked me into buying the machine for $186 on credit.*

In these cases, the reactions are much the same, the feeling of being tricked by a high-pressure salesman. In each instance, a purchase was made at a price higher than the anticipated one.

The "switch sale" is by no means limited to sewing machines. A 28-year-old Negro housewife told the following story about a phonograph sale:

> I saw an advertisement in the paper *for a $49 Hi-Fi set.* The ad said: "Phone for free demonstration," so I did. The salesman came

a few days later, bringing a set that was different from the one I saw advertised. I told him it wasn't the set I saw in the paper, but he said it was, so we hassled for a while. He kept high-pressuring me, saying he had one in the car he knew I would like. So finally, I told him to bring it up. He did, and played it for me.

I asked him to leave it so my husband could hear it, but he said "no." Then I asked him to come back later when my husband would be home and he said "no" again. Well, I decided to gamble and signed the papers. [Later they mailed a coupon book. The set came to $175.]

He asked me for a down-payment, so I gave him my old radio and got $10 off. *And right after that, my husband came in. He didn't want the set, but the salesman told him we couldn't return it.* Later my husband examined the set. The salesman had said it contained four woofers and two tweeters, but my husband found out they didn't exist. We called the store, but they said we couldn't change it, so we had to pay the full amount.

Once the set stopped working. We phoned the store and got free repairs. *But the second time the set broke down, we called the store and were told that the company no longer dealt in Hi-Fi sets, only in sewing machines.*

One law of the commercial jungle facing the low-income consumer is vividly dramatized in this irreversibility of the credit transaction. Tacit in all dealings with ethical merchants is the right to exchange merchandise if the customer is not satisfied. Not so in the low-income market. Once the signature is obtained on the contract, the sale is consummated. It should be noted that the husband returned in time to register his displeasure to the salesman. But the concept of the satisfied customer is foreign to such hit-and-run transactions. Even when the couple discovered that the phonograph did not measure up to the salesman's claims, they were still unable to exchange it. As we shall see, this is not an isolated occurrence. Other families also discovered that the principle of exchange does not apply to them. The "run-around" this couple received when seeking service is also fairly typical. The explanation given seems quite thin, and yet it was apparently enough to free the store from the complaining customer. The incident also illustrates the way "easy credit" breaks through traditional constraints upon consumption. However reluctant at first, this housewife was still able to indulge her impulse to buy without consulting her husband.

Bait advertising was reported by a 37-year-old Negro mother living on welfare. She had seen a newspaper ad, placed by a 125th Street furniture store, announcing the reupholstering of couches with good material for $49.95:

> I phoned them and they sent out a salesman. I told him I saw the ad and wanted my couch covered for $49.95. I asked him to show me the material. He pulled out some patterns and looked at them and said, "These aren't so hot. I really want to give customers something they'll be satisfied with." Then he flipped to the higher-priced patterns—*but I didn't know they were higher-priced then*. I picked out a pattern and asked him how much. He told me $149. *But I only had $49 in cash and wanted to pay only in cash, so I told him that this was too high. He praised the material so much, talking about its quality and durability, that I finally told him that if I could get an account I'd take it. He gave me a contract. I just took a quick look and signed it.* They sent for the couch and returned it two weeks later. The work on the seams of the pillows was awful. . . . Six months later, the wire in the spring popped out the side and the other side had a pointed end on it.

By now the elements of the process are familiar: the "bait ad," the high-pressure salesman, the purchase of a much more expensive item, and, as often happens, dissatisfaction with the merchandise. Of particular interest in this case is the fact that the woman had every intention of paying cash when she responded to the ad but was converted into a credit buyer in spite of her intent.

A 45-year-old white housewife reported the "switch sale" in connection with encyclopedias:

> About four years ago I saw an encyclopedia advertised on TV. I called for a salesman and he showed me a set, but it wasn't worth the money. He then talked me into buying a more expensive set.

Like other victims of bait advertising, this woman encountered further difficulties. Although promised an annual yearbook for $3.00, she never received it or recovered her money.

The idea of the unusual bargain takes other forms besides bait advertising. Sometimes the consumer is "hooked" by the promise of free merchandise. A 30-year-old Puerto Rican husband told us that he had once received a phone call from someone who promised him a present:

> The man brought a wastepaper basket as the present and he also had with him a vacuum cleaner which he demonstrated. *He talked me into buying the vacuum cleaner even though I thought the price was too high.* I felt "high-pressured."

Another variant of the "something for nothing" appeal is based on the principle of the "pyramid club." Consumers are promised a refund if they help the salesman find a certain number of customers. One instance, reported by an 18-year-old Negro housewife, involved the added inducement of an outright monetary gift:

> My mother sent the vacuum cleaner salesman here. He said that he would give me $5 just to talk to me. Then he said that if I got him nine more sales I could have the vacuum cleaner free. I wasn't able to find any customers and I can't work the vacuum cleaner with all its attachments. I don't want it and I've stopped making the payments on it.

Here we see an example of the great disparity between the more traditional logic of these consumers and the law of installment buying. Whether or not the consumer wants the merchandise has no bearing on the merchant's right to payment once the contract is signed.

The "contest" theme is a popular one in the exploitation of consumers. A 32-year-old Negro housewife told us that she entered a contest by filling out a coupon in a Third Avenue store:

> Later I was told I won first prize—$30 off on a set of silverware. A man came four different times with different silverware—some used, some with pieces missing. He told us to keep the set for the time being, and that he would return with the set we wanted. Before we ever received the set we ordered, they sent a final notice to pay or my husband's salary would be garnisheed. My husband told his boss who told him to take the silver back to the place and leave it. My husband did take it back, but the man refused to give him a receipt.

Another Negro housewife told of a puzzle contest tied in with the purchase of encyclopedias:

In different comic books my husband found puzzle-contest ads. The prizes were for $10,000, $5,000, and $1,000, plus a lot of other prizes. Over a period of about two years, while he was solving different puzzles, he was required to buy a book a month for $1.98 each. My husband bought twenty of these books. After he got the whole set, he wrote to find out about his position in the puzzle contest. In return he received more puzzles to solve. This went on for some time. Then the firm stopped sending puzzles. And they never did answer any of his letters asking about the contest.

It is apparent that these schemes are able to work because of the naivete of the consumers. This reader of comic books undoubtedly worked on the additional puzzles in good faith.

Some salesmen misrepresent themselves as officials of the Housing Authority. As we noted earlier, some families found themselves buying sink panels from men they thought were Housing-Authority employees. The 18-year-old housewife victimized by the vacuum-cleaner salesman was also a victim of this practice:

Soon after we moved in, a man came saying he was part of the housing management. He installed the cabinets under the kitchen and bathroom sink. Then he told me they cost $19. I thought he meant *both* cost $19, but I found out that they were $19 each. They're not worth it. But I didn't do anything about it.

Another woman, a 37-year-old Puerto Rican, signed a contract for a set of encyclopedias thinking that she was filling out Housing-Authority forms:

When I first moved, a man who said he was the manager asked me to sign some papers. *It turned out I signed for encyclopedias thinking I was signing some housing authority forms* as a new tenant. I went to the Legal Aid Society to complain. The case is still in court. My husband was threatened with a garnishee by the encyclopedia company. [*She said the company went out of business. The account has been taken over by KIP, Inc., and they are the firm suing the family for $96.*]

This incident points up more than the practices of unscrupulous salesmen. It also shows the complex web of business institutions involved in credit transactions which the traditional consumer finds so difficult to understand.

As we shall see, other interviewees also had the notion that the firm they were dealing with had gone out of business and that some other party had taken over the account. More likely, the original firm sold the contract at a discount to a credit agency, a practice of which many low-income consumers are only dimly aware.

MISREPRESENTATION OF PRICES

The preceding incidents illustrate various schemes through which low-income families are pressured into buying. Other incidents exhibit another fairly common form of duplicity: the misrepresentation of price, particularly in credit transactions. Although the merchant is required by law in New York State to enter both the cash price and the finance charges on the installment contract, some circumvent this law either by not explaining the terms of the contract or by not sending the customer his copy of the contract until sometime after the sale is consummated. In several instances we found that the consumer did not learn the full cost of his merchandise until he received the payment coupons some time after the sale. This practice is illustrated by the following typical episodes:

[41-year-old Puerto Rican husband, welfare family] I was cheated on a TV set I bought. At first the price was supposed to be $220. After I signed the contract I found out that it was really $300. *But then it was too late.*

[34-year-old Puerto Rican housewife] I was told by the salesman that the credit price for the Hi-Fi set was $299. *When I got the payment book, I found out that I had to pay them $347.*

[28-year-old Negro housewife] I heard an ad on the radio about a special bargain on washing machines for only $100. After I ordered it and had it installed, I got a bill for $200. I said I wouldn't pay it and they took it away. *I paid a $50 down-payment, and they never gave it back to me. I'm just glad I did not have to pay the balance.*

In the last case, we see that the misleading price appeared in an ad. The consumer made the purchase over the telephone, and therefore the true cost was not revealed until after the installation. It should also be noted that the misleading advertisement led to the loss of a $50 down-payment. The vulnerable position of many low-income consumers is suggested by this woman's feeling of relief that she did not lose even more money.

The manner in which salesmen lie to families about the cost of goods is revealed by another incident involving a door-to-door salesman selling washing machines:

[Husband and wife, aged 33 and 27, Puerto Rican] A salesman came to the door about three months ago and showed us a pamphlet with pictures of washing machines. He said it would be simple to buy it on credit. We met him at the furniture company, *where he showed us the machine and said it would not cost more than $290. So we signed the papers and didn't have to pay any cash.* When the machine was installed it didn't work.

We called the store three times and were promised a mechanic, but he never came. *And we got a credit-payment book in the mail for $462.66,* saying we were supposed to pay $18 a month. [*They also received a sales slip, and on this bill there is a typed statement to the effect that a down-payment of $29.30 was made by Mr. R. Both Mr. and Mrs. R. deny any cash payments.*] A month later we got a statement saying that payments were overdue and we would have to pay 93¢ more. We don't want this machine and they're going to sue us.

In this incident the true price was almost 60 per cent more than the one quoted by the salesman. Perhaps the mysterious down-payment credited to this family was made by the peddler-intermediary in order to reassure the merchant.

A number of families told us that peddlers frequently misrepresented the price of their merchandise, quoting lower prices initially and then demanding higher ones on later visits. Typical of these accounts is the story of a 36-year old Puerto Rican mother on welfare:

In March, 1960, a peddler knocked at my door and *insisted so much that I said I'd take a lamp for $29.* I gave him a $3 deposit. When he came back with the account book the next week, *the price had gone up to $42.* I said I wouldn't pay it. *So he took away the lamp, but he never gave me back the $3.*

Again we see the loss of a down payment as the outcome of this practice.

In the following case, a peddler's effort to mislead the customer about the price of a wrist watch was less successful:

[26-year-old Negro husband] I bought a wrist watch from a salesman who came around to the place where I work. He said it cost $45. I signed a little slip of paper . . . didn't even read it. A few weeks later I got a payment book through the mail saying I owed $73, even though I had made a $15 down-payment. I sent the $30 I still owed with a letter explaining that that was all I owed on the $45 watch—not the $73 listed in the book. I never heard from them again. The watch was no good. It lasted only a few months. I had it fixed and it still didn't work right. After that, I never buy from those guys again.

The following incident reveals several forms of exploitation on the part of a furniture store dealing with a Puerto Rican woman who had just come to this country:

This happened when I came to this country eight years ago. I went to a furniture store. They were offering two tables as a gift for people who would buy furniture. *I bought $500 worth and two tables were given to me. When the bill came, it was from a finance company, not the store; and it was for $900, not the $500 price they told me at first.* I went to the store and they told me that I was paying a service charge, credit charge, transportation and so forth, *plus the cost of the two tables. I told them that they were a gift. They said they were worth $75 and the tables offered as a gift were another kind. I asked them to let me see them but they told me they ran out of them.* The Welfare took over here and told me not to pay them anything. They should contact the Welfare Office. I do not know what happened. The store never called me again. I guess the Welfare paid them.

Perhaps misrepresentation of cost to this degree no longer happens. Certainly this practice was made illegal by the passage of the "all goods bill" by the New York State legislature in 1957.[2] Yet merchants seem to have ways of getting around the law.

As several cases have shown, misrepresentation of price can lead to the loss of down-payments when the families refuse the merchandise. But this is not the only way in which

---

2. Among other provisions, this law places a limit on credit charges, requires that the cost of credit as well as the cash price be entered on the contract, and that a copy of the contract be given to the consumer at the time of the sale. Dr. Persia Campbell, State Consumer Counsel during Governor Harriman's administration, was largely responsible for drafting this widely hailed progressive measure.

consumers can lose money in the low-income market. In one incident, a young Puerto Rican couple lost what they had paid on their furniture when the store with which they were dealing sold out to another one:

My wife and I bought some furniture and for the first few months we paid our money to the store. Then the store sold out, so we had to start paying the second store. (The second store noted what they had already paid in their payment book, but it did not appear in the store's own records.) *The store told us they were going to take us to court if we didn't pay $150 more. But I'd rather pay the extra money than go to court and lose any days of work, because I just got my job and don't want to risk it.*

It is difficult to tell from this account whether the original furniture store did in fact go out of business or whether this transaction also involved the sale of the contract to a credit firm. The attitudes of this couple are not atypical. Fear of losing a job often lies behind the apparent apathy and resignation of these consumers when they encounter difficulties.

SUBSTITUTION OF GOODS

Not only are prices misrepresented in the low-income market, but so is quality. Some families were sold reconditioned merchandise that had been represented as new, and others received merchandise inferior to that ordered.

The sale of used merchandise as new is of course illegal. Yet, as we noted in Chapter 2, some merchants hinted that their competitors engaged in this practice. The following reports indicate that this does indeed happen. A 36-year-old Puerto Rican mother on welfare gave this account:

I bought a TV set from a First Avenue store. *It was a used set which was sold as new.* After seven days it broke down. The store took it back and returned it in two weeks. It broke down again and they took it for thirty days. They brought it back and it broke down one week later. They took it away again and I *asked for a refund because there was a guarantee of ninety days which had not run out. But they wouldn't give me back my $100 or bring me another TV.* I went to the store several times but with no results.

A basic inequality in the merchant-consumer relationship is pointed up by this incident. When the low-income consumer fails to live up to his obligations of payment, the merchant is able to utilize the law to protect his rights. When the merchant fails to respect a guarantee, however, the consumer is more likely to lose his initial investment than to obtain justice. In part, this is due to his ignorance of the laws which protect him and the agencies which can help him. But this inequality also partly stems from the merchant's superior resources. He can turn the job of collecting over to lawyers, collection agencies, and the courts. The consumer, on the other hand, must invest his own time in at least initiating legal action, time which, as we have seen, he cannot easily take from his job.

In another incident the sale of a used TV set as new was confirmed by a repairman. A 39-year-old Puerto Rican mother living on welfare had this experience:

I got a new TV set and some beds for $452.67. The TV alone was $280. It broke down after two years, and I paid $30 for repairs. *The TV repairman said that the set was a reconditioned one in a new cabinet.*

The substitution of merchandise is illustrated by an incident told by a 26-year-old Negro husband:

We've spent more money repairing the TV than it cost. *The store sent a different one than we asked for and it didn't look new.* We complained to the store and they offered a trade for $25 on another one.

Another example of delivering the "wrong" item was provided by a 53-year-old white mother. In this case only a part of the equipment was delivered.

A peddler high-pressured my daughter into ordering a Hi-Fi from the catalogue he had. He then delivered a pick-up instead of a phonograph. He kept insisting that my daughter had marked a pick-up, and he wouldn't exchange it. [She has already paid $167 which is twice the current market price for this item.]

Substitution of merchandise frequently happens in furniture purchases. A 39-year-old Puerto Rican husband reported:

I ordered furniture in November, 1959. It was supposed to be delivered in December, but it didn't come until January, 1960. *Then they sent furniture that I hadn't selected. I tried to get the store to take it back but they wouldn't do it.* I had to keep the furniture. Then in February I got a letter from a credit corporation in Valley Stream, N.Y., saying that all payments had to be made to them and not to the store. *The store was closed.*

It should be noted that this man, like many others, interpreted the sale of his contract to mean that the store was no longer in business. This misunderstanding of the merchant's credit arrangements contributes to the consumer's belief that there is nothing he can do about his problem. In other words, the sale of contracts by the merchant results in absolving him of his responsibility toward the consumer even though under the law he is still responsible for the terms of the transaction.

A 29-year-old white housewife had a similar experience:

The bureau was supposed to be new. I raised hell with him. He gave me a different one from the one I saw in the store. *I went back the same day. But he wouldn't take a thing back.*

The delivery of goods inferior to those contracted for is illustrated by other incidents involving furniture:

[Young Puerto Rican couple] We were cheated on the bunk beds and youth bed we bought from a store on Third Avenue. We paid $200. *They offered spring mattresses, but they sent cotton mattresses. We complained, but the store insisted, and we had to accept their story.*

[34-year-old Puerto Rican housewife] I paid $44 for linoleum I bought from a peddler. *He showed me a sample, but the linoleum he brought was of a poorer quality.* I told him what I wanted, but he gave me something else. I complained, but he wouldn't do anything about it.

Some families were victims of the TV repair racket which received much publicity several years ago. Repairs made with used components involve extraordinary expenses as can be seen from the stories of two victims who happened to deal with the same company. A 42-year-old white housewife, who produced the bills for her repairs, gave this account:

We got a circular for TV repairs that was dropped in our mailbox. Since our TV set broke down about then, my husband phoned the TV repair service. The circular said that the first visit was free. The first time the repairman came he said a small tube had burned out, so he put in a new one and *charged for it*. We paid cash and were given a receipt with a 90-day guarantee on the tube. A few days later the set broke down again. We called the repair service again, and this time he said we needed a new picture tube. He put one in, but after a few days the new tube went dark. When the repairman came back the third time he took the chassis to the shop and left the picture tube on the floor. He brought the set back again, put in a new tube, and then we paid the second bill. The first bill was $32.58; the second was $54.81. The set worked for a few days and then it went dark again. We were so disgusted we called another man. *This one told us that it wasn't a new tube and it wasn't the RCA tube the bill said it was.* This man charged only $3.00 and told my husband to get in touch with the District Attorney's office. We went there but they told us that if the receipt didn't say it was a new tube, they couldn't help us.

A 40-year-old Puerto Rican mother living on welfare also dealt with this company and showed the interviewer her bills:

I received this circular and called the _____ TV Repair Service. They picked up the set, fixed it, and charged $77.68. *They did not put in a new tube* and I had to have it repaired at another store for $60, at still another store for $40, at another for $18, and finally another man who charged $7. I spent $203 for repairs on my set. A loan from a finance company for the $78 repair came to $105. *The total cost to repair the TV was $230.*

It is difficult to believe that the repairs were made in as rapid succession as her story implies, but even if spread over several years, the costs are exceptionally high.

THE ANONYMITY OF CREDIT TRANSACTIONS

Several families responded to the question about cheating by describing pots-and-pans salesmen who sold them poor-quality merchandise at exorbitant prices. The details of these stories are similar. The salesman shows up either with the goods or with a catalogue. He stresses the unusually low payments, gets the housewife to sign a contract, extracts a small down-payment, and then disappears. Sometime later the family receives a payment book from a finance company and frequently learns only then that the set of pots and pans will cost as much as $60. What is striking about these accounts is the anonymity of the transaction. Several interviewees reported that they tried unsuccessfully to find out the name of the store from which they had bought the merchandise. The high-pressure techniques of these salesmen as well as the theme of anonymity are illustrated in this report by a 30-year-old Puerto Rican husband:

This happened about four or five days after we moved in. My wife was home and a man knocked at the door. He was selling pots and he pressured my wife to look at them. He said that they would cost only $5 a month and that he would leave her a piggy bank so she could save for other things. Then he told her to "sign here," and when all the payments were made she'd get a present. He then asked her if he could just leave the pots for a second while he went downstairs. But since she was signed up he never came back. We got a coupon book and mailed $5 each month to a bank in New Jersey. . . . *I don't know the name of the store but I guess it's somewhere in Fenway, New Jersey. I have no records of it.*

[Another young Puerto Rican husband gave a similar account:] A salesman came around selling aluminum pots and pans. They're not worth a damn. I gave him a dollar down and then the bank sent me a book and I had to send in payments. *Some bank in New Jersey. I tried to find out the store's name, but I couldn't.* The set cost $60— $5 a month for twelve months.

These incidents illustrate the various ways in which merchants take advantage of low-income consumers. They show the high pressure tactics, the substitution of goods, the exorbitant prices and the shoddy merchandise that are commonplace in the low-income market. In the next chapter, we will consider one further consequence of this system; the pressures and legal entanglements that face the consumer when he fails to maintain payments.

CHAPTER 11

Consumer Problems II: Consequences of Missed Payments

MANY CONSUMERS have almost no idea
of the complex set of legal conditions embodied in the contracts they sign. The penalties that can be brought to bear
on them, such as the loss of possessions already paid for,
the payment of interest on money owed, the payment of
lawyer and court fees, are matters that some families become
rudely aware of only when—for whatever reasons—they miss
their payments.

Underlying the credit problems of many families is the
unexpected emergency that sharply curtails income: The
breadwinner becomes ill or loses his job; suddenly the
family finds that the "easy payments" are no longer easy.
When this happens, they are apt to learn about the complex
set of conditions governing their credit transactions. A
27-year-old Negro husband, armed with the contracts, sales
slips, and payment books of his transactions, told this story:

I first bought a bedroom set. I still owed money on it when I
wanted a living room set. I went back to the store and bought the
living room set on credit. *At that time I was working and making
good money. That was two years ago. Six months ago I got sick and*

155

stopped working. And so I couldn't pay anymore. I went to the store and told them to pick up the living room set. *They said they would take it back but they would also take the bedroom set too.* But I'd already paid for that. The bedroom set cost $583.57. I paid every month and still owed $178.57 when I bought the living room set which cost $439.94. When I got sick in April, I still owed $288.51. Last week they sent a summons saying I have to pay $440, not $288. *We have to pay but what I'm going to do is pay the $288.51, not the $440.*

This young man is by no means atypical in his failure to understand that he is liable for the interest charges on his debt as well as court costs and legal fees.

A 37-year-old Negro mother, separated from her husband, expressed confusion over the role of third parties in collecting a department store debt which went unpaid because she was out of work:

I had an $80 bill. *I then stopped working and couldn't pay for a year.* I went back to work and told the store I was ready to pay again. They told me that the account was turned over to a collection lawyer. I called up the lawyer and he told me to send him the money but to make it out to the store at $10 a month. I sent him three payments. *Then I got a letter from a collection agency saying that now I had to pay them. I made one payment to them, but I found it all confusing. I promised myself I'd save the money and then go to the store and pay them the balance.* But then I was out of work again and so I still haven't paid the bill.

Her confusion over the role of collection agencies is expressed in her plan to save the money and give it directly to the store. Her determination to pay off the debt whenever she is employed may not stem only from a sense of moral responsibility. An additional motive, revealed by some families, is that debts must be paid in order to restore their credit rating in the community.

In the following incident, missed payments, resulting from illness and subsequent loss of job, led to threats of physical harm from a travel agency. A 31-year-old Puerto Rican woman separated from her husband told this story:

I went to a travel agency called the "Emma Lou." I wanted my sons and sister to come from Puerto Rico. I had to pay $237. At that time I was working and paying. *But I got sick and couldn't pay any more*. The Welfare told me that I should go and tell them that if they wanted to get paid they should contact the Welfare office. *The people from the travel agency threatened me. The wife of the owner nearly slapped me. What a nightmare.* They did not contact the Welfare and I am paying now little by little.

Although loss of a job can force families to fall behind on payments, it also happens that *missed payments can lead to the loss of a job*. A number of employers are unwilling to go to the trouble of deducting payments from their employee's pay checks and will fire any who are garnisheed. This is illustrated by the experience of a middle-aged Negro couple:

We got into trouble with our first set of furniture. It cost $450. We paid $250 and were paying $17 a month. Then we missed two payments and they garnisheed my husband at the hotel. His boss said, "Straighten them out or else you're fired." We went to the store and offered them $75. They said they wanted more—they wanted every cent—and wouldn't take the $75. My husband went to Relief for help and they tried to get the store to take the $75 but the store refused. Then the Relief people told us not to pay them. *So my husband got fired from the hotel.* He then went to work at a laundry and *was garnisheed. We're still paying for it. We were cheated because we'd already paid $250, but on the garnishee we're paying $490, although the furniture was originally valued at $450.*

Refusal To Maintain Payments

Failure to maintain payments does not always stem from the consumer's inability to pay. Ironically, he may stop paying because the merchant has failed to live up to *his* obligations. When dissatisfied with the shoddy merchandise they receive, some families retaliate for the merchant's bad faith by withholding payments. But this logic, which may well make sense in a traditional society and even in dealings with ethical merchants in our bureaucratic society, does not apply in the low-income marketing system. As most of these families soon learned, the contracts they signed precluded this form of redress.

In these cases, the consumer is subjected to a kind of

double jeopardy. Not only is he stuck with faulty merchandise but, by stopping payments, he becomes subject to the full range of legal controls and added charges. The following incidents illustrate unsuccessful attempts at withholding payments to correct a wrong:

[28-year-old Puerto Rican husband] I bought a set of pots and pans from a door-to-door salesman. *They were very poor quality and I wanted to give them back but they wouldn't take them. I stopped paying and told them to change them or take them back. I refused to pay.* Then they sent me a letter from an adjustment service. *They started bothering me at every job I had.* Then they wrote to my current job and my boss is taking *$6 weekly from my pay and sending it to pay this.*

[21-year-old Negro housewife] We were cheated on the Hi-Fi. A salesman for a Long Island company came around. My husband was home and we had some company. The salesman had a catalogue full of pictures of sets. My husband picked out a model and ordered it right then and there. The guests were all excited over the purchase. Two days later the salesman came back and he had the wrong model. He said it was a better one and we took it. My husband signed a contract, and the salesman gave him a coupon book. The price on this model was the same as the one we originally wanted. Altogether it cost us $366, with a down-payment of $5 or $10 and payment at $11.50 a month. We sent almost $200 by money orders. Then the plastic knob on the set broke and we called to have it fixed. Then the whole set fell apart. The turn-table wobbled and the sound was turned down. *When they didn't come to fix it we stopped paying, and we told them we wouldn't pay them until it was fixed. Two months later a man came at night, saying he was the Marshal. We said we wouldn't pay until they fixed it, so the young boy with him took the set.* That's all we've heard of it.

[49-year-old white housewife] We bought a TV set about ten years ago because of an announcement on the radio. I called and made an appointment for the store salesman to come to my home. I was to pay $15 down, $11 per month, and I would get thirty days free service. I don't remember the actual cost. After two weeks, the set began to cause trouble, so the store installed a new tube, which lasted for about two weeks. Then the store repairman serviced it again. After the thirty-day service period was over, we had trouble again, and I had to pay the charge this time. I sent the set to the factory and got it repaired. Soon the set broke again, and this time I called another service man who said the set had a basic fault. So I called the store, but they wouldn't do anything.

*I stopped paying and wrote to the Better Business Bureau, but I
didn't get any answer.* Payments were two to three months behind
by this time. *The bank I bought the set through began serving court
papers.* [Contract had called for a Traveller set but she had received
an Admiral] I went to court, but since I was on welfare at the time
I couldn't even afford $1 a week. So a man came to repossess the set.
I wouldn't let them do this, so then two men came, bringing with
them a policeman who had a warrant. My husband let them take
the set away, and *that was the end of the matter.*

As we shall see, the matter does not always end with
the repossession. Had this family not been on welfare at
the time it would still have been liable for the balance of its
bill after the sale of the repossessed set.

In the following incident, the idea of withholding payments did not originate with the consumer, but rather was
recommended by legal counsel. But even so, the consumer
was not able to obtain satisfaction. Thus a young Negro
housewife reported:

Door-to-door salesman named George sold us a stereo set and furniture when we moved. Later on he came with a TV set. *He said it
was a new set. We didn't see it until it was delivered.* It played sat-
isfactorily for two months. Then it went on the bum, and the TV
repairman said it was a reconditioned set as indicated by the "jumper
on the picture tube." We called the store and were told that the set
was a new one. We phoned a second time and then got the run
around [i.e., "manager was out" or "manager on vacation."] So we
took the problem to Legal Aid. Up to this time we were paying $20
a month. *The salesman never gave us a contract.*
The store mailed us a payment book and each time we mailed a
payment we had to enclose the book. Legal Aid contacted the store
and they told them that it was a new set. The storekeeper agreed to
come over and look at the set, but he never showed up. *We went
back to Legal Aid and Legal Aid told us to write a letter saying
that the store would get no further payments unless "some sort of
satisfactory arrangement is made."* While Legal Aid was considering
the case, we didn't make any payments for about six months. We
never got an answer to our letter. The store went bankrupt and turned
its account over to another furniture company. The new store said:
"If you pay all your back payments, we'll send out a repairman and
nothing more." So we went back to Legal Aid, and they told us that
there was nothing Legal Aid could do. We figured that Legal Aid
wasn't interested any longer. Then the new furniture company found

out Legal Aid would not do anything, and *two weeks later we were garnisheed.* My husband did not appear in court. *He received no summons or anything. They just sent the garnishee to his job. He found out about the garnishee when his boss called him in.* He's continued paying through garnishee ever since.

This also points up the inequality in many of these transactions. In spite of fraud by the merchant and the family's efforts to enlist the law in its cause, the law operated only to enforce the family's obligations to the merchant.

A similar account was given by a 40-year-old Negro housewife who, in order to please her daughter, made the mistake of buying an overpriced watch from a peddler.

In 1955 a salesman came to the door selling wrist watches. I had promised my daughter I would get her one. We were both home and my daughter pleaded with me to buy the watch. So I agreed to buy it for $60. I gave him $3 down and I got a payment book in the mail. *About a month later I had the watch appraised in a 125th Street store and I found it was worth only $6.50.* I called up the company and said *I wouldn't pay for it and they should come and get it. They told me I had to pay or they'd take me to court. And I said, "fine, take me to court and I'll have the watch there."* Next thing I know about this, I get a court notice of Judgment by Default from Brooklyn Municipal Court for $69 balance, $3 interest, $5 "costs by statute," $14 court costs. *The total cost of the watch was $91.*

Here we see a good example of the exorbitant prices charged by peddlers. As this woman discovered, the wrist watch was priced at almost ten times the amount she would have had to pay in a store. With the addition of legal fees, the final cost came to almost fifteen times the store price.

One further detail in this case should be noted. The housewife was eager to present her case in court, but only learned of the court proceedings when she was notified of the judgment by default. This calls attention to a general problem confronting low-income consumers. However meritorious their cases may be, they automatically lose out if they fail to appear in court. As we have seen, a number of consumers in this group only learned of the court action taken against them after the fact, when, for example, they were informed by their employer that they were being garnisheed. Under the law, the consumer is given seven days to answer the summons issued him and if he does not reply in that time, a judgment by default is entered.

Judgments by default are quite frequent in cases involving low-income consumers; probably a majority of the cases end this way. Often, the consumer is at fault; he may not fully understand the nature of the legal actions taken against him; he may be reluctant to take time off from work; the court may be located some distance from his home, as in the case of this East Harlem woman who would have had to go to a Brooklyn court; or he may simply forget. But many times the consumer's failure to appear in court is the result of his *never receiving the summons.* In these actions, the summons is drawn up by the plaintiff's lawyer who hires a process server to deliver it to the defendant. Process servers sometimes evade their assignment. This happens with sufficient frequency that a special term has developed in legal circles to refer to it, "sewer service." Instead of finding the defendant, the process server simply throws the summons away. Low-income families are likely to be victims because they are not apt to know how to protect their rights.

Merchants are well aware that judgments by default are common and take advantage of this fact. However poor the merchant's case may be, he can count on winning a certain proportion simply because the consumer does not show up to defend himself. This is another aspect of the poor fit between these more traditional consumers and the role they are expected to play in our bureaucratic economy.[1]

Repossessions

At the beginning of chapter 10 we noted that twenty-seven families had had goods repossessed. The incidents related by a number of them point up further aspects of the law governing installment buying, such as the fact that the consumer runs the risk of losing much more than the merchandise directly involved in the credit transaction;

---

1. In the concluding chapter, we shall review in more detail the legal procedure in consumer cases.

they also suggest that extralegal tactics are sometimes employed under the guise of legal procedure.

One interviewee, a 36-year-old Puerto Rican, managed to avert a repossession, but only after a harrowing experience with a marshal:

> My wife bought three lamps on West 14th Street. *Because she was not able to make a payment we still owed $32, but they increased it to $80.* The Marshal came with a policeman and *they wanted to take the TV instead of the lamps.* I wouldn't let them. *I had $36 in my pocket and when they pushed me* (I had the baby in my arms) *my wallet fell out. They grabbed the wallet and took the $36.* They left a paper saying I had to pay $10 which I sent. First I went to a lawyer, but he wanted $100, and so at his suggestion I sent the $10.

Apart from the physical violence, it should be noted that the agents of the law tried to remove a TV set, not the lamps for which the money was owed. This is by no means illegal. Under the law, any property of the defendant, other than items essential for living (beds, chairs, etc.), can be attached and sold in order to make good the unpaid debt.[2]

The willingness of some families to incur unusually heavy installment debts and their failure to anticipate emergencies is pointed up by another incident involving repossession. A City Marshal also figures prominently in this account given by a 40-year-old Negro housewife:

> In 1953, before we moved to the project, we had bought a TV and refrigerator for a total of $1600, including service, installation, and interest. We paid $790 on time. We were evicted from our old apartment, so we put the TV and refrigerator in storage. *Then my husband had a heart attack and was out of work. I was sick at the same time,* so we missed three monthly payments, which were about $31 each. We made our payments to a bank which was financing for the store. We went to the store and told them that we had moved and told them where the merchandise was. *Three weeks later a Marshal came to the apartment. He said that he must repossess unless some payment was made, at least $5 or so. I paid the Marshal $10.* A few days later I phoned storage and they didn't know anything. Then the storage house sent a note saying that the TV and refrigerator

---

2. Should the proceeds of the public auction exceed the debt, the Marshal is required by law to return the excess money to the consumer.

had been repossessed. *I phoned the Marshal, and he said not to worry "since you paid me $10 it won't be auctioned."* When we paid the Marshal, he said he would be back for another payment in two weeks. *The two weeks went by and then I phoned the store and they said the items were auctioned. I waited for the Marshal to come back, but he never showed up.* Later, I learned from a friend of my daughter, who works in the credit department of a department store, that I was listed as owing $383 to the store.

Another incident points up the severe consequences that follow missed payments. A young Puerto Rican couple fell behind in payments on a watch purchased from a door-to-door salesman. The missed payments resulted in the loss of three major appliances in no way connected with the purchase of the watch:

A man came to the door selling watches. I bought one for $139. [Mr. C. exhibits a receipt for a watch, dated March 2, 1960. Three payments were noted. The balance was $118.] *When I lost my job I told the collector that I would begin payments again when I got a new job.* But the collector stopped coming, and I got a summons. So I called the store and explained. They said I had to keep up payments. Last Saturday, July 30th, two Marshals came with a "levy." [*Plaintiff:* _____ *Sales Co. Inventory: One Hi-Fi; one TV; one washing machine.*] The auction will be Saturday, August 6th, if I don't pay $25 by then and the balance at $5 per week.

The loss of these three major appliances rather than the watch is partly explained by the fact that the husband had pawned the watch and "it was just my luck to have lost the ticket." These actions suggest that the respondent is not a responsible consumer, but the removal of three major appliances would seem to be a heavy price to pay for such irresponsibility.

Mr. C. turned to the local Democratic club for help. They advised him to pay the Marshal $15 immediately and to send him $3 a week thereafter for his expenses. But Mr. C. told the interviewer, "I don't have the $15 to pay the Marshal."

The loss of goods in no way connected with the credit transaction is illustrated by yet another incident. A 32-year-old Negro housewife explained how a relatively minor purchase from a high pressure peddler led to the loss of a television set, radio, and bicycle:

A salesman came by soon after we moved in. I told him, "We don't want to buy anything because we moved and still owe a lot of money on the furniture." The salesman said he would leave whatever we bought for two weeks and we wouldn't have to pay; "After that, pay me one or two dollars a week," he said. He showed us a catalogue listing lots of things, from clothing and fur coats to sewing machines and TV sets. *The salesman told me that for $29 I could have one spread for the master bed, two pairs of drapes, and five scarves for the dressers. I didn't sign anything.* He just left the set here. After two weeks the "head salesman" came by and asked where my husband worked. I said I didn't know. He gave me a payment book and said I had to pay $1 or $2 a week. Some weeks a collector would come by. When the collector came he wanted $8, but he would take whatever I had. Around the last payments, the company sent letters saying, "pay in three days or we will take the spread back." Then the "head salesman" came by and I had no money and told him to wait until the weekend. The salesman threatened me with the Marshal and a lawsuit. He said, "The Marshal will come and take out all your furniture."

A month later the salesman returned with a Marshal and two policemen. The salesman said, "we came to get $52." I told him I didn't have it, and asked if I could phone my husband but they wouldn't let me. I asked, "Why $52?" and the salesman said; "That's what the Marshal and the lawsuit cost." The Marshal said, "if you make the first payment and then make an arrangement, we'll start bringing the things back." *They took a TV, radio, and two-wheel bike.* After that payment, we got the bike back. *We paid the balance, but never got back the TV or radio.* I called the store but they were nasty over the phone and said I still owed. I said I didn't owe any more.

One day the salesman came and asked me to sign for the TV. *The TV was downstairs, but I said I wouldn't sign until I saw it. He brought it up and it wasn't the same one.* I said I wanted my own TV back, because this one was all torn and broken. He wanted me to sign without even seeing it. *He called again and said that they had sold my set and that was why they were trying to give me another one. Then they just stopped calling.* My husband went to the store and found out the store had moved. He then went to Legal Aid and they told him that without the Marshal's slip, the record of what was taken, they couldn't help him. They said the money orders were insufficient proof. *I couldn't find the slip and so they've got the TV and the radio and the money too.*

Not the least interesting detail in this long account is the wife's insistence that she never signed a contract. If true, then it is difficult to understand how the subsequent events could have taken place within the law. Perhaps more than any other incident this one shows clearly the hardships which can result from succumbing to the high-pressure door-to-door salesman. It must be remembered that this family's problems all stemmed from a reluctant purchase of a rather inexpensive item. As the woman notes at the beginning of her story, she tried to tell the salesman that she did not want anything, for she was already heavily in debt.

Apart from the unscrupulous practices of merchants, many of these incidents show the ineffectiveness of these families as consumers. Some are gullible to an extraordinary degree, susceptible to the appeal of easy credit, ready to assume heavy installment debt provided the payments are small, and completely lacking in foresight and resources. When emergencies arise, such families become hopelessly trapped in debt. This kind of consumer is illustrated by a young Negro couple who experienced a chain reaction of indebtedness. As told by the 30-year-old wife, this incident also suggests a connection between marital instability and the irresponsible use of credit:

My husband was the one who started the debts. The first thing he bought on time was a car in a used car lot. *He bought it just for pleasure in 1954, even though at the time he kept losing jobs.* I didn't cosign for the car because I don't get mixed up with his purchases. The original price of the car was $500, the down-payment, $10. He had the car about two months and had paid about $80. Then he missed payments for about three weeks and the car was towed away without notice. Payments had been made to a discount company which was handling the credit. I telephoned the company, and they told me that if I sent $50 they'd return the car. I did, and then received a notice in the mail saying the car was going to be auctioned. *They kept the $50 and said nothing about it.* My husband didn't go to the auction since he couldn't have bought the car back anyway. *Then we received a notice saying the car was sold for $35.*

The company told us we owed $800 in all on the car that cost $500, because of interest and legal fees [$800 less the $80 in payments and less $35 auction price]. *I went to Legal Aid which said nothing could be done. Since my husband was out of work, they garnisheed by brother-in-law's salary.* He was paying $7.50 a week, and when my husband started to work he added $10 a week to the payments. My brother-in-law wanted a job with the Police Department but couldn't get it so long as his salary was being garnisheed. This was in 1956, when we still owed about $100 on the car. *So we took out a loan for $500 in order to pay off the debt on the car so my brother-in-law could get the job.* We paid off the car. [Her husband claimed that the rest of the $500 was to cover the cost of a washing machine and a new couch bed they needed. It was also to be used to pay a $20 bill which remained on a TV set bought at the department store.] *Instead of paying off the store and buying these things, my husband spent all the money getting things for his girl friend.* My husband and I were separated on and off during that time [1956], and I was working on the side and paying the rent. The finance company tried to collect on the loan, but I couldn't pay. They threatened to garnishee my husband when he went back to work, but they had to wait until the department store debt was paid off. After we received the loan, my husband opened a new account at the department store, and he now owes $200 on it. After three years of missing payments, they've added another $100 to his bill. In 1959, the department store threatened to repossess all the furniture unless we started paying. The store sent a lawyer, and we're now paying the store $20 a month without fail. The balance still to be paid off is $129. *I don't know what the finance company bill will come to, and I dread their coming around.* We'll just have to hold off on that debt until the department store bill is paid.

The problems of this family are extreme, but undoubtedly there are many others faced with the same almost insurmountable task of climbing out of their installment debts.[3] The exorbitant markup on goods sold to low-income

---

3. The discovery that they can obtain credit is apt to make some families almost completely irresponsible as consumers. A young white housewife who had opened a revolving credit account in a department store was allowed to purchase up to $300 of merchandise on credit. This she promptly did. Maintaining the payments on this account became so difficult that she and her husband took out a loan from a finance company to pay this debt. This of course transformed her into a good credit risk from the viewpoint of the store. After the bill was paid, she received an announcement from the store in the form of a mock $300 check stating that she had this amount of credit. Presumably flattered by this offer, she returned to the store and again bought $300 worth of merchandise on credit. Since this happened a few days before the interview, we can only surmise that she has since made another trip to the finance company.

consumers is suggested by the fact that their $500 car could only bring $35 in the public auction. This incident also shows how persons other than the consumer—in this case the brother-in-law—can become entangled in these credit problems.

Stresses and Strains in the
Low-Income Marketing System

Each episode reported in this and the preceding chapter can be viewed as a case of the breakdown of a system of exchange that is inherently unstable because it rests upon the consumer's poor credit status and his ignorance. Each of these foundations can easily crack. The risk factor becomes evident in the breakdown resulting from missed payments. But often this is not independent of the consumer's lack of sophistication. As we have seen, some consumers become overextended because they have been victimized by the high-pressure salesmen who urge too great a debt burden on them. And sometimes the failure to maintain payments is a consequence of the merchant's trying to exploit the consumer's ignorance. When this is discovered, the consumer may stop payments.

When missed payments are the cause of the breakdown, the consumer is left with no alternative but to leave the low-income market. As a known bad debtor, he can no longer play the role of consumer.

Since the system also rests upon the consumer's ignorance, this too contributes to its instability. As we have seen, the exchange system becomes strained when events suddenly make the consumer aware that he did not know what he was doing. He realizes that he has been exploited when the merchandise he buys falls apart, not after a few years (which he might consider legitimate), but in a few months or even a few days. Or the discovery may come from the repairman who finds that the ostensibly new appliance is actually a used one. Or again, the consumer may come to recognize exploitation through accidental comparative shopping. He sees the merchandise he has bought at prices much lower than he had to pay, or his friends tell him he was charged too much. (Only the consumers who feel that they could have obtained better terms react to these discoveries with indignation. Some continuing customers of peddlers know they pay more but are not indignant, presumably because they feel they have no alternative.)

The breakdowns which result from the consumer's initial ignorance often represent a first step toward greater sophistication. When these consumers leave the low-income market, they do so because they have broadened their shopping horizons.

The idea of learning through exploitation was implicit in many incidents (for example, the frequent references to having been "tricked") and can be illustrated by two others. A 55-year-old Puerto Rican husband said:

I once bought a refrigerator for $240. The bill was passed on to a finance company and I ended up paying over $400. *I decided to leave it be, but now I look over everything very carefully before I buy.*

A second example of sophistication acquired through exploitation is typical of many experiences of the families in this study:

One woman who was particularly disgusted with the system [of buying on time from peddlers] said that she paid $5 for a rug this way, and later saw one exactly like it in a department store for $1.98.

This is not the voice of one of our interviewees; rather, it is the voice of a New York City housewife, in 1904.[4] That this consumer pattern among the urban poor of sixty years ago is still with us today should give us pause. Although many consumers are driven out of this system of marketing or leave it voluntarily, the system is still sustained by the forces which brought it into being in the first place—poverty and ignorance.

4. This incident was reported in Louise Bolard More, *Wage-Earners Budgets: A Study of Standards and Cost of Living in New York City* (New York: Henry Holt and Co., 1907), p. 146.

Just as there were vast numbers of urban poor sixty years ago, so we find vast numbers in New York City today. And as the incidents of these chapters make amply clear, many of them, particularly the more traditionalistic ones, are subjected to crass exploitation. Exposed to misleading advertising and ruthless salesmen, they are pressured into buying shoddy merchandise at exorbitant prices. Confused by the multitude of credit institutions, they are easily put off by the merchant who wants to evade his responsibilities. Given some protection by the law, they are too naive, too uninformed, too intimidated to know their rights or to exercise them when they do. As a result, the laws designed to protect them as well as the merchant often operate as an aid to the merchant's exploitation of them.

CHAPTER 12

Coping Patterns:
Apathy, Ignorance,
and Ineffectiveness

THIS CHAPTER focuses on a question that was implicit in the previous one: what do low-income families do about their consumer difficulties? How many are aware of the professional assistance available to them, and how many actually make use of such help when they are confronted with a consumer problem?

More than ever before, American society has developed institutions for applying expert knowledge and skill to the solution of human problems. There are few human problems today the potential solutions to which do not lie within the province of some profession or body of professions. Consumer problems are no exception. Consumers can obtain expert advice on which brands are the best buys, what choices to make in view of their particular needs, and how to stretch their dollars when shopping for food. Most importantly for our purposes, they can get professional help when they encounter difficulties with merchants. Lawyers and public and private agencies are ready to assist consumers in trouble.

Studies of the matter have found, however, that the use of professional services varies considerably from one social class to another. Several studies, notably those of Earl L. Koos, have shown that working-class people take their various problems to professionals far less often than people in the other social strata.[1] These differences are not only a matter of economics, for in most communities many professional services are available to the poor without charge. But before these services are used, people must recognize that a problem exists, must know that there are experts who can handle it, and must feel secure in the company of the professional men and women who provide the service.

From earlier studies, we conclude that most low-income families are ill-prepared to cope with their consumer problems. Not only are they more often subject to such troubles than are middle-class consumers, but they are not as likely to know what to do about them. This was intimated in many of the episodes cited in the previous chapter, and is confirmed even more forcefully by the statistical data.

The families who reported that they had been cheated were asked what they did about their problem. *Half of them did nothing at all;* they did not even complain to the merchant. Another 40 per cent tried to deal with the merchant themselves. *Only 9 per cent sought professional help.* Before considering further statistical data bearing on this issue, let us examine these reactions more closely.

Reactions to Troubles

Apathy.—Inaction—generally the most prevalent response —was especially characteristic of the families who discovered that they had been greatly overcharged. In these cases, consumers were apt to blame themselves for having been taken in. After all, they had agreed to the price quoted by the salesman. But the apathetic response was by no means

---

1. Earl L. Koos, *Families in Trouble* (New York: Kings Crown Press, 1946); *The Family and the Law* (Rochester, New York: National Legal Aid Association, 1952); *The Health of Regionville* (New York: Columbia University Press, 1954).

limited to cases of overcharging. Some families who were deceived about the price of their appliances, who were victims of substitutions, who were sold defective merchandise, or who were sued by merchants also did nothing about their problems.

Inaction does not necessarily result from the belief that nothing can be done. Recall, for example, the young Puerto Rican husband who was afraid he would lose his job if he took the time to file a complaint against the store that was forcing him to pay more than he owed. His apathy stemmed not so much from ignorance of where to get help, but rather from the difficulty of getting there.

In most cases, however, apathy signifies the consumer's belief that he can do nothing about the problem. The housewife who lost a $50 down-payment as the result of a misleadingly advertised washing machine was *relieved* that she did not lose even more money. This sense of resignation was forcefully expressed by a 28-year-old Puerto Rican head of a household who had been on Welfare for eight years. He described an incident in which he had been badly cheated, and when asked what he had done about it, he replied:

> No, we didn't do anything because we can't say anything. We poor against a powerful rich. [The interviewer noted that this was said humbly, not aggressively.]

Patterns of Self-Help.—As professionals in all fields know, many people try inappropriately to solve their problems by themselves. This is especially the case with consumer problems. We found that almost all of those in our sample who did take action tried only to deal directly with the merchant. Most of them had either been sold defective merchandise or had been sent goods different from what they had ordered. When they discovered the problem, they complained to the merchant; but as we saw in the last chapter, these complaints seldom brought satisfaction. Goods are not easily exchanged in the low-income market, and guarantees are not always respected. Flimsy excuses—"we don't handle that any more"—or the sale of the contract to a finance company are often enough to absolve the merchant of his responsibilities. When their complaints go unheeded, these consumers usually resign themselves to their problems in the belief that nothing more can be done.

We have noted that one form of direct action taken by some families is to stop payments in the hope that this will make the merchant live up to his obligations. But, as we have seen, this common-sense solution makes singularly little sense in the world of installment contracts. Instead of gaining retribution, the consumer is apt to find his troubles compounded by the legal pressures brought to bear on him.

Seeking Professional Help.—The experiences of most of the small minority who sought professional help were presented in the last chapter. Some contacted the Legal Aid Society; others called the Better Business Bureau; a few contacted private lawyers; one person visited the District Attorney's office; and another turned to the local Democratic Club.[2] In most of these cases, the consumers gained little satisfaction. As a result, some became quite cynical about the effectiveness of community agencies.

One clue to why these low-income consumers may not get much help even when they do take their problem to a professional is provided by the incident reported at length on p. 164. This couple had their TV set and radio removed by a Marshal when they missed payments on a small purchase from a peddler. To quote again from the end of the wife's account:

> . . . [My husband] then went to Legal Aid and they told him that without the Marshal's slip, the record of what was taken, they couldn't help him. They said the money orders were insufficient proof. *I couldn't find the slip* and so they've got the TV and the radio and the money too.

2. The demise of the political machine as a powerful force in our society is perhaps suggested by the fact that so few of these families turned to political organizations for help. (Later, we shall raise the question of whether some functions once performed by the political machine are now going unmet.)

The consultation with Legal Aid came to no avail in this instance because the consumer had lost a document essential to his cause. This is scarcely an isolated case. The relatively simple matter of keeping records—almost second nature to the sophisticated consumer—is apt to be foreign to the more traditionalistic consumer.

Not all families were frustrated in their attempts to receive satisfaction from merchants. A few pressed their claims successfully. When the merchant refused to act on their complaints, they made effective use of community agencies. Their experiences follow:

[A 44-year-old Puerto Rican housewife] I bought covers for the living room furniture. When I washed them they shrank and their color faded. I called the store. The store took them and opened them at the seams to fix them but they still weren't right. When I went back again, he said he was busy. *So I went to court. He got a summons and I got half my money back.*

[A 27-year-old Negro housewife] I bought furniture that fell apart. Store refused to do anything about it so *I went to Legal Aid and got half my money back from the store.*

[A 31-year-old Negro housewife] I saw a coat in a small store on 14th Street for $80. I put a $15 deposit down. Then in a store a couple doors down I saw the same one for $50. I went back to get my money back. The salesgirl said she would have to see the boss. I went back five times in a row. He wasn't there each time. *I finally found out the owner's name and then I went to the Small Claims Court and I got him to pay me the $15 back.*

As these accounts indicate, some low-income consumers are knowledgeable enough and aggressive enough to pursue their rights. Unlike most, they have learned how to cope with problems that arise in the urban marketplace.

We need not rely only on the anecdotal material in assessing the adequacy of attempts by these consumers to cope with their problems. More systematic data can be brought to bear on at least one question: Whether they have any knowledge of sources of help.

Knowledge of Sources of Help

Whether they encountered difficulties as consumers or not, all interviewees were asked: "Where would you now go for help if you were being cheated by a merchant or salesman?"

The aggregated answers to this question at once indicate a major barrier to the use of professional services by these consumers: *Almost two in every three (64 per cent) replied that they did not know,* the rest mentioning a variety of sources. By far the most frequently cited agency was the Better Business Bureau, with ninety-five mentions—referred to by more than half of those who had some notion of where they could get help. The Legal Aid Society was next in order, with twenty-two mentions. The Small Claims Court was cited by fourteen people, and another fourteen said they would go to a private lawyer. Nine mentioned the police, six said they would take their problem to a Spanish newspaper, and five said they would turn to the Settlement House. One mentioned the local political club, and one said he would seek help from his priest.

Nowhere is the handicap imposed by these consumers' traditionalism more clearly indicated than on this issue of knowing about professional sources of help. For example, the newest group of migrants, the Puerto Ricans, are not nearly as well informed as the Negroes and whites. Only 24 per cent of the Puerto Ricans had some idea of where they could get help with a consumer problem. The highest proportion of knowledgeable families is found among the Negroes—50 per cent. Among whites, the figure is 41 per cent.

The inhibiting role of traditionalism is further suggested by the measure of shopping scope. Those who felt at home in the more bureaucratic "downtown" stores had less difficulty naming sources of help than those who shopped primarily in the neighborhood. This can be seen from Table 12.1, which shows the results separately for each

Table 12.1—Knowledge of Sources of Help According to Shopping Scope
(Per Cent Knowing of a Source of Help)

| | SHOPPING SCOPE | | | | | |
	Narrow		Intermediate		Broad	
Entire Sample	24	(193)	34	(140)	56	(131)
Whites	28	(46)	39	(36)	61	(33)
Negroes	41	(32)	39	(41)	63	(60)
Puerto Ricans	17	(115)	27	(63)	42	(38)

racial group as well as for the total sample. It will be noted that the pattern for the entire sample is repeated within each racial group.

The link between knowledge of professional services and the consumer's traditionalism is brought out most clearly in the extent of the household head's formal education. This is shown in Table 12.2. Knowledge of sources of help increases sharply with formal education, and this overall pattern holds true for each racial group. Puerto Ricans who have had the benefit of a high school education are almost as knowledgeable as white and Negro high school graduates. In fact, Table 12.2 helps explain why so few of the Puerto Ricans in our sample know about these community facilities. Most of them have only an elementary school education.

Table 12.2—Knowledge of Sources of Help According to Education of Household Head
(Per Cent Knowing of a Source of Help)

	Elementary School		Some High School		High School Graduate	
Entire Sample	21	(220)	43	(155)	66	(79)
Whites	24	(51)	42	(36)	72	(25)
Negroes	40	(35)	50	(60)	65	(34)
Puerto Ricans	15	(134)	36	(59)	60	(20)

Having seen the importance of formal education, we now consider the educational value of experience. It might at first seem that the consumers who encounter difficulties are the very ones least likely to know what to do about their troubles. But it is also possible that in the course of their difficulties, families come to learn about professional sources of help. Their troubles may lead them to consult their friends and acquaintances and so learn of a community agency that can help them. The possibility of a connection between problems and learning how to solve them was suggested in a few of the incidents. (It will be recalled that some families learned that they had been sold used TV sets from the repairman who then directed them to a public agency.) Some evidence of this process is found in Table 12.3.

Table 12.3—Relationship Between Consumer Problems and Knowledge of Sources of Help

(Per Cent Knowing of a Source of Help)

	No Consumer Problem		Had Consumer Problem	
Entire Sample	33	(186)	38	(278)
Whites	36	(67)	48	(48)
Negroes	46	(43)	52	(90)
Puerto Ricans	24	(76)	25	(140)

The experience of a consumer problem is related to knowledge of professional help, but only among the whites and Negroes, not the Puerto Ricans. As the newest migrants, Puerto Ricans may be too insecure or too intimidated to find out what they can do about their problems. Or perhaps their friends and acquaintances are of little help, for they, too, do not know where to turn.

Table 12.3 documents again the inequities in the merchant-consumer relationship. It can be assumed that all merchants know of professional services that can be used when they have trouble with their customers. But most consumers who encountered difficulty with merchants did not know of such available help.

We have been examining the low-income consumer's *knowledge* of sources of help. Whether he actually turns to these agencies when he has a problem is another matter. It would seem that many do not. Although more than a third of the sample could name a source of help, and those who had difficulties were somewhat more knowledgeable than the others, only 9 per cent of those in trouble, as we have seen, actually sought help from community agencies. Obviously, factors other than ignorance of professional services prevent these families from seeking professional help. The question must be raised whether the community agencies—as they are now organized—are adequate to meet the needs of these consumers. Many of these families find it difficult to get to the courts and to other public and private agencies capable of assisting them. These agencies tend to be located some distance from the consumers' homes, and they dispense their services during the hours when many of the consumers must be at work. Furthermore, these agencies are bureaucratically organized with all the formality and impersonality that this implies. In his analysis of the political machine, Merton notes, "In our prevailing impersonal society, the machine, through its local agents, fulfills the important social *function of humanizing and personalizing all manner of assistance to those in need.*"[3] It seems ironic that the merchants in low-income areas—the exploiters if you will—are more prepared to organize their services to fit the special requirements of these consumers than are the public agencies designed to deal with their troubles.

---

3. Robert K. Merton, *Social Theory and Social Structure,* rev. ed. (New York: The Free Press of Glencoe, 1957), p. 74.

CHAPTER 13

Conclusions: Theoretical Observations and Practical Recommendations

THE OBJECTIVE of this book has been to describe the consumer practices we have found among low-income families and to estimate the proportion and kinds of families that have major consumer problems. This concluding chapter examines the main findings of the study from a broader perspective. It directs attention to the conditions underlying the consumer problems of low-income families and suggests courses of action that might alleviate some of the difficulties facing them.

Bases of the Low-Income Marketing System

The problems of low-income consumers stem from the same set of forces that have created that special system of sales-and-credit—the quasi-traditional economy—catering to their wants. Any program of action must therefore take into account the conditions that have brought this system into being.

As we have seen, this marketing system is in many respects a deviant one, in which unethical and illegal practices abound. Nevertheless, it can persist because it fulfills social functions that are presently not fulfilled by more legitimate institutions. The system's paramount function is to allow those who fail to meet the requirements of the impersonal, bureaucratic economy to become consumers of products costing substantial sums. Families with almost no claim to credit—the welfare family, for example—are nevertheless able to buy major durables in this market. Through the various mechanisms we have examined, the poorest risks are shunted to a special class of merchants who are ready to accept great risk. A close association probably exists between the amount of risk that merchants in this system are willing to accept and their readiness to employ unethical and illegal tactics. It may even be that under the present marketing arrangements in our society, unethical practices are an inevitable consequence of serving the wants of the poorest risks. Society now virtually presents the very poor risks with twin options: of foregoing major purchases or of being exploited.

Of course, the poor risks are always free to do without the goods that are available to them only in this special system of marketing. But—and this is as much a part of the misfortune of the low-income consumer as the exploitative merchant—consumption in our society, as in many others, is more than a matter of getting and having material conveniences. Equally important, Americans in all walks of life are trained to consume *in order to win the respect of others and to maintain their self-respect*. These social pressures to consume are perhaps inevitable in a society characterized by a rising standard of living. As was observed by the French economist, Emile Levasseur, more than half a century ago:

In fact the [American] laborer does spend more than [the laborer] in France. But it is because he desires to, and because he must adjust his life to a higher standard of living *in order not to be looked down upon by his fellows.*"[1]

Compounding the force of a rising standard of living is the fact that most low-income families (many of which belong to minority racial and ethnic groups) have little opportunity to base their self-respect and the respect granted them by others on occupational, educational, or other accomplishments. And this poverty of opportunity may only reinforce the significance of consumption in that pattern which we have called "compensatory consumption."[2]

The power of this special marketing system rests on more than its readiness to give credit to poor risks. The local merchants and peddlers—unhampered by bureaucratic procedure—are able to personalize their services. This has particular importance for those low-income families who come from more traditionalistic cultures and are consequently intimidated by the impersonality that pervades the major downtown stores. When they do venture into the more bureaucratic marketplace, some of these consumers, because of their manners, dress, and language problems, find themselves greeted with suspicion rather than with carefully contrived courtesy. By catering to the traditionalism of their customers, the local merchants and peddlers undoubtedly attract many who meet the formal credit requirements of the more legitimate economy but who find its social atmosphere cold, remote, and repelling. Their

---

1. Emile Levasseur, *The American Workman*, American Translation by Thomas S. Adams, edited by Theodore Marburg (Baltimore: The Johns Hopkins Press, 1900), p. 396. [Italics supplied.]

2. Apart from these general conditions inducing low-income families to consume beyond their means, it is possible that the transitional character of their neighborhoods intensifies the problems of the consumers we have studied. As Cloward and Ohlin have pointed out, urban renewal programs result in high turnover of population and thus weaken local social organization. Social norms, which in stable communities regulate the behavior and impulses of their members, tend to break down in such areas. This loosening of social constraints might contribute to greater irresponsibility in the use of credit. See Richard A. Cloward and Lloyd E. Ohlin, *Delinquency and Opportunity* (New York: The Free Press of Glencoe, 1960), pp. 208-210.

attention to social relations, as well as accepting great risk, help the neighborhood merchants to develop their "captive markets."

The consumer's traditionalism also makes for the *dys*-functions of the system. The local merchants not only cater to traditional values, they exploit them for their own ends by imposing upon their naive customers terms of exchange that are far worse than those they could obtain if they knew where and how to shop.

Courses of action directed at the dysfunctions of the low-income marketing system will be effective only if they take account of the functions of that system. Two correlative kinds of action must be considered: changing the consumer through education and changing the marketing system through legislation.

The Role of Consumer Education

Educational campaigns are attempts to modify attitudes and behavior through the dissemination of knowledge and information. Which practices of low-income consumers, then, are most likely to be changed by newly acquired knowledge? How should the messages be communicated in order to reach the intended audience? And what institutional arrangements are necessary to supplement information if consumer practices are to be changed?

THE GOALS OF CONSUMER EDUCATION

In view of the powerful social forces creating their wants, it is doubtful whether low-income consumers will derive much satisfaction from the pious injunction: "do without." Consumer aspirations may be moderated but not obliterated. Nor is there any necessity for these low-income families to abandon the hope of having the major durables now standard in American households. Even so, this still leaves considerable room for an educational campaign directed toward the where and how of shopping. We have noted repeatedly that low-income families are vulnerable to exploitation not only because they are poor risks but also because they lack sophistication in shopping. As matters now stand, many families acquire such sophistication only through the grim experience of having been thoroughly exploited. Trial by error can be replaced by less painful programs of consumer education.

Short of persuading these families not to consume, the most desirable change in their shopping patterns would be to get them to buy for cash instead of credit. The findings have shown that "easy credit" plans are frequently hard, not easy, and in any case, are very expensive. Yet this educational goal is also apt to meet with only limited success. For many families, not buying on credit is tantamount to not buying at all. We have only to recall that many low-income families consider buying on time a bad idea, but do so anyway.

A more realistic goal of consumer education would be to try to extend the shopping horizons of these families. In Chapter 2, we met the merchant who made the worried observation that the Negroes were beginning to show signs of "shopping around." If low-income consumers can be taught to "shop around," the inequities in the system of exchange, now so heavily tilted in the merchant's favor, would be greatly reduced.

Many of the episodes recounted in Chapters 10 and 11 indicate that these consumers need to be taught not only where to shop, but also what to look for when they get there. Some of their problems could be avoided, for example, if only they knew how to distinguish between new and used merchandise, between current and obsolete models of appliances, between poorly built and substantially constructed furniture.

Another realistic goal of an educational campaign would be to inform these families of the community agencies that can help them with their consumer problems. The study disclosed that most families are totally ignorant of the Legal

Aid Society, The State Banking and Finance Department, the Small Claims Court, the Attorney General's office—in short, the community agencies equipped to deal with consumer problems.

REACHING THE INTENDED AUDIENCE

Many educational campaigns fall short of their goals because they fail to reach their intended audience.[3] This is particularly apt to be the case for campaigns which try to convert audiences to a position that is contrary to the one they currently hold. Studies have shown that the intended audience does not spontaneously expose itself to messages that run counter to its attitudes, beliefs, and practices. Fortunately, this form of resistance is not inherent in the present case. Many of these families shop where they do partly because they do not know of alternatives. They do nothing about their problems because they think nothing can be done.

The chief problem of an educational program for low-income consumers is not so much breaking down resistance to messages, but finding the appropriate media for communicating to these consumers. One obvious approach would be the dissemination of easy-to-read literature. Easily-read messages stating clearly the difference in cost between credit and cash purchases, between the cost of store credit and the peddler's credit, and between credit in neighborhood stores and in downtown stores might have some effect on shopping habits. Publicity directed at the complications that can and do result from dealing with peddlers might make some people wary of dealing with them and more willing to leave their apartments to shop. And literature listing the agencies prepared to help consumers might reduce the bewilderment of those who encounter trouble.

3. See Herbert H. Hyman and Paul B. Sheatsley, "Some Reasons Why Information Campaigns Fail" in Elinor Maccoby, Theodore M. Newcomb and Eugene L. Hartley (eds.), *Readings in Social Psychology*, 3rd ed. (New York: Henry Holt and Co., 1958).

But the findings of communication research and theory make it doubtful that information campaigns depending only on impersonal media of communication will be enough to have a great impact on the low-income audience. Face-to-face contacts are an important adjunct to the mass media. Direct, personal contact clarifies and reinforces messages and provides social support for the intended change in behavior.[4] Just as the local merchants have learned to personalize their services, so it is necessary to personalize the efforts to help these consumers. The messages of educational campaigns would be much more effectively communicated if informed people were readily available to advise these consumers. This suggests the need for consumer counsellors and perhaps consumer clinics close at hand to people living in low-income areas. Settlements would be particularly appropriate institutions for incorporating such services since they have had long experience in extending personal help to the poor, as has been noted by Koos in his study of working-class families trying to cope with their troubles. Koos found that relatively few turned to the many specialized welfare agencies. But they were not at all reluctant to take their problems to the workers of settlement houses.

The services offered informally by the personnel of these agencies [Settlements and Neighborhood Houses] were so varied and *so easily obtained* that families turned to them readily. . . . The families which made use of the settlement facilities regarded the personnel not as professional workers but rather as fortunately-placed friends.[5]

---

4. The importance of face-to-face contact in effecting changes in attitudes and behavior has been demonstrated by the work of Kurt Lewin and his students. See for example, Kurt Lewin, "Group Decision and Social Change," in Maccoby *et al., op. cit.* The role of interpersonal communication in reinforcing the mass media has received considerable attention in studies carried out by the Bureau of Applied Social Research. For a summary of these studies as well as the report of an empirical study dealing with this topic, see Elihu Katz and Paul F. Lazarsfeld, *Personal Influence* (New York: The Free Press of Glencoe, 1955).

5. Earl L. Koos, *Families in Trouble,* pp. 82–83.

Local consumer clinics free of bureaucratic trappings would also have easy access to these families.[6]

The findings of this study help to pinpoint the groups most in need of consumer advice. As we have seen, the move to public housing creates many consumer needs. Families in the early stages of the life cycle and relatively large families are especially active consumers of durable goods. Consumer counsellors might emulate the peddlers to the extent of calling on such families at their homes, thus reaching some of them before they become overburdened with consumer problems. It might also be possible for the Housing Authority to provide some counselling to its new tenants. This would only be emulating some enterprising merchants, for families reported to us that they were contacted by furniture stores shortly *before* they moved into public housing.[7] Prospective tenants of public housing would therefore be a prime group for receiving more disinterested advice from consumer counsellors.

INSTITUTIONAL ARRANGEMENTS
SUPPLEMENTING KNOWLEDGE

The problem of getting information to low-income consumers has led us to consider such innovations as consumer

6. Sources of personalized help for the urban poor are probably not as prevalent today as they were a few generations ago. In its early days, social work was primarily concerned with the needs of the immigrant poor. The Settlement House movement was then at the core of the profession. The only other institution designed to help the immigrant poor was the political machine. With the curbing of immigration in the twenties and the extension of welfare services by the state in the thirties and forties, the political machine and the Settlement House movement have both been curbed. In recent decades, social work has become more professionalized and its efforts are now focused on casework dispensed through bureaucratic agencies. This study is a reminder that institutions like settlement houses are still much needed today. In place of the European immigrants of a few generations ago, our large cities now have migrants from rural areas and Puerto Rico.

7. How the merchants obtained the names of prospective tenants is something of a puzzle, and the Housing Authority has made every effort to insure that this information is not obtained through a leak in its organization. Arrangements apparently exist between merchants and some moving companies whereby the movers sell names of clients to the merchants. This might explain how some prospective tenants become known to merchants.

counsellors and clinics. But the need for new institutional arrangements extends beyond the matter of communicating information. Families may receive expert advice, but whether they act upon it depends also on whether realistic alternatives are readily available to them. For example, efforts to get families to save their money and buy for cash are more likely to succeed if more savings banks can be induced to locate in low-income neighborhoods and if credit unions can achieve a foothold in the housing projects.

Similarly, the goal of enlarging the shopping horizons of these families can be better achieved if the more reliable merchants—the large department stores and discount houses, for example—also compete for the low-income consumer. Perhaps these enterprises can be induced to re-examine their policies. Are they aware of the new customers they might attract if they would make low-income consumers feel more at home in their stores? Of course, there are limits beyond which these enterprises cannot compete with the merchants now operating in the low-income market. Local merchants, for example, may offer credit terms which violate the principles of a sound and ethical business. But the more ethical merchants could undoubtedly make bigger inroads on the low-income market than they are now doing.

More effective institutional arrangements are particularly needed by the consumers who encounter difficulties with merchants. The widespread ignorance of the existence of community agencies is not the only problem. The institutions now providing these services tend to be inaccessible and too impersonal to meet the needs of many of these consumers. Until these facilities are developed to the point where they —like the local merchants—are readily accessible to low-income families, most of these consumers will not receive the professional services they need.

Throughout we have assumed that consumer habits can be changed, provided that sound consumer knowledge is accompanied by realistic alternatives to current practices. But it should be recognized that desirable alternatives may not be feasible for many of these consumers, particularly the poorest risks. If their desires for durable goods are as resistant to change as we suspect, it is possible that (in the absence of effective alternatives to their present shopping habits) educational efforts will only increase their discomfort. Such families might resist efforts to inform them of their exploitation, for this knowledge would only make visible to them the horns of their dilemma: forfeiting the compensatory gains they now derive from consumption or facing exploitation in the low-income marketing system.

Consumer Protection Through Legislation

Apart from efforts to change the attitudes, knowledge, and practices of the low-income consumer, consideration should be given to modifying the system of marketing in which he now finds himself.

Nowhere are the laws protecting the rights of consumers in time sales as fully developed as in New York State. Nevertheless, this study has found that even this advanced legislation does not meet the needs of many low-income consumers. The problem lies not so much in the failure of the legal structure to establish their rights as in the failure of these consumers to understand and to exercise their legal rights. The legal structure is based on a model of the "sophisticated" consumer, not that of the "traditional" consumer prevalent among low-income families. It assumes, for example, that the consumer understands the conditions to which he is agreeing when he affixes his signature to an installment contract. But we have seen, time and again, that this assumption does not hold for many of these consumers. Some have no understanding of the principles of a chattel mortgage. They do not realize that they are still liable for a debt even after their merchandise has been repossessed. The law that entitles the merchant to sell repossessed merchandise and deduct the sales price from the debt is not readily understood by the family that finds it still owes money even though it no longer has the merchandise. And some families have no understanding of their obligation to pay interest on their unpaid debts. Still another area of confusion for many low-income families is the legal provision which entitles the merchant to sell the contract to a credit agency. As we have seen, a frequent result of this practice is to free the merchant of his obligations to the consumer, not because the law gives him this right, but because the consumer misunderstands what has happened.

Not only do these consumers have difficulty understanding their rights, they are also poorly qualified to know when their rights have been violated. Merchants are able to pass off reconditioned merchandise as new, for example, because their customers are too inexperienced to know the difference.

The present legal structure thus falls short of its goals because its image of the low-income consumer is not correct. As a result, it unwittingly favors the interests of the merchant over those of the consumer by permitting deviant practices which take advantage of the consumer's ignorance. We have already noted one such practice, the institutionalized evasion of "sewer service." Still another evasion of legal procedure often follows upon the judgment against the defendant. At this point the law requires that the property of the defendant be attached. Only when the defendant does not have property that can satisfy the debt can his salary be garnisheed. The responsibility for carrying out the court's judgment rests with the City Marshal. City Marshals (there are forty-five of them in Manhattan) are appointed by the Mayor. They are essentially the collection agents of the law. (Unlike civil servants, they are not paid salaries; instead their income is derived from fees. The procedure is for the plaintiff, or rather his lawyer, to get in touch with a Marshal of his choice.) They are supposed to satisfy the judgment by attaching the defendant's property and arranging for its sale. If the defendant does not have any property that can meet the debt, the Marshal will return the judgment to the court as "unsatisfied." Then, and only then, does the law permit a garnishment. In practice, City Marshals sometimes neglect to investigate the defendant's property. Instead, they return the judgment as unsatisfied, and move directly to the next step, the garnishment. It is the combination of "sewer service" and this practice on the part of some Marshals that accounts for the fact that consumers sometimes never learn of the action taken against them until their employers notify them of the garnishment. And by that time it is often too late for the consumer to protect his job, let alone his rights in the legal action.[7]

It is instructive to contrast the legal machinery dealing with the consumer defendant with that dealing with the juvenile defendant. Enlightened public opinion has led to the emergence of legal arrangements for juvenile offenders which, if biased at all, favor the defendant rather than the plaintiff. The juvenile defendant is regarded as not fully responsible for his actions. The environmental pressures which shape his behavior are taken into account when his behavior is assessed. The emphasis is upon rehabilitation rather than retribution; the first offender is frequently let off with a warning, and the courts try to provide the defendant with professional services to aid in his rehabilitation. The findings of this study suggest that some of the general assumptions made about the juvenile defendant also apply to many low-income consumers. They,

---

7. In 1964, the law was changed; the creditor now has the option of obtaining a garnishment order without first attaching property. But abuses of the law still persist. The City Marshal is required to send the defendant a notice of garnishment twenty days prior to sending the garnishment order to the employer. The purpose of this law is to give the defendant a chance to settle the debt and thus avoid trouble with his employer. But many of those whose wages are garnisheed claim that they never receive this notice. Moreover, "sewer service" is still a serious problem in New York. In 1966, Attorney General Lefkowitz held hearings about this and considerable evidence was presented showing that "sewer service" is widespread in consumer and landlord-tenant cases; yet efforts to change the law to improve service of process have so far failed.

too, are not fully responsible for their actions. Poorly educated, intimidated by complex urban society, bombarded
with "bait advertising," they are no match for high-pressure
salesmen urging heavy burdens of debt upon them. Perhaps legal machinery can be instituted, which takes these facts
about low-income consumers into account.

Since many problems of low-income consumers stem
from their being pressured into credit commitments beyond their means, the question arises whether this activity
can be controlled by legislation. Under the present system,
the merchant alone makes the decision whether or not to
extend credit; and as one merchant put it, "extending
credit is not our responsibility, it is our risk." Since the
merchant does not accept the responsibility and many low-
income consumers lack the training for responsibility, how
can responsibility be built into the system? One solution
would be to establish by law minimal credit requirements
that must be met by all consumers. The merchant now does
not feel particularly responsible because he knows he can
count on the law to back his claims against the defaulting
debtor. If the merchant were unable to have legal redress
against customers who fail to meet the requirements of
reasonable risks, he would scarcely be as eager to pressure
such families into buying on time.

Another way of changing the low-income marketing system would be to enact laws regulating prices. If the merchants were forced to accept lower markups than they now
enjoy under their "number" system of pricing, they would
be unable to offer the "easy credit" plans they now do.

It is possible, however, that even if such laws were
feasible, they would not fully accomplish their intended
objectives. Instead of forcing poor risks to curtail their
consumption because the merchants would no longer extend them credit, such laws might only stimulate deviant
patterns worse than those now in effect. For example, as
their credit in local stores dried up, more families would
probably turn to the peddlers, who depend almost entirely

upon personal, rather than legal, controls. Enforcing laws pertaining to peddlers is not an easy matter, for these men are highly mobile and not readily apprehended. Also, some families might turn to loan sharks for the money that would enable them to buy for cash. Obviously, there is no simple solution to the ills of the low-income marketing system. But this should not deter efforts to reduce the abuses of the system through legislation.

In the final analysis, the consumer problems of low-income families cannot be divorced from the other problems facing them. Until society can find ways of raising their educational level, improving their occupational opportunities, increasing their income, and reducing the discrimination against them—in short, until poverty itself is eradicated—only limited solutions to their problems as consumers can be found.

Table of Indices

The Interview Schedule

FIRST, we would like to get an idea of who lives here, their ages and so forth.

1. Who is living in the apartment now?
   a. Who is the head of the family?
   b. How are they related to the head of the family?
   c. What are their ages? (DO NOT ASK AGE OF HUSBAND OR WIFE NOW.)
         (CIRCLE PERSON WHO IS RESPONDENT)

RELATION TO HEAD	AGE	RELATION TO HEAD	AGE
(1) Head_____	____	(5) _____	____
(2) _____	____	(6) _____	____
(3) _____	____	(7) _____	____
(4) _____	____	(8) _____	____

2. (IF INCOMPLETE FAMILY, ASK)
   a. Is your husband (wife) living?   Spouse deceased_____
                                              Separated or divorced_____
   b. How long ago did he (she) pass away?
         (OR)
      How long ago were you separated?   _____

3. a. Do you have any children under 17 who are not   No _____
living in the apartment? (IF YES) how many?   Yes _____

  b. Do you have any children *over* 17 who are not   No _____
living in the apartment? (IF YES) How many?   Yes _____

4. How long have you been living in this project?   _____

5. How long have you been living in this apartment?   _____

6. Did you live in this neighborhood before you   Yes _____
moved to the project?   No _____

Now, some questions about shopping.

7. Did you ever buy anything from someone who called   Yes _____
you on the phone or wrote you a letter?   No _____
(IF YES) What happened? _____

8. Do you have any friends or relatives who work in stores   Yes _____
or factories who help you to get things cheaper?   No _____
(IF YES)   a. Who? _____
          b. What sort of things? _____

9. Do you have a system for keeping track of how   Yes _____
you spend your money?   No _____
(IF YES)   What is it? _____

10. Have you ever seen a magazine   Yes _____
called *Consumer Reports*?   No _____

  (IF YES)   Do you ever check *Consumer Reports*   Yes _____
          when you want to buy something?   No _____

11. Some people get talked into buying things by
salesmen that they really don't want.   Yes _____
Does this happen to you?   No _____

  (IF YES)   Does it happen fairly often   Fairly often _____
          or only once in a while?   Once in a while _____

12. Some people like to do a lot of shopping
around no matter what they buy. Others   Shop around _____
make up their minds quickly and don't   Decide quickly _____
look around too much. Which do you do?   Depends _____

13. Do you find yourself buying things   Yes _____
that you don't really need?   No _____

  (IF YES)   Does this happen fairly often   Fairly often _____
          or only once in a while?   Once in a while _____

14. How many times have you gone to a Stanley
party or some other kind of demonstration party?   (No.) _____

15. Do you prefer to shop in neighborhood stores   Neighborhood _____
    or in big downtown (uptown) stores?   Depends _____
    (IF NEIGHBORHOOD   Downtown _____
       OR DOWNTOWN)   No Difference _____
    Why do you say that? _____

16. Has anyone recently asked you for advice   Yes _____
    on something that they wanted to buy?   No _____
    (IF YES) Who? What did they want to buy?   _____

17. Do you think it is a good idea or a bad idea   Good _____
    to buy things on the installment plan?   Bad _____
                                                          Depends _____
    Why do you say that? _____

18. *Before* you moved to this project, did you ever buy
    anything on credit from someone who brings the
    things to your apartment? (IF RESPONDENT
    DOES NOT SEEM TO UNDERSTAND, USE
    WORDS LIKE "door-to-door salesmen," "ped-   Yes _____
    dlers," etc.)   No _____

19. *Since* you've been living in this project, have you   Yes _____
    bought anything from such a person?   No _____
    (IF NO)
    a. Have such people tried to sell you things?   Yes _____
                                                               No _____

    (IF YES TO QUESTION 19a)
    b. Why didn't you buy from them?   Poor quality   _____
                                               Too expensive _____
    (SKIP TO QUESTION 38)   Other (specify) _____

    (IF YES TO QUESTION 19)

20. Which of the following have you bought in this way?
                          Sink attachment (cabinets)   _____
                          Lamps or mirrors   _____
                          Slip covers or linoleum   _____
                          Sheets, blankets, bedspreads   _____
                          Clothing for children   _____
                          Clothing for wife or husband   _____
                          TV, vacuum cleaner, washing
                              machine, or sewing machine   _____
                          Encyclopedias   _____
                          Bibles or other religious articles _____

21. Do you *now* owe any money to such a person?   Yes _____

                                                                No _____

(IF NO)

a. When was the last time you bought something
   from such a person?   _____

b. How many such salesmen did you deal with?   One   _____

                                                       Two   _____

                                          Three or more _____

c. How did you happen to meet him (them)?

                                          Rang bell _____

                      Through friend, neighbor _____

                              Through family _____

d. Do you think you might buy   Yes _____
   from such a person again?   No _____

                                                   Depends _____

Why   (OR)   Why not?   DK _____

(SKIP TO QUESTION 38)

(IF YES TO QUESTION 21)

22. How many of these people do you now   One   _____
    owe money to?   Two   _____

                                                     Three _____

23. Do you remember how much you owe him (them)?   1st man $_____

                                                   2nd man $_____

                                                   3rd man $_____

24. What do you pay him (them) each time?

                                              Varying

                1st   man $_____ per _____   _____

                2nd man $_____ per _____   _____

                3rd man $_____ per _____   _____

(IF MONEY OWED TO MORE THAN ONE MAN ASK)

a. How many of these men have you bought   One   _____
   more than one item from?   Two   _____

                                                     Three _____

b. Why don't you do all your
   business with one man?   _____

Let's talk about the one you've bought
the most things from.

25. How long have you been dealing with him?   _____

26. Who does the buying from him, you or your
    husband (wife)?

                                              Wife _____
                                           Husband _____
                                              Both _____

27. How did you happen to meet him?

                                         Rang bell _____
                       Through friend, neighbor _____
                                            Family _____
                                   Other (specify) _____

                       _____

28. Do you know other people who buy from him?   Who?
                                                No _____
                         Yes, friends, neighbors _____
                                      Yes, family _____
                                  Other (specify) _____

                       _____

29. Have you recommended him to anyone?   Who?
                                                No _____
                         Yes, friends, neighbors _____
                                      Yes, family _____
                                  Other (specify) _____

                       _____

30. Does he charge extra if you miss a payment?   Yes _____
                                                        No _____

31. Does he charge more than you'd have to   More _____
    pay at a store, less, or about the same?   Less _____
                                                        Same _____

    a. How do you know this?   _____

32. Do you like the quality of his goods?   Yes _____
                                                        No _____
                                                    Depends _____

33. What happens when he sells you something that is   Yes _____
     no good? Will he take it back or fix it?   No _____
                         Never happened, DK _____

34. Does he spend time chatting with you about   Yes _____
     everyday things when he comes around?   No _____

35. Do you think he's honest in   Yes _____
     his dealings with you?   No _____
                     DK _____

36. Has he ever done any special favors for you?   Yes _____
                     No _____

     (IF YES)   What kind? _____

37. Do you plan to go on buying from him?   Yes _____
                     No _____
                     Depends _____
     a. (IF NO) Why not? _____
                     DK _____
     (IF YES OR DEPENDS)
     b. Is he a nicer person to deal with than   Yes _____
        the salesmen you find in stores?   No _____
                     No difference _____
     c. Suppose you could get credit at a store,   Yes _____
        would you still buy from him?   No _____
        Why do you say that? _____
     d. Suppose you could pay cash, would you   Yes _____
        still buy from him?   No _____
        Why do you say that? _____

Now let's talk about food shopping.

38. Where do you buy most of your food?

                         Supermarkets _____
                         City markets _____
                     Independent grocer _____

39. How often do you go shopping for food?   _____ per _____

40. About how much on the average do you spend
     for food? $_____ per _____

41. Compared with a year ago, do you have   More _____
    more money now to spend on food,   Less _____
    less money now, or about the same?   Same _____
    (IF MORE OR LESS) Why is that? _____

42. Do you have milk delivered to your door?   Yes _____
                                                    No _____
    (IF YES) Why? _____
    (IF NO)
    Do you buy milk at the milk station   Yes _____
    here in the project?   No _____
    (IF NO) Why not? _____

43. Do you always pay cash at food stores or   Always cash _____
    do you sometimes buy on credit?   Credit _____
    (IF CREDIT)
    a. How high do you let your food bill go? $_____
    b. Do you owe any money *now* to a food store? Yes _____
                                                    No _____
    (IF YES) How much? $_____
    c. What's your main reason for buying food on credit? _____

    _____

    d. Would you buy at that store if you   Yes _____
       didn't need the credit?   No _____

44. a. Where do you (does your wife) usually get your
       (her) clothes? (NAME OF STORE OR SOURCES) _____

    _____

    b. Do you (does she) get most of your
       (her) clothes here in the neighbor-
       hood or do you (does she) go out of
       the neighborhood?   In neighborhood _____
                                             Out of neighborhood _____

45. a. Where does your husband (do you)
       buy his (your) clothes?   _____

    _____

    b. Does he (do you) get most of his
       (your) clothes here in the neighbor-
       hood or does he (do you) go out of   In neighborhood _____
       the neighborhood?   Out of neighborhood _____

46. a. What about the children's clothes? Where do you get them?_____

_____

 b. Do you get most of their clothes   In neighborhood _____
 here in this neighborhood?   Out of neighborhood _____

47. Do you ever buy second-hand clothes?   Yes _____
   No _____

48. Does any member of your family now have   Yes, wife _____
 a credit account at a store where you buy   Yes, husband _____
 clothing?   No _____
 (IF NO)
 a. Do you always pay cash for clothes or   Always cash _____
 do you sometimes buy clothing on credit?   Credit _____
 (IF YES: HAVE CREDIT ACCOUNTS)
 b. In which stores? _____

_____

 c. How much do you now owe the store for clothes? $_____
 d. How much did you pay the store last month for clothes? $_____

STORE	AMOUNT OWED	PAYMENT LAST MONTH
_____	$_____	$_____
_____	$_____	$_____

49. During the past year, have you been able to get all   Yes _____
 the clothes that you need for yourself and your family?   No _____
 (IF NO) Why not? _____

(ASK FOLLOWING OF VLADECK FAMILIES WHO HAVE
MOVED IN *BEFORE* 1950. FOR ALL OTHER FAMILIES, SKIP
TO QUESTION 51.)

50. In the last five years, have you bought any   Yes _____
 furniture for your apartment?   No _____
 (IF NO, SKIP TO QUESTION 61. IF YES)
 a. What did you buy?

	Set	Pieces
Living room	_____	_____
Kitchen	_____	_____
Master bedroom	_____	_____
Children's bedroom	_____	_____

b. Did you buy this new or second-hand?   New _____
                                                       Used _____

c. Did you buy the furniture in this   In neighborhood _____
   neighborhood or somewhere else?   Out of neighborhood _____

d. Did you pay cash or did you buy it on credit?
                                              Store credit _____
                                           Cash—savings _____
                                          Cash—borrowed _____

(IF CREDIT)

e. Are you still paying for it?   Yes _____
                                                        No _____

(IF YES)

f. What are the payments? $_____ per _____

g. How much do you still owe? $_____

           (SKIP TO QUESTION 61)

51. Did you have your own apartment before you moved to this project?
                                               Own apartment
                                               Nonproject   _____
                                               Project transfer _____
                                               Relative's apartment _____
                                               Furnished room _____

(IF OWN APARTMENT)

a. How many rooms did you have in that apartment?   _____

b. Was it furnished or unfurnished?   Furnished _____
                                                Unfurnished _____

(IF UNFURNISHED)

c. Did you bring any furniture with you from your old apartment
   when you moved into this project?

(CHECK ALL THAT APPLY)

| | None _____ | |
	Set	Pieces
Living room	_____	_____
Kitchen	_____	_____
Master bedroom	_____	_____
Children's bedroom	_____	_____

52. What furniture did you have to buy *at the time you were moving into this project?*
(CHECK ALL THAT APPLY)

	None Set	Pieces
Living room	_____	_____
Kitchen	_____	_____
Master bedroom	_____	_____
Children's bedroom	_____	_____

53. Did any furniture salesman contact you about buying furniture *before* you moved into this project?

Yes _____
No _____

(IF YES) Did you buy from him?

Yes _____
No _____

(IF NO FURNITURE BOUGHT AT TIME OF MOVE, SKIP TO QUESTION 58)

54. Did you have enough time to buy the furniture you needed when you first moved in?

Yes _____
No _____

(IF NO) Why not? _____

55. Did you buy new or used furniture at that time?

All new _____
Mostly new _____
Mostly used _____
All used _____

56. What did the furniture that you bought then cost all together?

$_____

57. Did you pay cash or did you buy it on credit?
(IF CASH) Was that money you had saved or did you have to borrow the money?

Store credit _____
Cash—savings _____
Cash—borrowed _____

58. Since you've been living here, have you bought any furniture?
(IF YES)
a. What did you buy?

Yes _____
No _____

	Set	Pieces
Living room	_____	_____
Kitchen	_____	_____
Master bedroom	_____	_____
Children's bedroom	_____	_____

b. Did you buy this furniture new or
  or did you buy used furniture?
New _____
Used _____
Both _____

c. Did you buy this furniture in this
  neighborhood or did you get it out
  of the neighborhood?
In neighborhood _____
Out of neighborhood _____
Both _____

d. Did you pay cash for this furniture or did you buy it on credit?
Store credit _____
Cash—savings _____
Cash—borrowed _____

59. Are you now making any payments for furniture?
Yes _____
No _____

(IF YES)

a. (CHECK ALL THAT APPLY. ASK RESPONDENT
  IF IN DOUBT)

           Payments on furniture bought for apartment
             lived in prior to move   _____
        Payments on furniture bought at time of move _____
         Payments on furniture bought since move _____

b. What are the payments? $_____ per _____
c. How much do you still owe? $_____

60. Are you satisfied with the furniture
  you bought for this apartment?
Yes _____
No _____
DNA _____

(IF NO) Why not? _____

61. Do you own an automobile?
Yes _____
(IF YES)
No _____
a. What is the year and make of the car? Year _____ Make _____
b. How long have you had it? _____
c. What did it cost? $_____
d. Are you still paying for it?
Paid cash _____
Paid up _____
Still paying _____

(IF STILL PAYING)
e. What are the payments? $_____ per _____
f. How much do you still owe? $_____

62. Do you own a ___?

	TV SET	PHONO	SEWING MACHINE	WASHING MACHINE	VACUUM CLEANER
	Yes	Yes	Yes	Yes	Yes
	No	No	No	No	No

   a. What type of TV?

     Console ____   Table ____

     TV-Phono ____   Portable ____

   b. What type of phono?

     Console ____   Portable ____

63. How long have
    you had it?   ____   ____   ____   ____   ____

64. Did you get it
    new or used?   ____   ____   ____   ____   ____

65. What did it cost? $____ $____ $____ $____ $____

66. How did you
    pay for it?

   Store credit   ____   ____   ____   ____   ____

   Cash—savings   ____   ____   ____   ____   ____

   Cash—borrowed   ____   ____   ____   ____   ____

   Gift or bought from
     friend, relative   ____   ____   ____   ____   ____

   (IF STORE CREDIT)

67. Are you still
    paying for it?   ____   ____   ____   ____   ____

   (IF STILL PAYING)

   a. What are the $____ $____ $____ $____ $____

     payments?   per____ per____ per____ per____ per____

   b. How much do
     you still owe? $____ $____ $____ $____ $____

68. Where did you get it?   69. (IF STORE) In this neighborhood?

   TV set   _____   Yes ____ No ____

   Phonograph   _____   Yes ____ No ____

   Sewing machine   _____   Yes ____ No ____

   Vacuum cleaner   _____   Yes ____ No ____

   Washing machine   _____   Yes ____ No ____

(ASK QUESTIONS 70-85 FOR MOST RECENT MAJOR PUR-
CHASE WITHIN LAST FIVE YEARS, INCLUDING AUTO-
MOBILE IF NO APPLIANCE. IF NO PURCHASES IN THIS
PERIOD, SKIP TO QUESTION 86.)

70. The most recent thing you bought is the _____

(Enter name of item)

71. What is the make of the _____? _____
What year model is it? _____
Do you know the model number
    or model name? _____
(CHECK HERE IF DATA COME FROM CONTRACT) _____

72. How long did you think about buying
it before you actually bought it? _____

73. Was there any particular reason why Yes _____
you bought it when you did? No _____
(IF YES) What? _____

74. Whose idea was it to buy the _____?

Wife _____
Husband _____
Both _____
Other (Specify) _____

75. Who did the actual buying?

Wife _____
Husband _____
Both _____
Other (Specify) _____

76. Did anyone else go along with you Yes _____
(him, her) to buy it? No _____
Who?
_____

77. Did you (your husband, wife) first ask anyone Yes _____
for advice about buying it? No _____
(IF YES)
a. Who? Anyone else? _____
b. What did you try to find out? _____

78. Did you (he, she) buy it at the first Single store _____
store you (he, she) went to or did you Several stores _____
go to different stores before buying it? Not bought in store _____

(IF ITEM BOUGHT ON CREDIT, ASK QUESTIONS 79-84)

79. If you could have paid cash for the _____   Yes _____
    would you have bought it at the same place?   No _____
    (IF NO)
    a. Where would you have gotten it?   _____
    b. You said before that the _____ cost $_____
                                        (Enter cost)

80. Was there a trade-in?   Yes _____
                                                      No _____

    (IF YES)
    a. Is that the price before or   Before _____
       after the trade-in?   After _____
    b. How much were you allowed? $_____

81. How long did they give you to pay it off?   _____
    a. How long did it (will it) actually take?   _____

82. Would the _____ have cost the same if you   Same _____
    had paid cash or would it have cost less?   Less _____
    (IF LESS)
    a. About how much would it have cost $_____
       if you had paid cash?   DK _____

83. Do you happen to know what the credit service   Yes _____%
    charge comes to in terms of a yearly interest   Guess _____%
    rate on the _____?   Don't know _____
                                    Does not understand _____

84. Has it been (was it) difficult for you   Yes _____
    to meet the payments on the _____?   No _____
    (IF YES)
    a. Did you ever have to miss any payments?   Yes _____
                                                     No _____

(ASK OF ALL WHO HAVE MADE A RECENT
MAJOR PURCHASE)

85. If you had it to do all over again, would you   Yes _____
    still have bought the _____ in the same way? No _____
    (IF NO)   What would you do differently?   _____
    (ASK OF EVERYONE)

86. Have you ever felt that you were cheated   Yes _____
    in something you bought?   No _____
    (IF YES)
    a. What happened?   _____
    b. What did you do about it?   _____

87. Where would you now go for help if you
were being cheated by a store or salesman? _____

88. Did you ever have anything that you   Yes _____
bought on time repossessed?   No _____
                                    Never bought on time _____
(IF YES)
a. What happened? _____
b. How many times has this happened?   (No.) _____
c. When was the last time?   _____

89. Was your husband's (your) salary   Yes _____
ever garnisheed or attached?   No _____
(IF YES)
a. What happened? _____
b. Is his (your) salary being garnisheed now?   Yes _____
                                                     No _____

(IF NO TO QUESTION 89)
c. Were you ever threatened with a garnishee?   Yes _____
                                                     No _____

(IF YES) What happened? _____

90. Did you ever have any (other) trouble   Yes _____
with stores or salesmen?   No _____
(IF YES) What happened? _____

91. Were you ever refused credit at a store?   Yes _____
                                                     No _____
(IF YES) What happened? _____

92. Are there any things that you feel you   Yes _____
should own that you don't own now?   No _____
(IF YES)
a. What?   _____
b. Which do you plan to get in the next year?   _____
c. Will you pay cash for it (them) or   Cash _____
will you buy it (them) on credit?   Credit _____

93. Do you *now* owe any money to a bank,   No _____
finance company, or credit union?   Yes, bank _____
                                         Yes, finance co. _____
                                       Yes, credit union _____

(IF NO)

a. Did you ever get a loan from   No _____
    a bank, finance co., or credit union?   Yes, bank _____
                     Yes, finance co. _____
                     Yes, credit union _____

(IF YES TO QUESTION 93a)

b. How long ago was that?   _____

c. What did you need the loan for?   _____

(IF NEVER BORROWED)

d. Did you ever *try* to get a loan from   Yes _____
    one of these places?   No _____

(IF YES) What happened?   _____

(IF MONEY NOW OWED)

94. How much did you borrow?   Source: _____ $_____
                                    _____ $_____

95. What were your reasons for getting the loan(s)?   _____

96. What are the payments?   Source: _____ $_____/_____ pymts
                             _____ $_____/_____ pymts

97. How much do you still owe?   Source: _____ $_____
                                    _____ $_____

98. Do you happen to know what the   _____ _____% DK_____
    interest rate is on the(se) loans?   _____ _____% DK_____

99. Since you first took out the loan have   Yes _____
    you gone back and renewed it?   No _____

(FOR THOSE BORROWING ONLY FROM FINANCE CO.)

100. Did you try to get a bank loan before   Yes _____
    you went to the finance co.?   No _____

(IF YES) What happened?   _____

(IF NOT) Why not?   _____

(ASK OF EVERYONE)

101. Are you now thinking of getting (another) loan?   Yes _____
                                          No _____

(IF YES)

a. Where?   _____

b. What for?   _____

102. Have you ever had to borrow money   Yes _____
    from a loan shark?   No _____

(IF NO)

a. Did you ever borrow from someone you knew   Yes _____
    where you had to pay extra for the loan?   No _____
(IF YES TO 102 or 102a)

b. Do you still owe money to such a person?   Yes _____
                                                      No _____

(IF YES)

c. How much did you borrow? $_____
d. How much do you still owe? $_____
e. What are the payments? $_____ per _____

103. When you need money, do you ever take   Yes _____
     things to pawn shops?   No _____

104. Do you now owe any money to relatives   Yes _____
     or friends?   No _____
     (IF YES)
     a. How much? $_____
     (IF NO)
     b. Could you borrow money from relatives or   Yes _____
        friends if you needed it?   No _____
                                                      D.K._____

105. Are you now helping out any relatives or friends Yes _____
     that are not living in the apartment?   No _____
     (IF YES)
     a. Who?   _____
     b. How much do you give them? $_____ per _____

106. Do you now owe any doctor or dentist bills?   Yes _____
                                                      No _____

     (IF YES)
     a. How much do you owe? $_____
     b. How are you paying it off? $_____ per _____

(PUERTO RICAN FAMILIES ONLY)

107. Do you owe any money to a travel agency   Yes _____
     for plane trips to Puerto Rico?   No _____
     (IF YES)
     a. How much do you owe? $_____
     b. What are the payments? $_____ per _____

108. When you consider all the money that you now owe
     to different places and people, like stores, salesmen,
     loans and doctor bills, how much money do you think
     you need to pay off *all* your debts? $_____

(IF NO DEBTS)

a. Were you in debt a year ago?   Yes _____
                                                          No _____

b. Were you in debt before you lived in the project?   Yes _____
                                                          No _____

(IF DEBTS)

a. Do you owe more money now than you did   More now _____
   a year ago, less now, or about the same?   Less now _____
                                                       Same _____

b. What about before you moved to the project?   More now _____
   Did you owe more money in those days than   Less now _____
   you owe now, less then, or is it about the same? Same _____

109. Which newspapers do you read almost every day?   None _____

_____

_____

110. Which magazines do you read regularly?   None _____

_____

_____

111. Do most of your friends live here in   Here _____
     the project or do they live elsewhere?   Elsewhere _____
                                                     No Friends _____

112. About how many families here in the project do you
     know by name?   (No.) _____

113. About how many families here come to visit
     you in your apartment?   (No.) _____

114. Do you have relatives living in N. Y. C.?   Yes _____
                                                            No _____

(IF YES)

a. Were you living closer to your relatives   Closer before _____
   before you moved here, or do you   Closer now _____
   live closer to them now?   Same _____

115. Do you or your husband (wife) belong   Yes, wife _____
     to any of the organizations or clubs   Yes, husband _____
     here in the project?   Yes, both _____
                                                           No _____

(IF YES) Which ones? _____

116. What about organizations and clubs   Yes, wife _____
     outside of the project? Do you or   Yes, husband _____
     your husband (wife) belong to any?   Yes, both _____
                                           No _____

     (IF YES) Which ones? _____

117. Do you like this apartment better than
     the one you were living in before you   Project apt. better _____
     moved to this project or did you like   Old apt. better _____
     your old apartment better?   No difference _____

118. Do you expect to move out of the project   Yes _____
     some day?   No _____
                                           DK _____

     (IF YES)

     a. Are you planning to buy your own home, move to another apart-
        ment, or what?

                                 Buy home   _____
                                 Co-op Apartment   _____
                                 Project Transfer   _____
                                 Non-project apartment _____
     b. When do you think you will move out?   _____
     (IF PLANNING TO BUY HOME OR CO-OP)
     c. Have you saved any money for the   Yes _____
        house (apartment)?   No _____

     (FOR FAMILIES WITH MALE CHILDREN NOT YET
     IN LABOR FORCE)

119. Would you rather have your boy(s) get a job   Get job _____
     when he finishes high school or would you   College _____
     rather have him (them) go to college?   Don't care _____
     a. Which do you think is more likely to   Work _____
        happen? That he'll (they'll) go to   College _____
        work or go to college?   Don't know _____

120. What do you think your boy(s) will do when
     he (they) grow(s) up?   _____
     a. What would you like to see him (them) do?   _____

121. Does your family income right now come from earnings, welfare, social security, or what?

(CHECK AS MANY AS APPLY)
Earnings   _____
Unempl. Benefit_____
Welfare   _____
Social Security   _____
Other pensions   _____
Other (what)   _____

(IF WELFARE)

a. How long have you been on welfare?   _____

(IF WELFARE, SOCIAL SECURITY OR PENSION FAMILY SKIP TO QUESTION 133)

122. (IF DOUBTFUL, ASK) Who is the chief wage earner?   _____

123. What kind of work does he (do you) do?   _____

124. Does he (do you) have a steady job or   Steady _____
     is it seasonal work?   Seasonal _____
     a. Is he (are you) working now?   Yes _____
                                                      No _____

125. Does he (do you) work in this neighborhood?   Yes _____
                                                      No _____

126. Does he (do you) work days or nights?   Days _____
                                                  Nights _____

127. Does he (do you) get paid every week,   Every week _____
     every two weeks, or what?   Every two weeks _____
                                              Every month _____

128. What is his (your) regular salary? $_____ per _____
     (INDICATE IF WIFE DOES NOT KNOW)

129. Does your husband (do you) belong   Yes _____
     to a union?   No _____

130. Does your husband (do you) plan to go into   Yes _____
     business for himself someday?   No _____
     (IF YES) What kind?
                                                       _____
     a. Does your husband (do you) plan to go into   Yes _____
        a different line of work some day?   No _____
     (IF YES) What?
                                                       _____

131. Since you've been married, has your   Yes _____
     family been on welfare?   No _____
     (IF YES) How long ago was that?
                                                       _____

(EMPLOYMENT OF WIFE WHERE CHIEF WAGE EARNER IS HUSBAND)

132. Do you (does your wife) earn any money now?   Yes _____
                                                                No _____

(IF YES)

a. Doing what? _____

b. Is that job in the neighborhood?   Yes _____
                                                                No _____

c. Is that full-time or part-time?   Full-time _____
                                                                Part-time _____

d. How much do you (does she) earn? $_____ per _____

(IF WIFE NOT WORKING NOW)

e. Have you worked in the last year?   Yes _____
                                                                No _____

f. Are you planning to work again?   Yes _____
                                                                No _____

   (IF YES)
   (1) When? _____
   (2) Doing what? _____

(ASK THE FOLLOWING OF ALL FAMILIES)

133. Is there anyone else who is living in the   Yes _____
     apartment who is working now?   No _____

     (IF YES)
     a. Who?   _____
     b. What does he (she, they) do? _____
     c. How much does he (she, they) make? $_____ per _____

134.a. Do you now get money from any family member   Yes _____
       or relative who is not living in the apartment?   No _____
       (IF YES)   How much does this come to? $_____ per _____

135. Compared with last year, is your family   More now _____
     income greater now, less now, or about   Less now _____
     the same?   About the same _____

136. Do you think that a year from now your   Greater then _____
     family income will be greater than it   Less then _____
     is now, less, or about the same?   About the same _____

137. What about five years from now? Do you   Yes _____
     expect that your income then will be much   No _____
     greater than it is now?

138. Do you or your (husband/wife) have a   Yes _____
     savings account at a bank or post office?   No _____

139. Have you or your (husband/wife) put   Yes _____
     any money into a Christmas Club?   No _____

140. Do you or your (husband/wife) have   Yes _____
     a checking account at a bank?   No _____

141. Do you or your (husband/wife) own   Yes _____
     any Government Savings Bonds?   No _____

142. Do you or your (husband/wife)   Yes _____
     belong to a credit union?   No _____

143. Do you have money saved up in any other place?   Yes _____
                                                       No _____

144. Does your family (do you) now have   Yes _____
     $500 or more in savings?   No _____
     (IF NO)
     a. Do you have $100 or more in savings?   Yes _____
                                                   No _____

145. Are you now making any payments on a life   Yes _____
     insurance policy for yourself and family?   No _____
     (IF YES)
     a. How many different policies do you have?   (No.) _____
     b. Are any of these endowment policies for   Yes _____
        the children?   No _____
     c. What are the payments? $_____ per _____
                                                   $_____ per _____
     d. Does a man come to collect the money or   Collection _____
        do you mail it in?   Mail in _____
     e. How much is the head of the family insured for? $_____

146. Are you and your family covered by   Only head _____
     health insurance such as Blue Cross, HIP,   Entire family _____
     or some other plan?   No _____
     (IF YES)   What kind? _____

147. Have you had to put off any medical care   Yes _____
     that you or your family need?   No _____
     (IF YES)   Why? _____

148. Have you had to put off any dental care   Yes _____
     that you or your family need?   No _____
     (IF YES)   Why? _____

149. Do you have any friends or relatives   Yes _____
that you would say are *very* well off financially?   No _____
(IF YES)
a. What do they do for a living? _____
b. How often do you see them? _____

150. Now, we'd like to ask you about how you spend your free time.
I'm going to read off a list of things and you tell me which ones
you've done in the last 3 months.

ACTIVITY	YES	No
1. Gone to the movies	_____	_____
2. Gone to a dance	_____	_____
3. Gone to a museum	_____	_____
4. Had friends visit you in your apartment during the evening	_____	_____
5. Read a book	_____	_____
6. Visited your relatives	_____	_____
7. Taken a trip out of New York City	_____	_____
8. Gambled on the numbers	_____	_____
9. Played cards for money	_____	_____
10. Given a party in your apartment	_____	_____
11. Had friends over to dinner	_____	_____
12. Talked about politics with your friends	_____	_____

(INDICATE WHETHER HUSBAND OR WIFE IS ANSWERING)

Male head _____

Wife (Female head) _____

Now we would like to ask you a few questions about your background.

F-1. Where were you born? (IF COMPLETE FAMILY:)
Where was your husband (wife) born?

	WIFE OR FEMALE HEAD	HUSBAND OR MALE HEAD
New York City	_____	_____
U. S. South	_____	_____
U. S. Other	_____	_____
Puerto Rico	_____	_____
Other (specify)	_____	_____

(IF NOT BORN IN N. Y. C., ASK)

a. Did you grow up in a city, small
town or a farm area?

	FEMALE	MALE
City	_____	_____
Small town	_____	_____
Farm area	_____	_____

b. How long have you been
in New York City?   _____   _____

F-2. What was your age at your last birthday?
(Your husband's / wife's?)   _____   _____

F-3. Do you remember what your father's
occupation was? (Your
husband's / wife's?)   _____   _____

F-4. What was the last grade of school that
you completed? What about your
husband (wife)?

	FEMALE	MALE
Elementary school or less	_____	_____
Some high school	_____	_____
Completed high school	_____	_____
Some college	_____	_____
Completed college	_____	_____

F-5. Do you belong to any Religious   Yes _____   _____
Organization? What about your   No _____   _____
husband (wife)?

F-6. Have you voted in any of the   Yes _____   _____
recent elections? What about your   No _____   _____
husband (wife)?

F-7. Now just a few more questions.
Suppose that next week you were to win a lot of money, say, $1,000.
What would you do with it?

F-8. Every family seems to have problems these days. What would you
say are the main problems facing your family right now?

F-9. Are there any questions you would like to ask us, or do you have
any comments you would like to make?

INTERVIEWER REPORT

R-1. Length of Interview _____. R-2. When did interview take place?

Morning _____
Afternoon _____
Evening _____

R-3. Who was present during the interview?

R-4. Was the respondent cooperative?

Very cooperative _____
Fairly cooperative _____
Not very cooperative _____

R-5. Was the respondent made anxious by queries about debts?

Yes _____
No _____

R-6. English proficiency:

	WIFE	HUSBAND
Good	_____	_____
Fair	_____	_____
Hardly any	_____	_____
Don't know	_____	_____

R-7. Ethnicity:

White: Jewish _____   Negro _____
       Italian _____   Puerto Rican and
       Other (What?) _____   other Spanish
       Undetermined _____   speaking _____
                                Oriental _____

R-8. Covering of living room floor:

Linoleum _____
Bare _____
Carpet _____
Don't know _____

R-9. Condition of furniture:

Excellent _____
Good _____
Fair _____
Poor _____
Don't know _____

R-10. Did you notice a telephone?   Black _____
       If so, was it black or colored?   Colored _____
                                                       Did not notice _____

R-11. What is your guess as to the   Protestant _____
       religion of the respondent?   Catholic _____
                                                           Jewish _____

R-12. Comments and impressions:

Index

Adams, Thomas S., 181n
Advertising, bait, 142, 144, 147–48
Age, of families studied, 8, 10–11; in relation to consumer activities, 45–48; shopping scope, 55–56; buying from peddlers, 67–69, 74, 77; credit accounts in department stores, 99; use of commercial loans, 99–100; dependence on credit, 102–104; of marginal families, 118–120; consumer problems, 141
Appliances, location of stores, 12; as compensatory consumption, 13; on credit, 15–16, 96–98; quality and prices of, 18–20, 81–93; reconditioned, 28; ownership of, 36–41; replacement of, 39, 42; purchased from peddlers, 60–62; consumer complaints about, 138, *see also* Durable Goods
Arendt, Wolfram, 12n
Attorney General, 184
Automobiles, 1, 13, 33, 36, 39, 45, 109, 165–66

Banks, 96, 99, 100, 105, 110–11
Bell, Daniel, 13n
Better Business Bureau, 159, 173, 175
Black Hillel, 23n
Bonds, United States savings, 110, 111
Bureau of Applied Social Research, 2, 185
Bureaucratic credit, 2, 58–59, 85, 89–90, 92–93, 98–99, 157–61

Campbell, Persia, 149n
Cash, for durable goods, 14, 54, 87–93, 96–98, 183

Caylay, Murray, 12n
Chain stores, 53–54, 85–93
Chinoy, Eli, 13n
Christmas Clubs, 110
City Marshall, 158, 162–64, 173–74, 189–90
Clark, Lincoln, 9n
Clothes, 54, 60, 98–99, 129–30
Cloward, Richard A., 181n
Columbia University, School of Business, 2
Community agencies, 170–84
Community participation of marginal families, 132–34, 136
Comparative shopping, 19, 92, 167–68
Compensatory consumption, definition of, 13; and purchases of durable goods, 41, 48; and prices paid for appliances, 92–93; racial differences in, 127–29; relation to occupation, 135–36; and poverty of opportunity, 180–81
Consumer activity, definition of, 2–4, 193; future purchasing plans, 41–44, 117–18, 135; relation to shopping scope, 56–57; and buying from peddlers, 68, 71–72, 77; relation to debts, 101–104
Consumer education, 87, 98, 121, 182–88
Consumer Finances, Survey of, 38–39, 96, 102, 107, 110
Consumers, low-income, 1–4; composition of, in study, 6–11; problems of, 12–15, 180–82; traditional shopping patterns of, 19–20; relation to local merchants, 29–31; as active purchasers, 44–48; shopping scope

221